Mary Austin: American Rhythm

Whitman's was the first clear + self-recognizing song of the road. Whitman was the type-genius like Mark Twain, Stephen Crane, Theodore Dreiser and Carl Sandburg, to group them by type, without respect to the quality of their performance. He was sensitive to the bigness which he mistook for universality, moved about a great deal, speculated freely, and was unclear in his conclusions; the American Type. His whole personality swaggered with what more or less dominated the movement of the American procession, the consciousness of being entirely adequate to the environment. America was a woman, and the poet, though slightly befuddled by her effect upon him, had proved his manhood upon her. But though he was sure, Americanly, that he was on his way, Whitman was by no means so deep in the wilderness as he supposed himself to be. He was seldom far from the rutted pioneer track, a place of chucks and wallows, dust choked in his time with the passing armies. Out of this dust, sweaty and raucous, we (continued)

hear him chanting, principally of what he sees so that his rhythms, more often than not, are mere unpatterned noises of the street:"... Bravuras of birds, bustle of growing wheat, gossip of flames, clack of two sticks, cooking my meals," etc.

It was the genius of Whitman not so much to be a poet as to be able to say out of what stuff the new poetry was to be made.

It was only when he occasionally turned aside into soli- tude that all the senses fused themselves in the spirit's heat. Only thus does his verse cease to be mere foot and eye record of his passage, and exhibits the true brand of the American strain: goal consciousness and pattern attained by balance and a system of compensating phrases.

Of this method it may be said that Whitman neither discovered nor invented it; but that to the limit of his capacity to respond, he was used by it. His capacity was on every side limited by his intelligence, which was adolescent & gamboling. What one suspects of Whitman admirers today is that the name is often invoked in justification of what the poet & poetaster alike of ink going on in themselves — the urge and recovery of the Democratic experience.

... My interest in Whitman swelled perceptibly in the discovery of how like the Indian's his method is, and how much less its emotional affectiveness.

Books by
EDGAR LEE MASTERS

A Book of Verses
Maximilian
The New Star Chamber and Other Essays
Blood of the Prophets
Spoon River Anthology
Songs and Satires
The Great Valley
Toward the Gulf
Starved Rock
Mitch Miller
Domesday Book
The Open Sea
Children of the Market Place
Skeeters Kirby
The Nuptial Flight
Mirage
The New Spoon River
Selected Poems
Lee, A Dramatic Poem
Kit O'Brien
Jack Kelso
The Fate of the Jury
Gettysburg, Manila, Acoma
Lichee Nuts
Lincoln — The Man
Godbey
The Serpent in the Wilderness
The Tale of Chicago
Dramatic Duologues
Vachel Lindsay
Invisible Landscapes
Poems of People
The Golden Fleece of California
Across Spoon River: An Autobiography
Whitman

Whitman

Walt Whitman
Sept: '87

From a copyright photograph, 1887, by G. C. Cox.

Whitman

Edgar Lee Masters 1868-1950,

NEW YORK
Charles Scribner's Sons
1 9 3 7

To

JOHN HALL WHEELOCK

Whitman

CHAPTER ONE

WHITMAN came of English-Quaker stock on his father's side, and Dutch-Welsh stock on his mother's. His Dutch blood undoubtedly predominated in his nature, at least in his own estimation. But when his wide humanitarian feelings are considered, his restless mental activity, and even his insatiable desire to know America and its people, which led him to some extensive travels over America, his Welsh blood cannot be ignored. He is inevitably linked by these characteristics with Jefferson and with Jackson. The New England poets, Whittier, Longfellow, and Lowell, had no such interest in America at large. Whitman's love of an audience, his passion to sing himself, and his egotism, are all Celtic traits.

He was born to be the poet of the American nation by the fact of his democratic passions and his comprehensive interests. Whitman when writing *Specimen Days* in 1882 seems to have consulted Savage's *Genealogical Dictionary*. From that he was of the opinion that the Whitman name in the Eastern States started with John Whitman, born in England in 1602. Leon Bazalgette, who went into this question with evident care, placed the origin of the American Whitmans with Abijah Whitman, born in England in 1560. This Abijah had three sons. One was Zechariah, born 1595, who sailed to America in the *True Love* in 1635, and settled in Milford, Connecticut. This Zechariah established the line of the poet, first through a son named Joseph. Joseph crossed over from Connecticut some time before 1660 and settled in Huntington, Long Island,

I

which was founded in 1653 upon land bought from the Indians. He was a man of many public employments. There is doubt whether it was he, or one of his sons, who bought the farm at West Hills, not far from Huntington, which became the Whitman homestead.

At any rate we go on now with clearness to the grandson of Joseph. This was Nehemiah Whitman, born in 1705. He married Sarah White, who used tobacco and opium, petted her slaves, and was masculine in character. She rode on horseback like a man, was profane, and sometimes offensive in her language, but of sterling character and great energy. She lived to be ninety years of age, dying in 1803. As the paternal great-grandmother of the poet she must have bequeathed to him some of her abounding vitality.

She had a son named Jesse, who was born in 1749 and died in the same year in which she died. Jesse married Hannah Brush; and their son was Walter Whitman, the poet's father, born in 1789 and died in 1855. Hannah Brush was an orphan who was reared by an aunt, Vashti Platt by name, living in the eastern part of Long Island. She was a school teacher, and a seamstress, reported as fair and strong, with some natural distinction, of intelligent mind and gay spirits. This paternal grandmother of the poet saw the Revolutionary War at first hand, in which many of the Whitmans, notable as rebels, took part. One of them, Nehemiah Whitman, was a lieutenant and was killed in the Battle of Brooklyn. The poet celebrated him in the poem "The Centenarian's Story"; while Major Brush, an uncle of Hannah, paid for his patriotism by dying in an English prison. The poet was fifteen when Hannah Brush died, and had heard from her many stories of the Revolutionary days.

The Whitmans were distinguished for long life and fecundity. They were a tall and vigorous breed. Bazalgette noted that Nehemiah Whitman, the great-grandfather of the poet, had twenty-two grandsons and granddaughters. In New England the Whitmans were at times ministers, professors, and some were graduates of Harvard and Yale. But in Long Island, as descendants in America always were who pushed on into the West, or afar from the original hive, they were farmers and workmen, without any trace of mental gifts. They labored and earned a competence. For more than a century the farm at West Hills furnished a good living to the family, blessing them with a kind of ease. They were hospitable people, of excellent reputation, devoted to their families. The West Hills farm was extensive at first, but along the years it diminished, and was largely fallen off when it came to the hands of the poet's father.

While the Whitmans were noted for their firmness of character, true to their English blood, the poet's maternal stock had the vitality and rich amiability of its Low Country origin. The poet's mother was Louisa Van Velsor, who was born in 1795. The Van Velsors stemmed from Garret Van Velsor, born in 1742 and died in 1812. He married Mary Kassabone, presumably a granddaughter of Old Salt Kassabone, as Whitman celebrated him in a poem. Bucke, Harned, and Traubel, the literary executors of the poet, certified to the probability of this relationship. These two had a son who became Major Cornelius Van Velsor, born in 1768 and died in 1826. He married Naomi, sometimes called Amy Williams, who was the daughter of Captain John Williams. The habitat of the Van Velsors was at Cold Spring, not far from the West Hills farm.

In 1881 after an absence of forty years Whitman visited the spots of his early life. He went to the Van Velsor site and in *Specimen Days* wrote of it as follows:

"Every spot had been familiar to me as a child and youth (1825-'40). Then stood there the long, rambling, shingle-sided house, with sheds, pens, a great barn, and much open road space. Now of all these not a vestige left; all had been pulled down, erased, and the plough and harrow pass'd over foundations, road spaces and everything for many summers, fenced in at present, and grain and clover growing like any other fine fields. Only a big hole from the cellar, with some little heaps of broken stone, green with grass and weeds, identified the place. Even the copious old brooks and spring seem'd to have mostly dwindled away. The whole scene, with what it arous'd, memories of my young days there half a century ago, the vast kitchen and ample fireplace and the sitting room adjoining, the plain furniture, the meals, the house full of merry people, my grandmother's sweet old face in its Quaker cap, my grandfather 'the Major,' jovial, red, stout, with sonorous voice and characteristic physiognomy, with the actual sights themselves, made the most pronounc'd half day's experience of my whole jaunt."

The poet's maternal grandmother, Amy Van Velsor, has come down to us as a woman of great sweetness of character and charm. She cared well for her children. She was of elevated spirituality, and of deep intuitive mind. The poet celebrated her with great tenderness. In one poem he wrote,

Behold a woman!

She looks out from her Quaker cap, her face is clearer and more beautiful than the sky.

If Amy Van Velsor was not a Quakeress, she was nevertheless strongly inclined toward the sect, which had been planted in Long Island in 1672. The poet in recording his visit to West Hills in 1881 had this to say concerning his mother:

"For there with all those wooded, hilly, healthy surroundings, my dearest mother Louisa Van Velsor, grew up—(her mother, Amy Williams, of the Friends' or Quakers' denomination—the Williams family, seven sisters and one brother—the father and brother sailors, both of whom met their deaths at sea). The Van Velsor people were noted for fine horses, which the men bred and train'd from blooded stock. My mother as a young woman was a daily and daring rider. As to the head of the family himself, the old race of the Netherlands, so deeply grafted on Manhattan Island and in Kings and Queens Counties, never yielded a more mark'd and full Americanized specimen than Major Cornelius Van Velsor."

Whitman was his mother's son. She exercised a profound spiritual influence upon his growing years, and they were in tender communication until her death in May, 1873, at which time the poet was prematurely old and broken down with paralysis. Spiritually there was a good deal of the Quaker in Whitman. His father was a friend of Elias Hicks, the Quaker preacher, whom Whitman heard as a boy, "more than once personally seeing the old man—and my dear father and mother faithful listeners to him at the meetings," wrote Whitman in 1888 in his tribute to the Quaker preacher. The poet's grandfather, Jesse Whitman, knew Hicks intimately. He also knew Thomas Paine, whom the poet was led in youth to admire by the attitude of his father, as later in New York City he learned much of Paine from an old man who was one of Paine's friends long before.

Walter Whitman, the poet's father, married Louisa Van Velsor in 1816. He had inherited the Whitman homestead at West Hills, where the Whitmans had lived since 1705. The poet was the third generation to be born in this house. He came into this world on May 31, 1819. His father was a carpenter and housebuilder by occupation, with the sluggish blood which belonged to the Whitmans, of large and powerful frame, and of a disposition which could become vehement when his temper was aroused.

No poet was ever born into an environment better adapted to the nourishment and development of his genius than was Whitman. He had the inestimable advantage of a home which had been in the family for long years. "A fine domain it was" wrote Whitman, "500 acres, all good soil, gently sloping east and south, about one tenth woods, plenty of grand old trees two or three miles off at West Hills, Suffolk County."

Today one can visit this spot in about an hour's ride from New York City, and look upon the shingled house still in substantial condition, and at the beautiful country of slopes and hills about it. The winds blow about here reminiscently, bringing scents of the sea and of the meadows. In writing of Long Island Whitman said that it had "plenty of sea shore, the horizon boundless, the sea air fresh and healthy, the numerous bays and creeks swarming with aquatic birds, the south side meadows covered with salt hay, the soil generally tough, but being abundantly supplied with springs of the sweetest waters in the world." To the south far off were the just visible waters of the Atlantic, to the north glimpses of Long Island Sound. No one fully appreciates how much nature meant to Whitman unless he carefully takes note of Whitman's familiarity with birds and vegetation, and with phases of the sea and of the sky.

Whitman took the dossier of years, diary jottings, war memoranda of 1862–'65, nature notes of 1877–'81, together with Western and Canadian observations, "all bundled up and tied by a big string" on the day of a sudden resolution, July 2, 1882, and began the writing of *Specimen Days*. At once his memory turned back to his father and mother, to his people there at West Hills. He was then ill and in comparative poverty, living at Camden, from which he repaired to a creek in the woods near by to get the sunshine and to ponder his life and the old days. Writing of Long Island he said:

"More in the middle of the island were the spreading Hempstead plains, then (1830–'40) quite prairie-like, open, uninhabited, rather sterile, cover'd with kill-calf and huckleberry bushes, yet plenty of fair pasture for the cattle, mostly milchcows, who fed there by hundreds, even thousands, and at evening (the plains too were own'd by the towns, and this was the use of them in common), might be seen taking their way home, branching off regularly in the right places. I have often been out on the edges of these plains toward sundown, and can yet recall in fancy the interminable cow-processions, and hear the music of the tin or copper bells clanking far or near, and breathe the cool of the sweet and slightly aromatic evening air, and note the sunset.

"Through the same region of the island, but further east, extended wide central tracts of pine and scrub oak (charcoal was largely made here), monotonous and sterile. But many a good day or half day did I have wandering through those solitary cross-roads, inhaling the peculiar and wild aroma. Here and all along the island and its shores, I spent intervals many years, all seasons, sometimes riding, sometimes boating, but generally afoot (I was always then a good walker), absorbing fields, shores, marine incidents, characters, the bay-men, farmers, pilots—always had a plentiful acquaintance with the latter, and with fishermen—went every summer on sailing trips —always liked the bare sea-beach, south side, and have some of my happiest hours on it to this day.

"As I write the whole experience comes back to me after the lapse of forty and more years—the soothing rustle of the waves, and the saline smell—boyhood's times, the clam digging, barefoot, and with trousers roll'd up—hauling down the creek —the perfume of the sedge meadows—the hay-boat, and the chowder and fishing excursions;—or, of later years, little voyages down and out New York bay, in the pilot boats. Those same later years, also, while living in Brooklyn (1836-'50), I went regularly every week in the mild seasons down to Coney island, at that time a long, bare unfrequented shore, which I had all to myself, and where I loved, after bathing, to race up and down the hard sand, and declaim Homer or Shakespeare to the surf and the sea gulls by the hour."

Then Whitman referred to the Van Velsor homestead, two or three miles from West Hills, there, as it was, on that solitary, picturesque road that wound up from Cold Spring Harbor. Around the child Whitman, around him later, as he roamed about his birthplace and up and down Long Island, were working people and farmers; while his own relatives were strong human beings without culture, long lived, moral without Puritanism, rational, hospitable and charitable, and full of that naturalness and goodness that better distinguished the strains of blood that flowed from Virginia and Tennessee and Kentucky into Illinois. For in truth Long Island was a kind of West in those days, it had taken on the religious and spiritual tone that Roger Williams brought into Rhode Island. Connecticut could be seen across the Sound. But there how different the people were, and the spiritual aroma of the land!

These are some of the influences that set Whitman apart, and kept him from being a New England poet, and made him the American national poet he became. He was thus of the West, while his imagination roamed the continent. Spiritually he placed himself at the center of America, and reached East and West to touch both oceans, as Jefferson did, through his heredity, environment and native genius. Lastly, Louisa Van Velsor Whitman is never to be forgotten. Whitman's love for her and her love for him filled him with magnetic power. Their relationship was not unlike that of Goethe and his mother. Nothing better can happen to a creative mind than this envelopment of maternal love, when it is so understandingly reciprocated.

CHAPTER TWO

As WHITMAN was to be a poet of people, of crowds, of American cities and of comrades, the pattern in his life turned true to his destiny when his father moved to Brooklyn, and left the West Hills farm. At the same time it is not likely that Whitman would have stayed on the farm, as Burns did. Eventually he would have taken to the streets of New York. It was 1824, when Whitman was five years old, that Walter Whitman, his carpenter father, took up the family residence in Brooklyn, a town then of about 10,000 people.

From 1824 to 1828 the family lived in Front, Cranberry, and Johnson Streets. In the latter Walter Whitman, the father, built what the poet called a "nice house, and afterwards another in Tillary Street." Both were mortgaged and were lost at last. The father did not prosper in the city; but this adversity seems not to have been sharp, and to have made no mark on the poet. He loved simple things, and simple fare and life. There was no delight greater for him than to sit in the kitchen, however humble it was, with his mother, and talk with her as she went about her domestic work.

At five years of age Whitman was a chubby, rosy boy. It was then that something happened by which Whitman touched hands with the Revolution in a way never to be forgotten. General Lafayette came to America, and on an occasion rode through the streets of Brooklyn. The school children turned out to welcome the man who had helped America to inde-

9

pendence, and who had been the friend of Washington. At the time a free public library was being built in Brooklyn, and Lafayette consented to lay the corner stone. The children were all about the excavation which had been made for the building; and the men who had gathered to witness the ceremony lifted the children so that they could see it. Lafayette was doing this, too; and he took up the five-year-old Whitman and pressed him to his breast, and gave him a kiss, then handed him down to safety by the excavation. Whitman preserved a memory of this to the last, and referred to it in *Specimen Days*.

The Whitman family in Brooklyn consisted of the father and mother and four children, a fourth having been born when they lived in Front Street. The poet was the second child of this group. The facts seem to indicate that at this time the carpenter father had embarked regularly upon the business of building houses, mortgaging them and then selling them. In 1830 the family had moved again and was living in Henry Street. Thus from the settled peace of West Hills there had come roving and change in the rural village of Brooklyn. Soon the poet-to-be put away his childhood dress and became a boy who went about the neighborhoods of the town, exploring them quite alone, and paying visits to the corner grocery store. He went upon the ferries where he was made much of by the ferrymen, as he watched the horses which trod in the center of the boat and furnished the power which propelled it. It was in his blood to be the carefree, wandering man which he became, living always as much as possible in the open air, and imbibing the influences of the sea and the lovely land of Long Island, which he roamed over all his youth.

He went to the public schools six years in all between 1824 and 1831, and attended Sunday School at St. Ann's Church. This was the only formal education he ever had, something that he never regretted, but rather rejoiced over. On occasion he went with his father and mother to hear Elias Hicks preach,

once in a ballroom on Brooklyn Heights. Then as before
mentioned there were the charming visits to West Hills. For
a poet of liberty and naturalism there could scarcely have been
a better training than came to Walt Whitman, the son of the
carpenter.

When Whitman was twelve years old (1831) he was employed in a lawyer's office, but conceived no ambition to become
a lawyer. He was given a desk by a window and his employer
started to help him with his handwriting and composition.
Through the kindness of this lawyer Whitman was given a
subscription to a big circulating library, "the signal event of
my life up to that time," Whitman recorded in *Specimen
Days.* "For a time I now revel'd in romance reading of all
kinds"; he wrote, "first the *Arabian Nights,* all the volumes,
an amazing treat. Then with sorties in very many directions,
took in Walter Scott's novels, one after another, and his
poetry." In his late days when talking to Traubel he commented on the influence of Scott and Cooper on his taste and
literary development.

"My taste," he said, "has been modelled on another theory—
in the school of Scott, of Cooper, of some others of the older
writers. How much I am indebted to Scott no one can tell—I
couldn't tell it myself—but it has permeated me through and
through. If you could reduce the *Leaves* to their elements you
would see Scott unmistakably active at the roots. I remember
the *Tales of My Landlord, Ivanhoe, The Fortunes of Nigel*—
yes, and *Kenilworth*—its great pageantry—then there's the
Heart of Midlothian, which I have read a dozen times and
more. I might say just about the same thing about Cooper, too.
He has written books which will survive into the farthest future. Try to think of literature, of the world of boys, today,
without *Natty Bumppo, The Spy, The Red Rover*—Oh *The
Red Rover*—it used to stir me up clarionlike: I read it many
times. Is all this old fashioned? I am not sworn to the old
things—not at all—that is, not to old things at the expense of

new—but some of the oldest things are the newest. I should not refuse to see and welcome any one who came to violate the precedents—on the contrary I am looking about for just such men—but a lot of the fresh things are not new—they are only repetitions after all: they do not seem to take life forward. Scott, Cooper, such men, always, perpetually, as a matter of course, always take life forward—take each new generation forward."

The volume of Scott that fell into Whitman's hands was a thousand-page one, of poetry. Considering that he inveighed so much against Old World culture and feudalism one would expect him to have had as little interest in Scott as Jefferson had, and to lament Scott's influence on America, as later eyes did who saw its working in the Southern states. It was only a romantic youthful interest after all, which was balanced and corrected by Shakespeare, the Bible and Homer.

Whitman did not stay long with the lawyer. He took employment as errand boy to a doctor in Brooklyn. Then at fourteen (1833) he became an apprentice in the composing room of a weekly paper called *The Long Island Patriot,* there to learn the printer's trade. Like Franklin and Greeley he was fascinated by the smell of printer's ink from the first; and from this time on, despite other occupations, the printing office was the place that most powerfully affected his imagination.

The proprietor of *The Patriot* was S. E. Clements, who took Whitman under his wing. It was not the machine age, but a time of leisurely employments, with plenty of opportunity for recreation and talk. Whitman while on *The Patriot* had for a fellow printer an old Revolutionary character who had seen Washington, and told the youthful poet of the heroic times when America was struggling for independence. Later Whitman worked on *The Long Island Star,* edited by Alden Spooner, who called him an idle boy, a characterization that stuck to Whitman. Those around him did not see that when he laid the scythe down and rested under a tree, or put down his composing stick and looked out of the window, his mind was working. It is impossible to read his journals and notes, his projections for poems and his observations on America, without seeing that his mind was always active, always seeking and exploring.

These school and printer's years did not find the farm at West Hills neglected. Whether he walked or rode from Brooklyn to West Hills he travelled frequently over the distance of something like twenty miles between them. In vacation days he went to see his grandparents, his gentle grandmother, the Quakeress Amy, and to make long visits with her. It was in these days that he was exploring the beautiful country of Long Island, taking note of the birds, the flowers and the weeds, the rocks and the creeks, the hills and the meadows. The sea laid a lasting spell on his imagination. He watched the ships from the shore along the southern coast of the island, and of himself wrote, "As a youngster I was in the atmosphere and tradition of many wrecks, almost an observer of one or two." He was so impregnated with the spirit of the sea, with its odors, its smells of seaweed and fish, that an old sea captain said of him, "I can smell salt water ten miles away in just seeing him." In these formative years he stored his mind with imagery of the sea, and it came forth in numerous lines throughout his poems.

From fourteen to sixteen he developed into a healthy strong youth of monstrous breadth and stature. He grew too fast, according to his own word, and was as "big as a man at fifteen or sixteen." He was of arresting handsomeness with his black hair, his bright, rosy complexion, and his large gray-blue eyes, heavy lidded and dreamy looking.

Undoubtedly he had chums, or boyhood friends, of happy relationship. But none stands out. There were no Arthur Hallams in his life; there were no boyhood sweethearts, such as Byron and Burns and Shelley had. He seemed to walk through these boyhood days with complete impersonality, interested only in nature, the sea, in crowds, ferrymen and farmers and workers. On the face of the records which we have Whitman's love for his mother was not undue, and if it prevented or delayed his psycho-sexual development it was in ways not easily unearthed. It was not a mother fixation, such as can be found in cases of the only boy, or the favorite boy, which he was, who becomes asocial as the result of a mother attachment, and wants the society of older persons.

If Whitman's love for his mother prevented him in fact from transferring his libido for her to other women it lies in such obscurity that it cannot be definitely revealed. It may have been one of the influences in his bachelorhood, co-operating with his literary occupations, his limited means, his passion for free-faring, and for freedom in general. But when he was fifteen and sixteen and so full of fresh life, so teeming with all his wonderful vitality and imagination it is strange almost beyond clear solution, that no girl came into his life. He acted very much as those youths do who are of neutral sexuality, being either ashamed in the presence of girls or considering them just another species of being in no wise to get excited about. His love for his mother does not explain this indifference to girls, for indifference it was, since it was neither one thing nor the other. It must be remembered, too, that Whitman had a genuine respect and admiration for his father, with which a mother fixation does not co-exist.

At sixteen Whitman was employed in a printing office in New York, and had become an omnivorous novel reader. He was also passionately devoted to the theatre, and was attending debating societies and taking part in the discussions. Now it was that he was crossing the Fulton Ferry from Brooklyn to New York to his work or his pleasure, as daily later when he was thirty and more he went back and forth on the Hudson River. In *Specimen Days* he reported that he sat in the pilot house where "I could get a full sweep, absorbing shows, accompaniments, surroundings. What oceanic currents, eddies, underneath—the great tides of humanity also, with ever shifting movements. Indeed I have always had a passion for ferries; to me they afford inimitable, never failing, living poems. The river and bay scenery, all about New York island, any time of a fine day—the hurrying, splashing seatides—the changing panorama of steamers of all sizes, often a string of big ones outward bound to distant ports—the myriads of white-sail'd schooners, sloops, skiffs, and the marvelously beautiful yachts —the majestic sound boats as they rounded the Battery and came along at 5, afternoon, eastward bound—the prospect far off towards Staten Island, or down the Narrows, or the other way up the Hudson, what refreshment of spirit such sights and experiences gave me years ago (and many a time since). My old pilot friends, the Balsirs, Johnny Cole, Ira Smith, William White, and my young friend Tom Gere—how well I remember them all."

Whitman wrote in *Specimen Days* that he was a little more than eighteen when he turned country school teacher "down in Queens and Suffolk Counties, and 'boarded around.' This latter I consider one of my best experiences and deepest lessons in human nature behind the scenes, and in the masses." In all he taught at the villages of Flushing, Babylon, Jamaica, Woodbury, Whitestone. In these days he was going over Long Island again and again, and to the farm at West Hills. We have some report on Whitman as a teacher. One of his pupils was I. H. Pratt who had this to say in a book entitled *Walt Whitman:*

"I went to school to him in the town of Flushing, Long Island. He taught the school at Little Bay Side. We became very much attached to him. His ways of teaching were peculiar. He did not confine himself to books, as most of the teachers then did, but taught orally—yes, had some original ideas all his own. I know about that, for I had heard of others who tried oral teaching. But the plans he adopted were wholly of his own conception, and most successful. He was not severe with the boys, but had complete discipline in the school. Before and after school and at recess, he was a boy among boys, always free, always easy, never stiff. He took active part in games of frolic. It seemed his object to teach even when we played.

"Whitman was very fond of describing objects and incidents to the school. He would not do this privately, but to all hands. He would give quite a good deal of time to any subject that seemed worth while. He was always interesting, a very good talker, able to command the attention of scholars, of whom, by the way, there were seventy or eighty. Our ages ranged sixteen, seventeen years old, yet many, too, were young shavers like myself. The girls did not seem to attract him. He did not specially go anywhere with them or show any extra fondness for their society.

"Walt was a good story teller. Oh! excellent; was both funny and serious. Did I say he had his own notions how to punish a scholar? If he caught a boy lying, he exposed him before the whole school in a story. But the story was told without the mention of any names. No punishment beyond that. He had such a way of telling his story that the guilty fellow knew who was meant. He would do this in the case of any ordinary offence; but, if the offence was grave enough, the whole school was taken into the secret.

"My memory of Walt is acute, unusually acute—probably because his personality had such a peculiar and powerful effect upon me, even as a boy. I had other teachers, but none of them ever left such an impress upon me. And yet I could not mention any particular thing. It was his whole air, his general sympathetic way, his eye, his voice, his entire geniality. I felt something I could not describe. What I say, others will also say. I think he affected all as he did me. They have admitted it, yet, like me, can give no definite reasons. No one could tell why. Their memory of him is exactly like mine. There must be something in it; it is not imagination.

"Whitman had dignity, and yet at the same time he could descend to sociability. The very moment he stepped across that school doorsill he was master. He had authority, but was not severe. We obeyed and respected him. One thing is sure. As far as Walt's goodness of character goes, you can report me pretty fully and as strongly as you choose. Even back in the school-days, those of us who knew him, his scholars there on Long Island felt, somehow, without knowing why, that here was a man out of the average, who strangely attracted our respect and affection."

Doctor Johnson, an English admirer of Walt Whitman, interviewed a Long Island farmer named Sanford Brown, who as a youth had been one of Whitman's pupils. He said:

"Walter Whitman, or 'Walt' as we used to call him, was my first teacher. He 'kept school' for 'bout a year around here. I was one of his scholars, and I used to think a powerful deal on him. I can't say that he was exactly a failure as a teacher, but he was certainly not a success. He warn't in his element. He was always musin' and writin', 'stead of 'tending to his proper dooties; but I guess he was like a good many on us— not very well off, and had to do somethin' for a livin'. But school teachin' was not his forte. His forte was poetry. Folks used ter consider him a bit lazy and indolent, because, when he was workin' in the fields, he would sometimes go off for from five minutes to an hour, and lay down on his back on the grass in the sun, then get up and do some writin'; and the folks used ter say he was idlin'; but I guess he was then workin' with his brain, and thinkin' hard, and then writin' down his thoughts. . . . He kept school for a year and then his sister succeeded him."

Whitman had passed by the chance to be a lawyer or a doctor. The ministry evidently never entered his head. If he had at this time any sympathy with Christianity, it was Christianity as an influence of revolution among the masses, not as asceticism. Very early in his life New England excited his distaste, and he expressed it later many times. As he was neutral about women so was he uncertain about what he should do with his life. He conceived neither convictions nor aspirations that drove him into a course. His young breast was stormed with powerful emotions, his restless mind carried him about. He walked and observed nature, he read and thought, he engaged in sports of strength and skill with other young men, always the leader in boisterous and magnificent vitality. He was handsome and admired. Some report him as an athlete, but that he was ever exactly that, or exactly of powerful muscularity may be questioned. He did have abandon and animation.

He had really touched in himself the springs of deepest interest when he learned the printer's trade at fourteen years of age, and so at about twenty years of age he founded *The Long Islander* at Huntington with his brother George as part owner, then about thirty years old. Whitman was manager, editor-in-chief, compositor and pressman. Despite these various duties he had time for games, and he loafed a good deal too. At this time his school-teaching was not ended, so that he had that to attend to. His brother George has left us pictures of Walt, of his abstractions, his inattention to the hour for meals, his habit of leaving the table to wander off somewhere. As an editor he played with a ring swinging on a string from the ceiling, which could be tossed and hooked on a hook in the wall, if skillfully directed; in which case a piece of pie or a nickel was the prize.

Whitman wrote of *The Long Islander* as follows: "I was encouraged to start a paper in the region where I was born. I went to New York, bought a press and type, hired some little help, but did most of the work myself including the press work. Everything seem'd turning out well; and (only my own restlessness prevented me establishing a permanent property there). I bought a good horse, and every week went all around the country serving my papers, devoting one day and night to it. I never had happier jaunts—going over to the southside, to Babylon, down the south road across to Smithtown and Comac, and back home. The experience of those jaunts, the dear old fashion'd farmers and their wives, the stops by the hay-fields, the hospitality, nice dinners, occasional evenings, the girls, the rides through the brush, come up in my memory to this day."

Here was that lust of life, that delight in the passions of the flesh, that capacity for sensation which was gathering material for *Leaves of Grass*. He was observed and remembered by the people of Huntington. They saw him in his giant physique, his brimming life, his disregard of money, his carelessness in the use of his time. They saw him too as a lover of books who liked to assemble in the printing shop the youths of the village and tell them stories and read poetry to them, probably from the great volume of Scott, and sometimes, it is said, his own, his yawp, as he called it then, which he was beginning to sound over the world. If he had any sweethearts the fact lies hidden. Every one has seen in his youth the young man who had no interest in women, who if he married later, did so as a matter of form, and because it was one of the things in life to do. This seems to have been the case with Whitman. He liked masculine association, he found with men sufficient outlet for his emotional nature. Yet, as he confessed, he was restless. Many another young man would have pursued that editorship at Huntington, and grown into a competence out of it, though it is clear enough that Whitman showed no brilliance as a journalist, neither then nor at any time in his life. He wrote no verses then and not for long later that had any distinction whatever. They were worse than mediocre. They were pure rubbish. Bryant at eighteen had written "Thanatopsis," Longfellow and Poe just out of boyhood had produced creditable or memorable poetry. Whitman was too full of surging thoughts and emotions, too undirected as yet, too wandering in space without an orbit, to find just the thing he wanted to say, and the medium adapted to saying it.

When Whitman was about twenty-two he abandoned *The Long Islander* and returned to New York City. The idea of becoming a writer, a poet, probably entered his mind at his fourteenth year, for he had printed "Sentimental Bits" in *The Long Island Patriot*. The germination of his genius as a poet will be considered later. Now it is in order to say that resuming his life in New York, he became laborer, journalist and printer, as well as gardener. For five years he worked as a compositor in the printing offices of New York, as a tramp printer, it might be said; for in the summers this casual-liver would go to Long Island, where he haunted the woods and the seashores. On these occasions he maintained himself by working as a gardener. It was then that he read Homer and Shakespeare, reciting from them to the sea.

Remembering these days when he wrote "From a Backward Glance O'er Traveled Roads," the preface to *November Boughs* of 1888, he said: "I have wondered since why I was not overwhelmed by those mighty masters. Likely because I read them, as described in the full presence of nature, under the sun, with the far spreading landscape and vistas, or the sea rolling in." To sit on the sandy shore at Babylon amid the whispering reeds, and to look afar at the sea silent, yet lisping at one's feet, is to understand the happiness of a lover of Homer reading the *Iliad* under such enchanting circumstances. So Whitman had delight. He fed to the full his capacity for æsthetic and sensual enjoyment.

But people and crowds must not be forgotten. Whitman's passions were nature and people. The ferries, Broadway and the opera and theatre engrossed him. From *Specimen Days* his own words tell the story: "Besides Fulton ferry, off and on for years, I knew and frequented Broadway—that noted avenue of New York's crowded and mixed humanity, and of so many notables. Here I saw during those times Andrew Jackson, Webster, Clay, Seward, Martin Van Buren, filibuster Walker, Kossuth, Fitz Greene Halleck, Bryant, the Prince of Wales,

Charles Dickens, the first Japanese ambassadors, and lots of other celebrities of the time. Always something novel or inspirating; yet mostly to me the hurrying and vast amplitude of those never-ending human currents. I remember seeing James Fenimore Cooper in a court room in Chambers street, back of the city hall, where he was carrying on a law case—(I think it was a charge of libel he had brought against someone). I also remember seeing Edgar A. Poe, and having a short interview with him (it must have been in 1845, or '6), in his office, second story of a corner building (Duane or Pearl street). He was editor and owner, or part owner, of 'the Broadway Journal'. The visit was about a piece of mine he had publish'd. Poe was very cordial, in a quiet way, appear'd well in person, dress, &c. I have a distinct and pleasing remembrance of his looks, voice, manner and matter; very kindly and human, but subdued, perhaps a little jaded."

Then there were the omnibus rides up and down Broadway. "One phase of these days," wrote Whitman in *Specimen Days,* "must by no means go unrecorded—namely the Broadway omnibuses, with their drivers. The vehicles still (I write this paragraph in 1881) give a portion of the character of Broadway—the Fifth avenue, Madison avenue, and Twenty-third street lines yet running. But the flush days of the old Broadway stages, characteristic and copious, are over. The Yellow-birds, the original Broadway, the Fourth avenue, the Knickerbocker, and a dozen others of twenty or thirty years ago, are all gone. And the men specially identified with them, and giving vitality and meaning to them—the drivers—a strange, natural, quick-eyed and wondrous race—(not only Rabelais and Cervantes would have gloated upon them, but Homer and Shakespeare would)—how well I remember them, and must here give a word about them. How many hours, forenoons and afternoons—how many exhilirating night times I have had—perhaps June or July, in cooler air—riding the whole length of Broadway, listening to some yarn (and the most vivid yarns ever spun, and the rarest mimicry—or perhaps I declaiming some stormy passage from Julius Cæsar or Richard, (you could roar as loud as you chose in that heavy, dense, uninterrupted street-bass). Yes, I knew all the drivers then, Broadway Jack, Dressmaker, Balky Bill, George Storms, Old Elephant, his brother Young Elephant (who came afterward), Tippy, Pop Rice, Big Frank, Yellow Joe, Pete Callahan, Patsy Dee, and dozens more; for there were hundreds. They had immense qualities, largely animal—eating, drinking, women—great personal pride, in their way, perhaps a few slouches here and there, but I should have trusted the general run of them, in their simple good will and honor under all circumstances. Nor only for comradeship, and sometimes affection—great studies I found them also. (I suppose the critics will laugh heartily, but the influence of those Broadway jaunts and drives and declamations and escapades undoubtedly entered into the gestation of 'Leaves of Grass.' "

We shall have to take Whitman's word for the poetical influence of these associations; but it would seem that the material he gathered through them was better adapted to the uses of DeMaupassant or Balzac or Dickens. Surely the opera and the theatre bore with equal influence upon Whitman's poetical growth. In *Specimen Days* he recorded, "All through these years, off and on, I frequented the old Park, the Bowery, Broadway and Chatham-square theatres, and the Italian operas at Chambers-street, Astor-place or the Bowery—many seasons was on the free list, writing for papers even as quite a youth."

He noted that he saw among others, Hackett, the younger Kean, Macready, old Booth and Charlotte Cushman; and such plays as Richard Third, Lear, Macbeth, Othello, The Tempest, and Hamlet. In opera among his special enjoyments were Somnambula, The Puritans, Huguenots, Faust, Ernani, Rigolleto, Lucia, William Tell, and many others, and such artists as Alboni, Grisi, the tenor Mario, and the baritone Badiali. At Castle Garden there were splendid seasons of opera.

And the Havana musical troupe came, where amid cool sea-breezes Whitman listened to a fine band and to the "unsurpassed vocalism of famous singers of the day in *Don Pasquale* and *Favorita*." Whitman also heard Jenny Lind when she came to America under the auspices of Barnum. He indulged in a fond reminiscence: "The Battery—its past associations—what tales those old trees and walks and sea-walls could tell!"

The youth of Whitman was a rich one: there were Long Island and the walks and the sea; there were the Broadway buses and the opera and theatre. There was the fascination of the newspaper office, of reading Cervantes, Homer, Ossian and Shakespeare, as well as novels. There was everything by way of delight and self-cultivation. But there was no romance.

CHAPTER THREE

THERE was something slovenly and disorderly about Whitman's mind. His habits of eating, and walking and reading and working were without system. Once he said that he wrote *Leaves of Grass* as "just so much let fly." He wrote many things that way, including *Specimen Days,* which despite its charm and its tang is without order and intelligible sequence at times. For instance he mentioned in those notes after speaking of Broadway sights, already quoted, that the years 1846–'47 saw him in New York working as writer and printer, "having my usual good health, and a good time generally." He passed from this to the omnibuses, then to the plays and operas. Then he wrote, "in 1848–'49 I was occupied as editor of the daily *Eagle,* newspaper in Brooklyn." Glancing forward and backwards the story can be assembled: how he haunted the libraries and museums. But the stuff does not come forth in fullness and in order.

Now, as a matter of fact, Whitman quitted *The Long Islander* at Huntington in 1840, and came to New York. Before this he had published in *The Mirror* of George P. Morris, a celebrated journal of the time. Settled in New York now he began to write for *The Democratic Review, The New World, Brother Jonathan, The Columbian Magazine, The American Review,* and *The Broadway Journal* edited by Poe, already referred to. From 1841 to 1845 the name of W. W. or Walter Whitman appeared frequently in these publications. Poe, Hawthorne, Whittier, Lowell and Bryant also wrote for *The*

Democratic Review. All of these men were older than Whitman, except Lowell; and all had more reputation, and were doing more creditable work.

Consider now that Whitman had had a marvellous youth in the country and by the sea; and that he had nursed his mind on Scott and Shakespeare and on Homer, and was still doing so. Then take into account the story he published in the August 1841 number of *The Democratic Review.* It was entitled *Death in the School Room* (*A Fact*). This ineffable performance at twenty-two years of age is in substance as follows:

Tim Barker, a young boy, was seen by Mr. Nichols' garden, and departing from it with something in a bag, which had been reported to Lugare, the schoolmaster. In point of fact Tim was the son of a poor widow, and was being helped by a well-to-do farmer, who was leaving potatoes for Tim and his mother by the Nichols' garden. That secret way had been adopted in order not to shame the poverty of the widow and the boy. The schoolmaster called Tim to the desk and questioned him. Not getting anything from the boy he started to bully him. He got nothing then, and sent the boy to his seat. At the close of school the master took his rattan and went to the boy who was sitting with his head down, and began to belabor him. The boy uttered no cry, and spoke no word. He was dead. He had died of fright during the afternoon.

Some samples from this story will give its quality: "And pray sir, continued Lugare, as the outward signs of wrath disappear'd from his features, what were you about the garden for? Perhaps you only received the plunder, and had an accomplice to do the more dangerous part of the job?

"I went that way because it is on my road home. I was there again afterwards to meet an acquaintance; and—and. But I did not go into the garden, nor take anything from it. I would not steal—hardly to save my life from starving."

This was the kind of Sunday School fiction which Bill Nye satirized so uproariously in the story of the grammatical boy.

Bazalgette is authority for saying that this story had a wide circulation, and made a sensation in those days when over in England Dickens was publishing the *Pickwick Papers* at twenty-five years of age and Thackeray was contributing *The Yellowplush Papers* to *Fraser's Magazine* at the same age, while in America Cooper twenty years before this time had won celebrity by his *The Spy* at thirty-three years of age. Whitman had learned little that equipped him for the writing of fiction from his omnivorous novel reading, perhaps for the reason that he had no gift for invention or for character depiction, and little gift of any sort. At this period of his life he was ridden by a moral consciousness, and was being swept along by the great tide of reformation in America, which did much to influence *Leaves of Grass,* a matter to be more carefully considered in another connection.

Meanwhile in these days there were the theatres and Broadway and the crowds. He joined an amateur dramatic company and essayed the rôle of an actor. If, as a coming poet and writer, he was not influenced by the ideas and methods of other writers, yet he did not use the very considerable material which he had gathered by now in any original or meritorious way. His places of study continued to be the tops of the buses, or in some secluded place by the sea. He also frequented the New York libraries, and attended the lectures of men like Emerson and Bryant. In time he grew to know Bryant and took many long walks with him. Whitman admired Bryant. He enjoyed Bryant's description of Europe—the architecture and the cities of Italy.

Back on Long Island when Whitman was seventeen the campaign of Van Buren for the Presidency came on, and he took part in that. He made a vivid impression as a political orator in those days at Jamaica. He was a Democrat and remained one fundamentally, despite the slavery question which later, as a moral factor, grew every year more insistent as it changed the political alignments of Whigs and Democrats.

In 1888 Whitman said, "Not the negro, not the negro. The negro was not the chief thing: the chief thing was to stick together. The South was technically right and morally wrong."

So it was that in 1836 Whitman saw, as Emerson did, that Negro slavery was not the only slavery. Later than this when Texas was the issue, and the slavery question again raised its menacing head, Whitman published a poem in *The New York Tribune* of June 14, 1850, then entitled "House of Friends" and later "Wounded in the House of Friends." One passage of this omitted from Whitman's *Collect* is as follows:

> Vaunters of the Free,
> Why do you strain your lungs off southward?
> Why be going to Alabama?
> Sweep first before your own door;
> Stop this squalling and this scorn
> Over the mote there in the distance;
> Look well to your own eye, Massachusetts —
> Yours, New York and Pennsylvania;
> — I would say yours, too, Michigan,
> But all the salve, all the surgery
> Of the great wide world were powerless there.

When America was being rounded by the acquisition of California and Lowell was pouring the denunciation of the *Biglow Papers* on the Mexican War, and its policies, Whitman wrote in in *The New Orleans Crescent,* "Folly all who see in the extent of the country, or perhaps in the Mexican War the secret of the Union's sure decay. Dissolution and decay are for the old, the worn out, the poor and feeble, among nations as among individuals."

Thus in these years before he went to New Orleans, which was in February, 1848, Whitman was involved in the politics of the hour. He frequented Tammany Hall, and became acquainted with the political figures there. In the campaign of Polk-for-President in 1844 he was an active participant. For the rest between the ages of nineteen and thirty-five, whether he was in New York or New Orleans, he was lost in the great streams of city crowds, learning about shops, houses, sidewalks, ferries, factories, taverns, religious assemblies, political meetings, carousings, hospitals, poor houses, and prisons —where he came in contact with the fakir, the beggar and the peddler, the thief and the ragged man, the old and the young, with outcasts and prostitutes. He also learned to know merchants, lawyers, doctors, scholars, actors, singers, and writers. But he liked best the farmers of Long Island, the mechanics, carpenters, pilots, printers, masons, deck hands, teamsters, and bus drivers of the city.

In addition to looking into foundries, shipyards, rolling mills, slaughter houses, factories, and wharves, and wherever labor was being performed, he had time for clam bakes and clam diggings by the sea, and for races and auctions, weddings, sailing and bathing parties, for christenings, and for church attendance at times. Thus he built up the material for his vast catalogues in which, when writing about America, he tried, by piling item upon item, to give a picture of the land which was always so deeply in his love. His Celtic blood was clearly manifested in his disposition to be among crowds, to talk with passersby, to search out new friends, to learn about people, and to fellow with them. John Burroughs wrote of him that his nature carried him "towards beings who have the qualities of things of the open air—the power of rocks, of trees, of hills."

There was something else: he loved the flesh of humanity, he wanted to be in affectionate touch with it, to feel it and to identify himself with it. This to him was more than books or culture, more than the life of thought, more even than poetry as an art. He wanted first-hand news of life. Many times he disparaged books which were written out of books, rather than out of the throbbing heart of life. No writer ever had closer and more constant contact with the stuff of life itself. In these years and in these ways he was a happy man, healthy and full of contagious mirth. He later said that he had a good time in every way, and he did.

He had everything except a woman's love. His sexual life at this period is hidden, or if partly revealed can be summed in his own words that he lived an all-around man. This must have been by casual experiences, for there are no Whitman love letters during these years of his great physical vitality. His giant body, the fresh rich blood that made his face ruddy and his spirits abounding, had no romantic expression.

Whitman was not done with that kind of trash which took form so melodramatically in the story of the school boy. Humanitarian ideas swarmed about him in the America of that day. There were the slavery question and the temperance question, and Whitman as a radical and an idealist could not escape their influence upon him. As Shelley abstained from wine and flesh so Whitman took up with causes, more or less, like the abolition of capital punishment, but in no way that showed a philosophy or great thought. In the November number (1842) of *The Democratic Review* he published a novel called "Franklin Evans or the Inebriate." At this time Whitman was working in the composing room of this paper. The novel was announced as having been written to order and paid for in advance. The author was heralded as one of the eminent writers of America.

Later Whitman confessed that he wrote this novel on the table of a saloon while drinking gin. It showed the effect of confused mentality, due to some cause or other, in its cheap style and manner of narrative. It is a thoroughly worthless production for a man at any age, and Whitman had come to twenty-three years. Traubel in the days of his association with Whitman at Camden, some twenty years later, tried to rescue this story from loss, but he had no encouragement from its author. However, it was out of these early ardors for new methods of teaching with no flogging, the lesson he really meant to inculcate in the story of the school room; out of sympathy with the unfortunate and the disinherited, out of devotion to living wages for laborers, to the rights of women, to other ennobling changes in American life, that Whitman evolved into the poet who spoke for the greatness of America, for beauty, for a higher spirituality, and for the Union at last. These early and absurd adventures into the field of creative work sprang from the rank soil which later produced the immortal flowers of his great poems.

In *Specimen Days* Whitman wrote, "In 1848, '49 I was occupied as editor of the 'daily Eagle' newspaper in Brooklyn." The truth was that he was so occupied in 1847, while in 1848, in February, he went to New Orleans to engage in newspaper work there. Whitman wrote as to *The Brooklyn Eagle,* "I had there one of the pleasantest sits of my life—a good owner, good pay, easy work and convenient hours."

C. H. M. Skinner contributed an article to the November, 1903 number of *The Atlantic Monthly* pointing out that Whitman did not have the temperament of a journalist. He was slow and leisurely, and given to repose. At this time Whitman was living with his parents in Myrtle Avenue, Brooklyn, more than a mile from the office of *The Eagle* near the Fulton Ferry. He walked back and forth from his house to the office, and loafed along the way, observing the sights of the town. Worse than that he absented himself from duty for whole days, while he went to swim in the ocean or to play around. It is hard to see that his advice on editorial policy was very valuable; but if it was, *The Eagle* was frequently denied it. According to Skinner, Whitman appeared at his desk between eleven and noon. Then he looked over the dailies; then he went for a lounge of an hour or two under the trees in the Battery, looking at the sea.

It is remarkable that *The Eagle* retained his editorship as long as it did, particularly as Whitman's writing was colorless and indifferent to the last degree. What he wrote was in the vein of the country weekly. His editorials were commonplace. He only became measurably alive when he spoke of liberty and honesty, when he combatted capital punishment, the brutal treatment of negroes, the luxury and hypocrisy of the churches, and the corruption of municipal politics. He gave interesting counsel on matters of hygiene, and the bath. He showed an interest in the City of Brooklyn. In an open letter to the city council and the mayor he adjured them to administer the city in a way to consult the rights of the individual in conformity with the real spirit of an American community. Nevertheless he was not a journalist. It was only because of the easy times, and perhaps on account of his own personality, and his wide acquaintanceship with newspaper men, that he was always able to pick up a job.

At last he was let out of *The Brooklyn Eagle,* and according to report it was because of something he wrote about the treatment of negroes. Whatever it was it was no loss to *The Eagle* when he departed from its editorship. He had had a chance at prosperity and position when he founded *The Long Islander.* He was fortuned again with the editorship of *The Eagle.* But he made slight use of these opportunities and was probably incapable of doing so. And now luck favored him again.

He had been about New York and Brooklyn for nearly a decade, mixing with joyous bands of fellows, temperate but loving a glass of beer slowly drunk, never intoxicated, but more sober as his associates grew stimulated. He had remained an Easterner, like New Yorkers of the present who have not been west of the Hudson River. He knew only Long Island and Manhattan Island. To be the poet of the continent he needed to see the West, and gather catalogues for *Leaves of Grass,* which had not as yet come into his slowly growing mind.

One evening in the early part of 1848 Whitman met a man from New Orleans who had come to New York to buy material for the starting of a newspaper in New Orleans. They had a drink together and after a brief talk Whitman was engaged as editor of the new journal, and given $200 to bind the employment. Whitman placed this event in 1849. In *Specimen Days* he wrote, "The latter year went off on a leisurely journey and working expedition (my brother Jeff with me) through all the middle states, and down the Ohio and Mississippi rivers. Lived a while in New Orleans, and work'd there on the editorial staff of 'daily Crescent' newspaper." This was all. Traubel, Bucke and Harned said that the details of this trip to New Orleans were not preserved. However, we do have a poem by Whitman entitled "Sailing the Mississippi at Midnight," a portion of which is quoted here:

> Vast and starless, the pall of heaven
> Laps on the trailing pall below;
> And forward, forward in solemn darkness,
> As if to the sea of the lost we go.
>
> Now draw nigh the edge of the river,
> Weird like creatures suddenly rise;
> Shapes that fade, dissolving outlines
> Baffle the gazer's straining eyes.
>
> . . . .
>
> Steady, helmsman! you guide the immortal;
> Many a wreck is beneath you piled,
> Many a brave yet unwary sailor
> Over these waters has been beguiled.
>
> . . . .
>
> But when there comes a voluptuous languor,
> Soft the sunshine, silent the air,
> Bewitching your craft with safety and sweetness,
> Then, young pilot of life, beware.

In January of 1887 when Whitman was an invalid at Camden he received a letter from New Orleans asking for an account of his stay in that city for publication in *The Picayune*. "We have been informed," the letter stated, "that when you were younger and less famous than now, you were in New Orleans and perhaps have helped on *The Picayune*."

Whitman replied: "I went down to New Orleans in 1848 to work on a daily newspaper, but it was not *The Picayune,* though I saw a good deal of the editors of that paper. But let me indulge my pen in some gossipy recollections of that time and place with extracts from my journal up the Mississippi and across the Great Lakes to the Hudson." Nothing, it is observed, about the trip down the Ohio and Mississippi to New Orleans.

He then went on to speak of the Mexican War and its stirring aftermaths in the country, and of New Orleans as a center of tumult, and as an entrepôt for "everything going and coming." He recalled meeting General Taylor and his staff at the theatre after talking with them the same day, and the "crowds of soldiers, the gay young officers, going or coming.

"One of my choice amusements during my stay in New Orleans," he wrote, "was going down to the old French Market, especially of a Sunday morning. The show was a varied and curious one; among the rest the Indian and negro hucksters with their wives. For there were always fine specimens of Indians, both men and women, young and old. I remember I nearly always on these occasions got a large cup of delicious coffee with a biscuit for my breakfast, from the immense shining copper kettle of a great Creole mulatto woman (I believe she weighed 230 pounds). I never have had such coffee since. About nice drinks, anyhow, my recollection of the 'cobblers' (with strawberries and snow on top of the large tumblers), and also the exquisite wines, and the perfect and mild French brandy, help the regretful reminiscence of my New Orleans experiences of those days. And what splendid and leisurely bar-rooms! Particularly the grand ones of the St. Charles and St. Louis. I used to wander a midday hour or two now and then for amusement on the crowded and bustling levees, on the banks of the river. The diagonally wedg'd-in boats, the stevedores, the piles of cotton and other merchandise, the carts, the mules, negroes, etc., afforded neverending studies and sights

33

to me. I made acquaintances among the captains, boatmen, other characters, and often had long talks with them, sometimes finding a real rough diamond among my chance encounters. Sundays I sometimes went forenoons to the old Catholic Cathedral in the French quarter. I used to walk a good deal in this arrondissement; and I have deeply regretted since that I did not cultivate while I had such a good opportunity the chance of better knowledge of French and Spanish Creole New Orleans people. (I have an idea that there is much and of importance about the Latin race contribution to American nationality in the South and Southwest that will never be put with sympathetic understanding and tact on record.)

"Let me say for better detail that through several months (1848) I work'd on a new daily paper, *The Crescent;* my situation rather a pleasant one. My young brother, Jeff, was with me; and he not only grew very homesick, but the climate of the place, and especially the water, seriously disagreed with him. From this and other reasons (although I was quite happily fix'd) I made no very long stay in the South."

Whitman's writing for *The Crescent* was not only without distinction, it was slovenly and worthless. It must have been his distinguished appearance, and the atmosphere of importance which he was always able to throw about himself, and perhaps the talk in New York of his stories—the exciting story about the school boy and the temperance novel—which deceived the man from New Orleans into believing that he was getting valuable talent in Whitman. But it was not long before the proprietor of *The Crescent* saw what Whitman was. The sleepy air of New Orleans did not quicken Walt's step or increase his laboring energy. He went into the police courts and wrote up the prostitutes who were brought to the dock, but in no vivid or original way. He saw slavery right under his eyes, on the wharves of New Orleans, where later, slave drivers brutally handled the Negro. Whitman was not stirred. Emory Holloway is authority for saying that Whitman, like Emerson, knew that there will always be slavery so long as man is not free within himself. If ever there was a man who lived along in a lethargy, save in the sense that he saw some things, it was Whitman. One night he went to the Terpsichore Ball, and there was introduced to a beautiful woman. He wrote an account of the ball and this espisode for *The Crescent,* "My head began to swim. I saw none but her. A mist surrounded all the others. She turned, I saw her face, radiant with smiles, ecstasy, delight. 'Tis she, I ejaculated." The long sought woman!

Then he was introduced by the man escort of the woman to her, only to find that the man was her husband. So he ended his report with a humorous half-satirical description of his own chagrin. This was the only woman in New Orleans, unless it was a woman whom he mentioned in a poem presently to be noticed. In a city of Spanish and Creole beauties, of license and play, of amorous opportunties, Whitman lived for some months, acting all the while like a peasant boy twelve years old. He wrote no letters about romances, for he had none; he made no diary entries about women. The Creole woman who served him coffee was as near to him as any woman he met. If he had any sexual adventures, however fugitive, no one ever knew anything about it. Whitman for that matter was markedly secretive about any matter that he didn't want known. But it is impossible that Whitman was ever romantically stirred, and that there should be no record of it. Traubel was at his side like a Boswell for several years, and got nothing from him on this subject. Emory Holloway, who searched the Whitman material with great thoroughness, found nothing of moment. Holloway contributed an article to *The Nation* in November, 1920, in which he said that what Whitman's intimacies were between 1841 and 1848 will never be known, that is, between the ages of twenty-two and twenty-nine. Later this writer in his book *Whitman: an Interpretation in Narrative,* wrote that Whitman's love affair in New Orleans was probably with an octoroon; but he gave no facts whatever for that conclusion. Much has been made of Whitman's poem, "Once I Pass'd Through a Populous City." This was not included in the first edition of *Leaves of Grass,* 1855, but appeared in the 1860–'61 edition. In point of fact it proves nothing on the subject of Whitman having a woman in his life in New Orleans; it proves scarcely anything on the subject of a transient affair. The woman mentioned might have been a prostitute, who welcomed Whitman generously from the streets of the city through which he was wandering leisurely and alone. In *Leaves of Grass* the poem reads:

Once I pass'd through a populous city imprinting my brain for
    future use with its shows, architecture, customs, traditions,
Yet now of all that city I remember only a woman I casually met
    who detain'd me for love of me,
Day by day, night by night we were together — all else has long
    since been forgotten by me,
I remember, I say, only that woman who passionately clung to me,
Again we wander, we love, we separate again,
Again she holds me by the hand, I must not go,
I see her close beside me with silent lips sad and tremulous.

This poem expressly records, it is to be observed, that he met the woman casually, that they were together for a time, that she clung to him, and would not have him go; but that he separated himself from her, leaving her in sorrow. All of this could have happened with a prostitute. Why did he leave her if he loved her? At the time he was making money as an editor, he was twenty-nine and without a tie or an obstacle in the world toward making her his wife. Why separate?

Emory Holloway ran this subject down, and evidently saw the original manuscript of this poem, which he quoted in an article in *The Dial* for November, 1920, as follows:

Once I passed through a populous city, imprinting my brain for
    future use with its shows, architecture, customs and traditions,

But now of all that city I remember only the man who wandered
with me there for love of me.

So it was not a woman! Holloway wrote that this poem, both
as originally written and as later published, belonged histori-
cally to the poem, "I Saw in Louisiana a Live-Oak Growing."
That reads so far as pertinent here:

I saw in Louisiana a live-oak growing,
All alone it stood and the moss hung down from the branches
Without any companion it grew there uttering joyous leaves of
    dark green,
And its look, rude, unbending, lusty made me think of myself,
But I wonder'd how it could utter joyous leaves standing alone
    there without its friend near, for I knew I could not,
And I broke off a twig with a certain number of leaves upon it
    and twined around it a little moss,
And brought it away, and I have placed it in sight in my room,
It is not needed to remind me as of my own dear friends,
(For I believe lately I think of little else than of them),
Yet it remains to me a curious token, it makes me think of manly
    love;
For all that, and though the live-oak glistens there in Louisiana
    solitary in a wide flat space,
Uttering joyous leaves all its life without a friend, a lover near,
I know very well I could not.

This too appeared first in the 1860–'61 edition of *Leaves of
Grass* among the *Calamus* poems. In a few years after this,
1868, Whitman made a memorandum unpublished at the time
of Holloway's article in *The Nation,* "depress the adhesive
(manly love) nature." This subject cannot be pursued here
without interrupting the present continuity. It will be taken
up again, and in its place.

Whitman had arrived in New Orleans in February, he left
on his return to New York on May 27. His brother Jeff may
have failed to be acclimatized yet Whitman himself had not
proven the right editor for *The Crescent.* If it was a woman
that he met as he passed through the populous city of New

Orleans he was very well ready to leave her, and never to mention her name, or to write her a line thereafter. Less than twenty years after this he became intimately acquainted with John Burroughs, and later with Traubel. They never had his confidence on this subject. Some of Whitman's biographers gloss this matter over by saying that Whitman's innate delicacy prevented him from speaking of his women. But innate delicacy is not violated by revelations to close friends, especially when made in tenderness.

In *Specimen Days* Whitman put the whole story of his trip to New Orleans and return in ten lines of type. In 1879 Whitman sent to Burroughs a map of the Missouri Pacific through-line on which he had traced his route to and from New Orleans, as well as his itinerary on his journey to the West in 1879. This map was reproduced in *Whitman and Burroughs Comrades,* by Clara Barrus, and was exhibited at the *Whitmania Exhibition* at the New York Public Library in 1925. This map pretty well follows the line of travel given by Whitman in his article to *The New Orleans Picayune* in 1887.

Here again Whitman was vague about dates, and it may be ascribed to the operation of his secretiveness, such as he showed on occasions. "Let me say for better detail," he wrote, "that through several months (1848) I work'd on a new daily paper, *The Crescent*. I made no very long stay in the South. In due time we took passage northward for St. Louis in the *Pride of the West* steamer which left her wharf just at dusk.

"Our voyage up the Mississippi was after the same sort as the voyage, some months before, down it. The shores of this great river are very monotonous and dull—one continuous and rank flat, with the exception of a meagre stretch of bluff about the neighborhood of Natchez, Memphis, etc. Fortunately we had good weather, and not a great crowd of passengers, though the berths were full. The *Pride* jogg'd along pretty well, and put us into St. Louis about noon Saturday."

This would be an interesting detail if he had said what day

of the week it was that the boat left New Orleans. The failure to do so shows Whitman's deficient historical faculty, and even journalistic talent. He went on: "After looking around a little I secured passage on the steamer *Prairie Bird* (to leave late in the afternoon), bound up the Illinois River to La Salle, where we were to take canal for Chicago. During the day I rambled with my brother over a large portion of the town, search'd after a refectory, and after much trouble succeeded in getting some dinner." That is all about St. Louis, at the time the largest city in that part of America. Chicago was than but a town of about 20,000 people.

Whitman continued: "Our *Prairie Bird* started out at dark, and a couple of hours after there was quite a rain and blow, which made them haul in shore and tie fast. We made but thirty miles the whole night. The boat was excessively crowded with passengers, and had withal so much freight that we could hardly turn around. I slept on the floor. The Illinois River is spotted with little villages with big names, Marseilles, Naples, etc.; its banks are low, and the vegetation excessively rank. Peoria some distance up [up from where?] is a pleasant town; I went over the place; the country back is all rich land, for sale cheap. Three or four miles from P., land of the first quality can be bought for $3 or $4 an acre."

As a matter of fact a good deal of the land around Peoria is hilly. One wonders where Whitman had time to explore the farm lands there while the boat was pausing. One wonders, too, why Whitman made no mention of Starved Rock, a picturesque object in the Illinois River north of Peoria, rendered historical by the fate of the Illini Tribe in the days of the Indians. But let us read on:

"Arriving at La Salle Tuesday morning we went on board a canal boat, had a detention by sticking on a mud bar, and then jogg'd along at a slow trot, some seventy of us, on a moderate sized boat. (If the weather hadn't been rather cool, particularly at night, it would have been insufferable.) Illinois is the most splendid agricultural country I ever saw; the land is of surpassing richness; the place par excellence for farmers. We stopt at various points along the canal, some of them pretty villages.

"It was ten o'clock A.M. when we got in Chicago, too late for the steamer; so we went to an excellent public house, the 'American Temperance,' and I spent the time that day and till the next morning looking around Chicago." This is all about Chicago. Harriet Martineau, Margaret Fuller and others left vivid descriptions of the Chicago of those days. They were thrilled with the life and bustle of the growing town. Whitman, evidently, was not impressed with this American phenomenon, the most dramatic of all the sudden rise of cities out of the soil which was prepared by Jefferson.

"At 9 the next forenoon," he continued, "we started on the *Griffith* . . . I was delighted with the appearance of the towns along Wisconsin. At Milwaukee I went on shore and walk'd around the place. They say the country back is beautiful and rich. (It seems to me if we should ever remove from Long Island Wisconsin would be the proper place to come to.) The towns have a remarkable appearance of good living, without any penury or want." Whitman then recorded the matter of a woman falling overboard, and then went on:

"Sunday morning June 11.—We pass'd down Lake Huron yesterday and last night, and between 4 and 5 o'clock this morning we ran on the 'flats' and have been vainly trying, with the aid of a steam tug and a lumbering lighter to get clear again. . . . Night before last we stopt at Mackinaw (the island and town), and I went up to the old fort, one of the oldest stations in the Northwest. We expect to get to Buffalo tomorrow." The boat was finally freed.

"We are off again—expect to reach Detroit before dinner. . . . We did not stop at Detroit." He liked the Canadian shore here. "While I now write we can see a little distance ahead the scene of the battle between Perry's fleet and the British during the last war with England. . . .

"June 12.—We stopt last evening at Cleveland, and though it was dark, I took the opportunity of rambling about the place; went up in the heart of the city and back to what appear'd to be the court house. The streets are unusually wide, and the buildings appear to be substantial and comfortable. We went down through Main Street and found, some distance along, several squares of ground very prettily planted with trees and looking attractive enough. Return'd to the boat by way of the lighthouse on the hill. This morning we are making for Buffalo, being, I imagine, a little more than half across Lake Erie. . . . We arriv'd in Buffalo on Monday evening; spent that night and a portion of next day going round the city exploring. Then got in the cars and went to Niagara; went under the falls—saw the whirlpool and all the other sights. Tuesday night started for Albany; travell'd all night. From the time daylight afforded us a view of the country all seemed very rich and well cultivated. Every few miles were large towns. Wednesday we arriv'd at Albany. Spent the evening in exploring. There was a political meeting (Hunker) at the capital, but pass'd it by. Next morning I started down the Hudson in the *Aida;* arriv'd safely in New York that evening."

So home again at last. This article was made up from notes which Whitman jotted down on this journey. Nothing more colorless, more commonplace than this record of a wonderful trip could be imagined. Dickens' *American Notes* show what can be done with the American scene of the time by a writer who observes, and who can set down what he sees.

Here now was Whitman back in Brooklyn at thirty years of age, without a profession, a printer by trade, a failure as a newspaper man, and out of a job. His father and mother were living in Brooklyn at this time, and with them his four brothers and his younger sister, all unmarried. The youngest brother had been born mentally defective. Walter Whitman, the poet's father, was now sixty years of age, and in bad health, and scarcely able to work at his trade. At this period of Whitman's life not much is at hand to say, for the reason that nothing much happened. In 1849 Whitman had a little print shop in Myrtle Avenue, in the front part of which he sold books. *The Freeman,* which he founded at this time, was edited in these rooms. It was first a weekly and then a daily, in which Whitman began to take up with radical ideas, which later pursued, led him to leave the Democratic Party. *The Freeman* lasted a year.

On September 4, 1848, *The New York Tribune* announced that Whitman was about to start a Barnburner paper. The Barnburners who flourished from 1845 to 1852 were opposed to the Hunkers, the regular body of the Democratic Party, taking issue with it on the matter of the extension of slavery and the banking institutions, both Jeffersonian ideas. These radicals were dubbed Barnburners in allusion to the Dutch farmer who burned down his barn to rid it of rats. So these reckless idealists would destroy the Democratic Party to eradicate slavery and the bank. The paper which *The Tribune* stated Whitman was about to start was abortive. The first issue was destroyed by fire, and there was the end.

But Whitman was very active politically just the same. He was chosen as a delegate to the Buffalo Free Soil Convention, and was on its committee from the Seventh Ward of New York. No doubt the walks and talks with Bryant sustained Whitman's new political feelings, if they needed it. For Bryant was an early and a pronounced opponent to the extension of slavery. Whitman was beginning to write political poems. On March 2, 1850, he published in Bryant's *Evening Post* over the pseudonym of *Paumanok* his "Song for Certain Congressmen," and in April of the same year his "Blood Money." Later, in 1851, he was writing a series of five articles for that paper. It remains here to be said on the subject of politics leading to events, even to war, which profoundly affected Whitman's life and career as a poet, that the Whigs got control of New York State through the Democratic defection caused by the Barnburners, and that in 1848 they elected General Taylor to the presidency. Whitman, however, did not pursue politics in any practical sense; nor did he follow newspaper work steadily as a profession.

It was now that Whitman took up his father's business of building houses and selling them, houses of two or three stories for laboring men. Between the building of houses he loafed down the wild coasts of Long Island, reading Homer and Shakespeare in the presence of the sea. While at work building a house he left in the morning like any other workman, with his dinner bucket, which his adoring mother had carefully filled for him. He came back in the evening to stray over into New York to see the sights of the city. Whitman made money at this business. He had luck in spite of himself. After a time he neglected his business, and by 1854 abandoned it entirely, along with all the money prospects which were ahead of him. He did this with utter gladness, for poetry was now definitely stirring in his blood.

His family did not understand him at all. He was simple, affectionate, but abstracted. His brother George wrote of him that Walt had no idea of money. He lay abed late, he would write a few hours, then go away for the rest of the day. If dinner was at one he would sit down at three. As the table was being set he would roam away, coming back in his own time. At times he would be down in Long Island for weeks. He had given up writing the sentimental stories, the mawkish stuff which he was producing at twenty-five. Already he was pondering the poems that were to go into *Leaves of Grass*.

In 1853 there was a Universal Exposition in New York, and Whitman spent many days looking over the works of art which had been sent to it from Europe, and at the objects of inventive genius. He had a wide wandering eye, which absorbed much, but not everything by any means. He did not have, at least not always at command, the articulate gift of expressing what he had seen, except by way of catalogues. By catalogues he managed to list everything that a given manifestation furnished. In this year of 1853 his father became ill and wanted to return to Huntington, there to die in his native locality. The poet took the old man there.

Much has been written of Whitman's psychology. It is a puzzling subject. Whitman was extremely reticent when he wanted to be. He had a way of chloroforming curiosity about himself by an expressive "Ah," something that his housekeeper at Camden, Mrs. Davis, noted with emphasis. His later egotism, which was monumental, and beyond any reduction by any reproof, opposition or satire, may have taken rise in childhood Narcissism. He grew up knowing that he had a fine body, and he loved his body always. He was admired along the way, and when he published *Leaves of Grass* he began to have the most extravagant devotees, all of which sustained his egotism. As a child and youth he was given to romancing, a faculty that was stimulated likely by Cooper and Scott. This grew into harmless mendacity at times, something to be mentioned in particular later.

There is too much of explanation of Whitman in terms of modern psychology, in Freudianism. One can call his poems of nakedness a survival of youthful exhibitionism. A simpler explanation lies in the influences of his free and barbaric innocent days in the country, by the sea, and in the fact of his own wonderful health and vitality. A human being cannot feel strong and happy without respecting and loving his own body, in which the miraculous forces of life and destiny are lodged.

Whitman's sex life is a more baffling matter, and perhaps every one is entitled to his own analysis of it. He ached with desire, he loved beauty in women, yet the contradiction is that he had nothing to do with them. The love he had for his mother does not explain this anomaly, this antinomy. That love was a profound, but quiet emotion; one that sustained his soul and even conducted him to the celebration of America. For at last the tumult of the time, the new ideas of a growing America, were adjutant to the Whitman mind that had been growing during these years. And with one thing and another, which the succeeding pages will attempt to make clear, Whitman took America for his love and his wife, in somewhat the same way as Vachel Lindsay did later. America absorbed all his emotional strength as an object of adoration, as a spectacle of the "dear love of comrades" achieving happiness for themselves and greatness for their country in a new ideal of enlightenment and brotherhood.

CHAPTER FOUR

EXCEPT for the popular revolution under Jefferson, if Hamiltonism had prevailed in 1800, the United States might have been as neutral in point of national individuality as Canada is, and very much more tinged with English ideas and culture than it became. And it might have produced more poets like Longfellow and the derivative lyricists and sonnet mongers of Knickerbocker New York. There could scarcely have been a Whitman save for the Declaration of Independence and the immense influence of Jefferson.

H. L. Mencken, whose word carries the weight of great authority, stated in his *The American Language,* 4th ed., that the "American in the seventeeth century already showed many of the characteristics that were to set him off from the Englishman later on—his bold and somewhat grotesque imagination, his contempt for dignified authority, his lack of æsthetic sensitiveness, his extravagant humor." It is true, as he wrote, that the Puritan was pushed aside to some extent by the sweaty proletariat, by soldiers and artisans in Boston; while in Virginia the ships came fast from England bearing an influx of ignorance. All this contributed to an American breed, to an American language. But as America has struggled with English ideas and culture, with an ever appearing Anglophilism, and that despite what Jefferson and others since Jefferson did, what would America have been if Hamiltonism had prevailed in 1800 and had sunk its roots deep down into the spiritual soil of the country? For Hamilton had no original ideas, but derived all his philosophy from the feudal and Tory past. His favorite character was Julius Cæsar; not Bacon, Newton and Locke, who were the objects of Jefferson's greatest admiration. How could the American stock of the seventeenth century and later have preserved its character against the political and cultural ramifications of a system of government based on taxation, upon which rested consolidated public credit, on which rested bank stock, and upon that bank notes and industrial stocks? Indeed how has America preserved itself against the considerable supremacy of that Hamiltonian system?

Marshall, in his *Life of Washington,* Vol. II, page 217, wrote that the Hamilton measures "contributed not inconsiderably to the complete organization of those distinct and visible parties, which in their long and dubious conflict for power have since shaken the United States to their center." That was true because Jefferson arose to destroy the Hamilton edifice. By that time the bank, funding, the tariff and other financial schemes had been written into the Constitution—and against its terms. Every one of these things had been copied from the English system. Hamilton and his party had no vision of a new land, a republic, an America. It was Jefferson who saw into the future, for which vision such superficial minds, of Anglophile color, as Theodore Roosevelt, Henry Cabot Lodge, and others like them, have called him a doctrinaire.

These men got their ideas from Hamilton, who wrote to John Jay in 1800 anent the probable election of Jefferson: "You, sir, know in a great degree the anti-federal party; but I fear you do not know them all as well as I do. It is a composition indeed, of very incongruous material; but all tending to mischief—some of them to the overthrow of the government by stripping it of its due energies [*sic*: the energies it had filched by judicial construction of the Constitution], others of them to a revolution after the manner of Bonaparte. I speak from indubitable facts." It was the creation of a capitalistic interest to oppose the agrarian interest that made the party division to which Marshall referred.

Jefferson saw that America offered the unique opportunity to try out the republican system; Hamilton wanted to make the government a copy of that of England. Jefferson originated the expression "the American states"; Hamilton shrank from using the word *republic*. Jefferson wanted to make the people the fount of power; Hamilton wanted the control to be with money. Jefferson traced his blood to Aristotle and Locke; Hamilton was the descendant of Machiavelli and Hobbes. The Declaration of Independence and the *Notes on Virginia* were expressions of the American mind. Hamilton wrote only of finance, and military and political organization to give power to the already strong and prosperous. There was nothing not materialistic in his programs.

Jefferson was concerned with such things as the Ordinance of 1787, with work which should make America different from Europe and an improvement over it. He wanted America a beautiful and intelligent civilization. Hence he spoke for a new political philosophy, for architecture, gardens, education, science, for peace and justice, and for a recapturing of the best in Athenian civilization. To Joel Barlow he wrote in 1806, "I have often wished we could have a philosophical society or academy, so organized that while the central academy should be at the seat of government, its members dispersed over the states, should constitute filiated academies in each state, publish their communications, from which the central academy should select unpublished what should be most choice." He saw that the law of New England was the principles of the Jewish law incorporated with some words of the common law, and like Whitman after him, he detected the anti-American influence of that law. It was the law of Laban and Jacob.

Jefferson was for the American language, for new dictionaries, for words taken into the body of speech—"Dictionaries are but the depositories of words already legitimized by usage," he wrote to John Adams in 1820.

Jefferson advocated equal rights, and the abolition of slavery. He saw that Negroes had the genius to imagine "catches," or tunes on the banjo, even if he did not see that the Negroes would contribute to the realm of music the only distinctively American tone and quality. Finally let Jefferson's First Inaugural be quoted in part to sum his philosophy, so American and so salutary: "Equal and exact justice to all men, of whatever state or persuasion, religious or political; peace, commerce and honest friendship with all nations, entangling alliances with none; the support of the state governments in all their rights, as the most competent administrations for our domestic concerns, and the surest bulwark against anti-republican tendencies. . . . These principles form the bright constellation which has gone before us, and guided our steps through an age of revolution and reformation. The wisdom of our sages and the blood of our heroes have been devoted to their attainment. They should be the creed of our political faith, the text of civic instruction, the touchstone by which to try the services of those we trust; and should we wander from them in moments of error or of alarm, let us hasten to retrace our steps."

Whitman without Jefferson and Jeffersonian Democracy is inconceivable. "These states," said Whitman, "conceal an enormous beauty, which native bards and rhymers manipulating syllables and emotions imported from Europe should justify by their songs, tallying themselves to the immensity of the continent, to the fecundity of its people, to the appetite of a proud race, fluent and free."

Charles A. Beard in his *The Rise of American Civilization,* Vol. I, page 778, well observed that Whitman voiced the democratic spirit, while Lowell, more or less indoctrinated with the Hamilton-Webster political philosophy, and torn by conflicting ideas, took up with current reforms of temporary interest, attacking the Mexican War and the acquisitions which followed it. That is the difference in one particular between Lowell and Whitman. Lowell was not a thoroughgoing Jeffersonian, which is to say he was not a complete liberal, or a mind of great vision.

Laws and constitutions are first the expression of a people, and then they are moulded by the people. Culturally there is the influence of ideas and the written word. Perhaps no one who prepared the way for Whitman did more than Noah Webster (1757–1843). He wrote in his *Dissertations on the English Language* published in 1789: "Besides this a national language is a band of national union. Every engine should be employed to render the people of this country national; to call their attachments home to their own country; and to inspire them with the pride of national character. However they may boast of Independence, and the freedom of their government, yet their opinions are not sufficiently independent; an astonishing respect for the arts and literature of their parent country, and a blind imitation of its manners, are still prevalent among the Americans. Thus an habitual respect for another country, deserved indeed and once laudable, turns their attention from their own interests, and prevents their respecting themselves."

In 1783 Webster brought out his *American Spelling Book,* which had an influence on the American Language which H. L. Mencken called stupendous. It had a vast circulation during the Revolution, and for a hundred years after. By 1889 it had a sale aggregating 62,000,000 copies, according to Mencken, and the *Biographical Dictionary of English Literature* placed its total circulation at 70,000,000 copies. The book had much to do in creating an American speech and in drawing America away from English precedent and practice, just as after the War of 1812 there was conscious effort to do this, especially by such writers as James Fenimore Cooper, who was one of Whitman's early admirations, as we have seen.

At the same time new names for towns and rivers and places

were getting a place in the American vocabulary. In New England there were *Cambridges, Bristols* and *Londons*. But commencing with Indian names, there was *Penobscot,* and as the West was opened up there arose *Mississippi,* first called the Colbert River—*Kalamazoo* and *Chicago,* and thousands of other indigenous names. The word *Mississippi* filled Whitman with delight. "Mississippi," he exclaimed, "the word winds with chutes—it rolls a stream three thousand miles long. Monongahela! It rolls with venison richness upon the palate." Whitman's poetry abounds in American names and words. Whitman wrote an interesting short article entitled "Slang in America," in which he said:

"Slang, profoundly consider'd, is the lawless germinal element, below all words and sentences, and behind all poetry, and proves a certain perennial rankness and protestantism in speech. As the United States inherit by far their most precious possession—the language they talk and write—from the Old World, under and out of its feudal institutes, I will allow myself to borrow a simile even of those forms farthest removed from American Democracy. Considering Language then as some mighty potentate, into the majestic audience-hall of the monarch ever enters a personage like one of Shakespeare's clowns, and takes position there, and plays a part even in the stateliest ceremonies. Such is Slang, or indirection, an attempt of common humanity to escape from bald literalism, and express itself illimitably, which in highest walks produces poets and poems, and doubtless in prehistoric times gave the start to, and perfected, the whole immense tangle of the old mythologies. For, curious as it may appear, it is strictly the same impulse-source, the same thing. Slang, too, is the wholesome fermentation or eructation of those processes eternally active in language, by which froth and specks are thrown up, mostly to pass away; though occasionally to settle and permanently crystallize."

In 1820 in a letter to John Adams, Jefferson wrote concerning neologies: "Dictionaries are but the depositories of words already legitimized by usage. Society is the workshop in which new words are elaborated. When an individual uses a new word, if ill-formed it is rejected in society; if well-formed, and adopted, after due time it is laid up in the depository of dictionaries."

Whitman was, from the first edition of *Leaves of Grass* a champion of new words and American expressions. He even partly invented some words, though not happily. He had at his command Noah Webster's dictionary, which was first published in 1806, and again in a second edition in 1828, and in a third in 1838, at the time when Whitman was in newspaper work, and beginning to write verses. There was little of stock poetical phraseology in Whitman's poetry even from the first. It was so transient, at least, that it need not concern us much. Webster's dictionaries were of immense influence on the development of an indigenous language for America. They, the Webster *American Spelling Book* and a confluence of influences, carried Whitman to his rightful place as one of the moulders of American speech. Once in talking to Traubel he said: *"Leaves of Grass* is only a language experiment—an attempt to give the spirit, the body, the man, new words, new potentialities of speech—an American—range of self-expression. The new world, the new times, the new peoples, the new vistas."

In the 1850's before Whitman wrote *Leaves of Grass,* when after his return from New Orleans he was running *The Freeman,* he seemed compelled to look about for a means of livelihood, and he contemplated the lecture field. It was then that he projected a lecture entitled "The Primer of Words—For American Young Men and Women—For Literats, Orators, Teachers, Musicians, Judges, Presidents, &c." He wrote this lecture out, and a few quotations follow:

"For me," he said, "I see no object, no expression, no animal, no tree, no art, no book, but I see from morning to night, and from night to morning the spiritual—Bodies are all spiritual —all words are spiritual—nothing is more spiritual than words. . . . In a little while in the United States, the English language enriched with contributions from all languages, old and new, will be spoken by a hundred millions of people: perhaps a hundred thousand words ('seventy or eighty thousand words'—Noah Webster, of the English language). . . . The Americans are going to be the most fluent users of words— words follow character—nativity, independence, individuality. . . . I see that the time is nigh when the etiquette of the saloons is to be discharged from that great thing, the renovated English speech in America. . . . These states are rapidly supplying themselves with new words, called up by new occasions, new facts, new politics, new combinations—far plentier additions will be needed, and of course will be supplied. . . . We are to justify our inheritance—we are to pass it on to those who come after us, a thousand years hence: American geography, the plenteousness and variety of the great nation of the Union—the thousands of settlements—the seacoast, the Canadian north, the Mexican south—California and Oregon—the inland seas—the mountains—Arizona—the prairies, the immense rivers. . . . What name a city has— what name a state, river, sea, mountain, wood, prairie has, is no indifferent matter. . . . All aboriginal names sound good. I was asking for something savage and luxuriant, and behold here are aboriginal words: Mississippi! . . . Ohio, Connecticut, Ottawa, Monongahela, all fit. . . . California is sown thick with the names of all the little and big saints. Chase them away and substitute aboriginal names. . . . Among names to be revolutionized: that of the the city of Baltimore. . . . Among the names that stand in need of fresh appropriate names are the great cities of St. Louis, New Orleans, St. Paul. . . . I say we have here now a greater age to celebrate, greater ideas to embody, than anything ever in Greece or Rome— or in the names of Jupiter, Jehovah, Apollo and their myths.

The great proper names used in America must commemorate things belonging to America and dating thence— Because what is America for? To commemorate the old myths and gods? To report the Mediterranean here? or the uses and growths of Europe here? No;—(Na-o-o) but to destroy all those from the purposes of the earth, and to erect a new earth in their place. . . . American writers are to show far more freedom in the use of words— Ten thousand native, idiomatic words are growing, or are today already grown, out of which vast numbers could be used by American writers, with meaning and effect—words that would be welcomed by the orator, being of the national blood—words that would give that taste of identity and locality which is so dear to literature."

In speaking of a dictionary, Whitman said: "The real dictionary will give all the words that exist in use, the bad words as well as any. The Real Grammar will be that which declares itself a nucleus of the spirit of the laws, with liberty to all to carry out the spirit of the laws, even by violating them, if necessary. . . . These States are rapidly supplying themselves with new words, called for by new occasions, new facts, new politics, new combinations. Far plentier additions will be needed, and, of course, will be supplied. . . . Many of the slang words are our best; slang words among fighting men, gamblers, thieves, are powerful words. . . . The appetite of the people of These States, in popular speeches and writings, is for unhemmed latitude, coarseness, directness, live epithets, expletives, words of opprobrium, resistance. This I understand because I have the taste myself as large, as largely, as any one. I have pleasure in the use, on fit occasions, of— traitor, coward, liar, shyster, skulk, doughface, trickster, mean cuss, backslider, thief, impotent, lickspittle. . . . I like limber, lasting, fierce words. I like them applied to myself—and I like them in newspapers, courts, debates, Congress. Do you suppose the liberties and the brawn of These States have to do

only with delicate lady-words? with gloved gentleman words?
Bad Presidents, bad judges, bad clients, bad editors, owners of
slaves, and the long ranks of Northern political suckers (rob-
bers, traitors, suborned), monopolists, infidels, . . . shaved
persons, supplejacks, ecclesiastics, men not fond of women,
women not fond of men, cry down the use of strong, cutting, beautiful, rude words. To the manly instincts of the
People they will be forever welcome."

Very many of Whitman's ideas had before his time been
circulated by Jefferson. For example, Jefferson wrote to Baron
Von Humboldt in 1813 as follows:

"The European nations constitute a separate division of the
globe; their treaties make them part of a distinct system; they
have a set of interests of their own in which it is our business
never to engage ourselves. America has a hemisphere to itself. It must have its separate system of interests, which must
not be subordinated to those of Europe. The insulated state in
which nature has placed the American continent should so
far avail it that no spark of war kindled in the other quarters of the globe should be wafted across the wide oceans
which separate us from them. And it will be so."

And this to Horatio G. Spafford in 1814: "I fear nothing
for our liberty from the assaults of force; but I have seen and
felt much, and fear more from English books, English prejudices, English manners, and the apes, the dupes, and designs
among our professional crafts. When I look around me for
security against these seductions, I find it in the wide un-
sophisticated minds, their independence and their power, if
called on, to crush the Humists (Tories) of our cities, and to
maintain the principles which severed us from England."

To J. Correa De Serra, Jefferson wrote in 1820: "Nothing
is so important as that America shall separate herself from the
systems of Europe, and establish one of her own. Our circumstances, our pursuits, our interests, are distinct; the principles of
our policy should be so also. All entanglements with that quar-

ter of the globe should be avoided if we mean that peace and justice shall be the polar stars of the American societies."

And to Horatio Gates in 1797: "I wish any events could induce us to cease to copy such a model [the British Government] and to assume the dignity of being original."

Such ideas as the earth belonging to the living were taken over from Jefferson by Whitman, by which is meant that Jefferson first entertained them and that they belonged later to Whitman as a Jeffersonian Democrat. Jefferson thus repudiated the land tenures of England:

"The will and the power of man expire with his life, by nature's law. Some societies give it an artificial continuance, for the encouragement of industry; some refuse it, as our aboriginal neighbors, whom we call barbarians. The generations of men may be considered as bodies or corporations. Each generation has the usufruct of the earth during the period of its continuance. When it ceases to exist the usufruct passes on to the succeeding generation, free and unencumbered, and so on, successively, from one generation to another forever." This was written in a letter to John Wayles Eppes in 1813.

Centralization in its injurious effect upon liberty was one of Jefferson's favorite preachments. To Joseph C. Cabell he wrote in 1816: "What has destroyed the liberty and the rights of man in every government which has ever existed under the sun? The generalizing and concentrating of all cares and powers into one body, no matter whether of the autocrats of Russia or France, or of the aristocrats of a Venetian Senate."

When Whitman addressed the states with the admonition to obey little and to resist much he expressed the same idea; even the Jefferson declaration that the roots of liberty needed at times to be refreshed with the blood of patriots and tyrants had Whitman's support. Jefferson's ideas about liberty, about England as the natural enemy of America, natural and inveterate, about the safety for America in preserving its farming interests, about labor, about free trade, were the ideas of Whitman too, for Whitman was a strong supporter of free trade, and of the people as the safest repository of power.

"I am not among those who fear the people," said Jefferson. Certainly Whitman was not either. To Thomas Leiper, Jefferson wrote in 1815: "Not in our day, but at no distant one we may shake a rod over the heads of all, which may make the stoutest of them tremble. But I hope our wisdom will grow with our power, and teach us that the less we use our power the greater it will be."

Whitman looked forward to this time and did all he could to establish his country in a position of enlightened supremacy, in a new leadership. "To save the republic is the first and supreme law," said Jefferson in his autobiography in 1821. Jefferson's free thinking was also Whitman's and both were devoted to Thomas Paine. To establish science in all its branches, and to repel the hue and cry against philosophy by stories of raw head and bloody bones taken from the Bible were equally ardent principles of Jefferson and Whitman. Both repudiated the belief that government, religion, morality and every other science were in the highest state of perfection in the ages of darkest ignorance, and that nothing could be devised more perfect than what was established by former generations of men.

Both of these Americans believed that America was the great hope of liberty in the world, that it was that Atlantis which Shelley celebrated in a chorus of *Hellas,* and that every smaller passion should be postponed to the great object of liberty. Whitman suspected New England and did not trust it to carry forward the American idea. In Jefferson's day New England talked secession from the Union because of its chauvinistic loyalty to England. Jefferson wrote to Doctor William Eustis in 1809 that the conduct of New England in this particular had distressingly impaired future confidence in the Northeast states. "In this as in all other cases," he wrote, "we must do them full justice, and make the fault all their own should the last hope of human liberty be destined to receive its final stab from them."

In Whitman's day the Southern states tried to secede, not through loyalty to England, but to devotion to what it conceived to be American principles. Whitman as a matter of legalism was with the South. But he was for the Union as the best hope of liberty, as Jefferson had been. He could not endure to see the American domain severed. It was an unendurable wound to his imagination, to his hopes of a new culture—a new theme in the world speaking for liberty and the progress of mankind, to have the Union divided.

As to slavery, while Jefferson inveighed against the European governments who kept down the laboring people by hard work, poverty and ignorance, taking from them "as from bees, so much of their earnings, as that unremitting labor shall be necessary to obtain a sufficient surplus to sustain a scanty and miserable life"—so Whitman did not look with favor upon a system which exploited the negro.

As Whitman was born during the administration of Monroe, in the Era of Good Feeling and Jeffersonian achievement, and developed to 1855, when he produced *Leaves of Grass,* through one of the most varied and transforming periods of American life, distinguished by movements and reforms both sane and wild, and by follies and fads, as well as by sound national aspirations, some attention must be paid to these years when Whitman was gathering his genuine powers and finding himself. Politically he became a free-trader and an expansionist. He was born to have faith in humanity and in the future of America, and he retained this faith to the end.

CHAPTER FIVE

POETS and creative thinkers make a nation by ideas and æsthetic leadership, while statesmen are at work upon it with laws and constitutions. Whitman consciously strove to mould America to his dream of greatness and nobility. He was doing this when Webster and Clay were trying to settle the vexing questions which arose over Texas and California. The land, the state lines, the negro problem, were quieted for the time by what these lawmakers and statesmen did. The nation which Whitman was sketching in his imagination at the time must still be created; and no one has arisen to present a better model for the republic of thought and life than he gave us.

Much that Whitman thought and expressed was in the very air of America from 1835 to 1855, the period of his preparation. The improvement of education, the resistance to Europe in music, art, literature, manners, the drama, and poetry; opposition to materialism and the vulgarity of the merchant code with slavery for one of its engines, the abolition of capital punishment, the curse of intemperance, the spiritual education coming from a worship of Nature, for Emerson had published his essay on "Nature" in 1836—these ideas were omnipresent in America. The grandiose talk of orators about the greatness of America took hold of Whitman when he was scarcely more than a boy, and he began to write poems and articles about it, as well as to figure notably at political meetings. From the first the great West enthralled his imagination. There could have been no great West without the Louisiana Purchase under Jefferson, without the treaty of Guadalupe Hidalgo in 1848, which brought to America Texas, New Mexico, California, Nevada, Utah, and Arizona; or without the treaty relating to Oregon in 1846.

This, then, is how the great West stood at the time Whitman was contemplating the country and meditating his poems. It was principally a domain, for when Whitman published *Leaves of Grass* the only states west of the Mississippi were Arkansas, Missouri, Iowa, Louisiana, Texas, and California. Such states as Minnesota and Kansas came into the Union later. What a domain in all of varied and climatic earth; with the mountain ranges of the Appalachian system, the Adirondacks of upper New York, the vast fertile plains of the Mississippi, the great Rocky Mountains and the table lands beyond them, the great rivers and the great lakes, the forests, the gold and silver in the hills, the inexhaustible resources of the land producing nearly everything used by man, and far away the waters of the Pacific!

Whittier might be content to write "The Barefoot Boy" and "Snowbound," Longfellow might choose the American theme of the Indian in "Hiawatha," Lowell might celebrate the "dear land" in a Pindaric ode—Whitman could not rest while trying to put all of America into poetry. He was driven into catalogues, which are a way of presenting to the eye of imagination the content of a vision. Above this, Whitman knew that the Revolution, which he had related to him by eye witnesses, was not a mere strife between England and the Colonies over the matter of tea, or even over the right to set up a new government, but that it was a historical struggle at one of those appointed times in the history of mankind when liberal forces take their stand against a conservative past. He knew that the new day required poetry to express it and to carry it forward. When he returned from New Orleans the country had about twenty-three millions in population; when he published

Leaves of Grass the population was about twenty-seven million. He prophesied an ever-growing land and he wanted to give it song by which to steady and advance its steps. It was this vision of Whitman that made him a great poet; it was not his poetical skill, not artistry, not even his own successful achievement. Over and over again later he said that he merely gave directions. He was never the Homer of America; at best he was our Hesiod, writing *Works and Days* in terms of what America was and meant, and what its rightful destiny was.

The Democratic ferment of Whitman's formative years was unexampled in the history of the world. Invention, the vast West, the ideals of the Revolution, the influence of Jefferson and Jackson—all these were among the thousand contributing forces. The states were multiplying in number, the cities were growing larger and richer. Canals came along to facilitate transportation and to reduce freight rates and thereby increase trade. Railroads were soon built. Men were laboring fourteen hours a day; but there was protest, and a labor union was arising to demand shorter hours and a better educational system.

Freedom of thought and free inquiry which had taken its rise with the Greeks, with Aristotle, and had wound its way to Frederick the Great, to Voltaire, Rousseau and the English deists, was making itself felt against the Bible whose account of creation contradicted the discoveries in geology and the investigations into zoology and anthropology. Science was heading toward Darwin and Huxley, just as the theory of evolution had been in the minds of thinkers since the days of Aristotle and later, of Leonardo. The work of Grotius, Locke, and Jefferson was bearing fruit in these stirring days, when at the same time steam was beginning to come into a mastery and men were hastening across the continent bringing back tales of wonder of the new country.

At this time, too, the Rappites were building a *New Harmony* near Pittsburgh (later Owen established a community town of that name in Indiana), while Karl Marx was European correspondent for Greeley's *Tribune,* to which Whitman was sending contributions, praised and encouraged by its admiring editor. Owen said that man had been a slave to a trinity of monstrous evils which had physically and spiritually tortured the whole race. These were the private ownership of property, the absurd and irrational systems of religion, and the marriage tie, which, he thought, ought to be made without ceremony and ended at the will of those concerned. Women were taking to the lecture platform, thereby shocking the moral community; but the subjects they discussed were still more shocking. They were asking for the abolition of marriage and for the right to vote and to hold office. Over the country there was agitation against imprisonment for debt and against capital punishment. Movements went forward for co-operation and reform in a hundred ways.

Even in Charleston *The Southern Free Press* was advocating no sect, no creed—and had taken on a championship for mechanics and working men. Among grotesque cults and party-formings were spiritualism and the anti-Masonics. These were but a few of the agitations in the air at the period when Whitman was at West Hills and in Brooklyn. It speaks well for the strength and sanity of his mind that none of them carried him away. His opposition to tea, tobacco, coffee, and to all stimulants in excess, was reasonable enough. Many of these radicalisms were shared by men fully as great as Whitman.

When Whitman's eyes at about ten years of age began to observe the earth scene about him, New York was a city of nearly 200,000 people. Sixteen packets plied regularly between that city and Liverpool, four others sailed to Havre. Trade in New York was growing by leaps and bounds and mercantile houses were springing up by the hundreds. Railroads were building in New York and New England and steamboats were plying all the rivers, especially the Hudson, the Ohio and the

Mississippi. It was a busy and colorful spectacle that engaged the rapturous eyes of young Whitman. One begins to see the genesis of his catalogues: the rafts, the traffic, the hammer of the carpenter, the noise of the machine shop.

In the 1840's Broadway was without good pavement, and was poorly lighted by gas. It was lined with Lombard poplars and was the great promenade of the city along which buses rumbled and cabs, hackney coaches, handcarts and phaetons streamed. Luxury was coming to the city too. All day long, up and down Broadway, there were sightseers and shoppers and foreign gazers taking in the new metropolis. Dickens observed this street and described it much better than Whitman did. Dickens saw the women in all colors, particolored silks and with radiant parasols. In that day, too, the bankers and speculators hastened to Wall Street while the lawyers wended their way to Nassau and Pine Streets. There were numberless cafés and restaurants. The streets were full of visitors from city and country going along side by side with newsboys, laborers, loungers, ladies, and dandies. This was Whitman's city, having risen in a few years after the adoption of the Constitution, and after Washington's farewell to his officers at Fraunces' Tavern. It was a city of stir and richness, of ermine-lined cloaks, luxurious furs, expensive feathers, and silk bonnets. It was the beginning of that materialism which Whitman castigated in his poetry and in his vigorous prose.

There were great hotels like the Astor House and fascinating restaurants like Niblo's. Theatres were numerous, such as the Park, the National, the Chatham, the Olympic, and the Franklin. And there was Barnum's Museum. Fine club houses adorned the city including the Kent for the lawyers, the Sketch Club for artists, the Bread and Cheese Club for literary and scientific men, and the Union for the aristocrats.

In this city of New York pigs roamed in the streets, a thing that Dickens described and abhorred. The business and residence sections were noisy with oystermen blowing their horns, and ragmen and old iron men pushing their carts and bawling with jangling bells. It was the day when Fanny Elssler captivated the city, when Ole Bull came to America, and when Poe was wandering about trying to sell his poems and his stories. The country was full of quacks. Mesmerism was flourishing. At Hartford Horace Wells was making his first demonstrations of nitrous oxide as an anæsthetic. Then came Charles T. Jackson with sulphuric ether to deaden pain for pulling teeth and for operations.

By 1824 Irving had published *Bracebridge Hall*, *The Sketch Book*, and *The Tales of a Traveler*. The *Life of Columbus* came out in 1828. By this time Marshall had published his *Life of Washington* and Jared Sparks was writing his history. *The Pilot* appeared in 1824, *Lionel Lincoln* and *The Leaguer of Boston* in 1825. *The Mohicans* came out in 1827, *The Red Rover* in 1828 and *The Wept of Wish-ton Wish* in 1829. These were ready for the growing Whitman when he began to read at sixteen. The *Quarterly Review* said that America could produce nothing of moment; yet Cooper was winning praise in England. Bryant in 1821 brought out his poems in a small volume of forty-four pages which contained "Thanatopsis," "The Yellow Violet" and "The Water Fowl." In five years this book sold only 270 copies and brought Bryant $15 profit. Hawthorne published *Twice Told Tales* in 1837 and *Mosses from an Old Manse* in 1846. Longfellow came along with *Voices of the Night* in 1838, Whittier with *Voices of Freedom* in 1836, and Lowell with *Poems* in 1848. At Craigenputtock, Carlyle, who exercised a very considerable influence on Whitman, was publishing *Sartor Resartus* (1831) and a little later was contemplating *The French Revolution*.

By 1832 transatlantic passage by steam became common, though that method had lapsed in 1819 when the *Savannah* had crossed the ocean with only measurable success. Junius Smith, an American living in London, was annoyed by the fifty-four days he spent in crossing from London to New York in 1832. He believed that the time could be reduced to fifteen days and he set about to organize a company to operate ocean steamships. By 1850, five years before *Leaves of Grass* was published, four steamships, the *Atlantic, Pacific, Baltic* and *Arctic,* were sailing from the New World to the Old. By 1844 the telegraph was a success, and in that year flashed the nomination of Henry Clay to the presidency from Baltimore to Washington.

Meanwhile there was the Free Soil Movement, the Union was beginning to be threatened, the gold craze of California took the country; and Mormonism and a thousand other American phenomena manifested themselves. All this was substance for *Leaves of Grass* when poetically distilled. During this time new magazines and publishing houses were coming into being under the influence of changed social conditions and as the result of better technique in printing. New York, which had about 30,000 people when Washington was President, had grown to half a million, and Chicago was pushing itself toward a small metropolis. It is difficult to overestimate the effect of Jackson and his leadership toward a powerful and emancipated America, obliterating as it did the Toryism of Hamilton and the compromising influence of the Old World under the historic meaninglessness of John Quincy Adams's Presidency. New England, clerical hierarchy, aristocracy, city finance, the imitation of England and monarchical standards, all received a set-back when Jackson led farmers, mechanics, and the populares to an assertion of the law against monopoly and the banks.

The period of Jackson's administrations and up to the middle fifties, when the safety of the Union became an absorbing occupation, was one, as Beard pointed out in his *Rise of American Civilization,* of lectures, public schools, circuses, museums, penny newspapers, propaganda of every kind, the agitation for woman suffrage, labor unrest, labor organization, phrenology, and other quackeries. It was, wrote Beard, "an age of shoemakers, carpenters, and sons of poor parsons writing poems and essays, of women erecting colleges, asserting rights and taking part in every phase of the American opera, grand or comic—the martial notes of the agitator mingling with the vibrant tones of the moralist preacher and educator—pioneers in opinion marching forward, sometimes inspired, often ignorant, and usually crotchety, to the conquest of the future America."

Emerson saw all this and he wrote that "madmen and women, men with beards, Dunkers, Muggletonians, Come-outers, Groaners, Agrarians, Seventh-Day Baptists, Quakers, Abolitionists, Unitarians," composed the tumultuous Democracy of America. At the same time he was striking at orthodoxy by resigning his ministry and elevating the culture of his country by *The American Scholar,* all before 1837 in which year he was thirty-four. Whitman contributed practically nothing to the thought of America in the decade between 1840 and 1850. He was surely of slow growth, and without haste or impatience, biding his time while other American writers were producing memorable work.

In *Specimen Days* Whitman said, "To sum up the foregoing from the outset (and of course, far, far more unrecorded) I estimate three leading sources and formative stamps to my own character, now solidified for good or bad, and its subsequent literary and other outgrowth—the maternal nativity-stock brought hither from far-away Netherlands, for one, (doubtless the best)—the subterranean tenacity and central bony structure (Obstinacy, wilfulness) which I get from my paternal English elements, for another—and the combination of my Long Island birthspot, sea-shores, childhood's scenes, absorptions with teeming Brooklyn and New York—with, I suppose, my experiences afterward in the secession outbreak for the third." Whitman seemed to take little interest in Rabelais, and yet Whitman learned much, just by living, that Rabelais had set down in his book on Pantagruel and Gargantua. "Wisdom cannot enter an unkind spirit, and knowledge without conscience is the ruin of the soul," wrote Rabelais. And also, "we

66

establish sovereign good not by taking and receiving, but by giving with both hands. . . . There is only one thing I dislike and that is contempt of the commonplace. [How Whitmanesque!] Abandon yourself to Nature's truths, and let nothing in this world be unknown to you."

Some of Whitman's friends thought that he had a sense of humor. What he included in his work, and what he failed to include, would have been different if his sense of humor had been livelier. When he attempted a jocular vein it was pretty awkward and lifeless. In *Whitman's Complete Works,* Volume IX, may be found a list of the books which he read as preparatory schooling to the writing of poetry. There are here whole pages of authors with merely the dates of their births and deaths—such as Felicia Hemans, H. K. White, Maria Edgeworth, Landor, and such writers as Scott and Carlyle. He recorded that he read Dante in the spring of 1859, and said, "mark the simplicity of Dante, like the Bible's different from the tangled and florid Shakespeare . . . Mark, I say, his economy of words—perhaps no other writer ever equal him." Of Milton he wrote, "the *Paradise Lost* is to us nonsense, anyhow, because it takes themes entirely outside of human cognizance, and treats them as Homer treats his siege . . . it is a poetical fanaticism, with a few great strong features, but not a great poem. . . . Think of a writer going into the creative action of the Deity. . . . The difference between perfect originality and second-hand originality is the difference between the Bible and *Paradise Lost.*"

It is to be gathered from this list that Whitman read Shakespeare, particularly the earliest plays, "Romeo and Juliet," "Richard II," and "Richard III." He jotted down numerous notes about Shakespeare's career. He also read Spenser, spelling the name *Spencer;* also Swedenborg and Swinton's translation of Rousseau's *Confessions.* Also, Corneille, Burns, Heldenbuch's *Book of Heroes,* the *Nibelungenlied,* Keats, notes on Shelley's life, Gower, and Chaucer whom he called as great as Spenser and very easily as human as Shakespeare. Further he listed Heine's poems which he denominated fanciful, ironical and melancholy with a dash of craziness. Also Ben Jonson and the Troubadors. Also Æschylus, Sophocles, Euripides, Aristophanes, Aristotle, Zoroaster, Confucius, Pindar, La Fontaine, Goethe, Schiller, Niebuhr, Von Strehleman, Goldsmith, Schlegel, Richter, Plutarch, Dryden, Lessing and Tasso. Among metaphysicians he included Kant, Fichte, Schelling, and Hegel.

Whitman had the literary mind which catches meanings and contents at a glance; and one feels that he did not go through all these books with studious care, or dwell long over any of them. Of course he read Ossian and the Bible. As he knew no language but his own he had to gather out of translations what he could of Goethe and Schiller and other writers in foreign languages. It seems impossible that he mastered any philosophy, whether Kant's or any other. He knew about Hegel from Gostick's *German Literature,* and likely from magazine articles. Whitman was accustomed to clip out and preserve from magazines and newspapers whatever caught his insatiable interest. Great stacks of these clippings and magazine articles were found in his rooms in the Camden house after his death.

Philosophically Whitman attached himself to Hegel, who was one of the German importations in the 'Forties, along with Kant—all this as the result of Carlyle's books and the transcendentalism of Emerson. Kant had taken up with the agricultural enthusiasms of Rousseau but that did not sway Whitman away from Hegel, for he remarked that Hegel only was fit for America. Also in his *Specimen Days* Whitman wrote: "What is the fusing explanation and tie—what the relation between the (radical democrat) Me, the human identity of understanding, emotions, spirit, &c., on the one side of and with the (conservative) Not Me, the whole of the material objective universe and laws, with what is behind them in time and space on the other side? Immanuel Kant, though he explain'd or partially explain'd, as may be said, the laws of the human understanding, left this question an open one. . . . But G. F. Hegel's fuller statement of the matter probably remains the last best word that has been said upon it up to date. . . . According to Hegel the whole earth (an old nucleus thought, as in the Vedas, and no doubt before, but never hitherto brought so absolutely to the front, fully surcharged with modern scientism and facts and made the sole entrance to each and all), with its infinite variety, the past, the surroundings of today, or what may happen in the future, the contrarieties of material with spiritual and the natural with artificial, are all to the eye of the *ensemblist,* but necessary unfoldings, different steps or links in the endless process of Creative thought, which amid numberless failures and contradictions is held together by central and never broken unity. . . . To politics throughout Hegel applies the like catholic standard and faith. Not any one party, or any one form of government, is absolutely and exclusively true. Truth consists in the just relations of objects to each other. A majority or democracy may rule as outrageously, and do as great harm as an oligarchy or despotism—though far less likely to do so."

Hegel's dialectical process, making change, thesis, antithesis and revolution the law of life, appealed to Whitman's conception of a tumultous democracy working itself into wisdom and good laws with government forces of spiritual evolution operating from within. In *Democratic Vistas* when Whitman was touching upon one of his hobbies, the belief that America would produce poets immenser than any of Jewry, Greece or Rome and greater than Shakespeare, he depicted them as being full of religious fire, luxuriant in the epic talent of Homer, "but consistent with the Hegelian formulas and consistent with modern science."

Whitman has scarcely had his dues as a critic of life and literature, particularly as those things are related to America. His richness, broadness and freshness cannot be too much praised, nor too closely studied. Though neither so learned nor so variously subtle as Emerson, Whitman no less generally and more suggestively belongs to the American scene. His various prefaces are immensely inspiring and packed with valuable thought. Here it is pertinent to quote what he wrote in "A Backward Glance O'er Traveled Roads," the preface to *November Boughs* in 1888, for it bears upon the germination and writing of *Leaves of Grass:*

"After continued personal ambition and effort, as a young fellow, to enter with the rest into competition for the usual rewards, business, political, literary, etc.—to take part in the great melee, both for victory's prize and to do some good —after years of those aims and pursuits, I found myself remaining possessed, at the age of thirty-one to thirty-three, with a special desire and conviction. Or rather, to be quite exact, a desire that had been flitting through my previous life, or hovering on the flanks, mostly indefinite hitherto, had steadily advanced to the front, defined itself, and finally dominated everything else. This was a feeling or ambition to articulate and faithfully express in literary or poetic form, and uncompromising, my own physical, emotional, moral, intellectual, and æsthetic Personality, in the midst of, and tallying, the momentous spirit and facts of its immediate days, and of current America—and to exploit that Personality, identified with place and date, in a far more candid and comprehensive sense than any hitherto poem or book."

Further in the same preface Whitman wrote: "For grounds for *Leaves of Grass,* as a poem, I abandoned the conventional themes, which do not appear in it: none of the stock ornamentation, or choice plots of love or war, or high, exceptional personages of Old-World song; nothing, as I may say, for beauty's sake—no legend, or myth, or romance, nor euphemism, nor rhyme. But the broadest average of humanity and its identities in the now ripening Nineteenth Century, and especially in each of their countless examples and practical occupations in the United States to-day . . .

"Think of the United States to-day—the facts of these thirty-eight or forty empires soldered in one—sixty or seventy millions of equals, with their lives, their passions, their future—these incalculable, modern, American, seething multitudes around us, of which we are inseparable parts! Think in comparison of the petty environage and limited area of the poets of past or present Europe, no matter how great their genius. Think of the absence and ignorance in all cases hitherto, of the multitudinousness, vitality, and the unprecedented stimulants of to-day and here. It almost seems as if a poetry with cosmic and dynamic features of magnitude and limitlessness suitable to the human soul were never possible before. It is certain that a poetry of absolute faith and equality for the use of the democratic masses never was . . .

"And whether my friends claim it for me or not, I know well enough, too, that in respect to pictorial talent, dramatic situations, and especially in verbal melody and all the conventional technique of poetry, not only the divine works that to-day stand ahead in the world's reading, but dozens more, transcend (some of them immeasurably transcend) all I have done, or could do . . .

"Without stopping to qualify the averment, the Old World has had the poems of myths, fictions, feudalism, conquest, caste, dynastic wars, and splendid exceptional characters and affairs, which have been great; but the New World needs the poems of realities and science and of the democratic average and basic equality, which shall be greater. In the center of all, and object of all, stands the Human Being, towards whose heroic and spiritual evolution poems and everything directly or indirectly tend, Old World or New . . .

"While the ambitious thought of my song is to help the forming of a great aggregate Nation, it is, perhaps, altogether through the forming of myriads of fully developed and enclosing individuals. . . . Without yielding an inch the working-man and working-woman were to be in my pages from first to last. The ranges of heroism and loftiness with which Greek and feudal poets endowed their god-like or lordly born characters—indeed prouder and better based and with fuller ranges than those—I was to endow the democratic averages of America. I was to show that we, here and to-day, are eligible to the grandest and the best—more eligible now than any times of old were. I will also want my utterances (I said to myself before beginning) to be in spirit the poems of the morning. (They have been founded and mainly written in the sunny forenoon and early midday of my life.) . . .

"Then still a purpose enclosing all, and over and beneath all. Ever since what might be called thought, or the budding of thought, fairly began in my youthful mind, I had had a desire to attempt some worthy record of that entire faith and acceptance ('to justify the ways of God to man' is Milton's well-known and ambitious phrase) which is the foundation of moral America. I felt it all as positively then in my young days as I do now in my old ones: to formulate a poem whose every thought or fact should directly or indirectly be or connive at an implicit belief in the wisdom, health, mystery, beauty of every process, every concrete object, every human or other existence, not only considered from the point of view of all, but of each . . .

"One main genesis-motive of the *Leaves* was my conviction (just as strong to-day as ever) that the crowning growth of the United States is to be spiritual and heroic. To help start and favor that growth—or even to call attention to it, or the need of it—is the beginning, middle and final purpose of the poems.

"*Leaves of Grass* indeed (I cannot too often reiterate) has mainly been the outcropping of my own emotional and other personal nature—an attempt from first to last, to put *a Person,* a human being (myself, in the latter half of the nineteenth century, in America), freely, fully and truly on record. I could not find any similar personal record in current literature that satisfied me. But it is not on *Leaves of Grass* distinctively as *literature,* or a specimen thereof, that I feel to dwell, or advance claims. No one will get at my verses who insists upon viewing them as literary performance, or attempt at such performance, or as aiming mainly towards art or æstheticism."

For a footnote in this preface, Whitman wrote: "The ferment and germination even of the United States to-day, dating back to, and in my opinion mainly founded on, the Elizabethan age in English history, the age of Francis Bacon and Shakespeare. Indeed when we pursue it, what growth or advent is there that does not date back, back, until lost—perhaps its most tantalizing clues lost—in the receded horizons of the past?"

This is an answer to the critics of Whitman, those like Santayana—who said that Whitman barbarously repelled the past. Once to Traubel Whitman said, "I know of course that the past is probably a main factor in that we are and know and must be."

Whitman prepared himself as an athlete would do for a great contest of strength and endurance, for the task of poetry. Once he set down in writing the resolution to abstain from every weakening and corrupting indulgence the better to clarify and spiritualize his mind. In Volume IX of his *Complete Works* may be found *Notes on the Meaning and Intention of Leaves of Grass.* These show what was in his mind when he wrote the poems. They may usefully be incorporated here to prove how far-sightedly he entered into the business of poetry. There is no parallel to this preparation in any literature of which we have a record.

"Great constituent elements of my poetry," he writes, are "Two, viz.: Materialism—Spirituality—The Intellect, the Esthetic is what is to be the medium of these and to beautify and make serviceable there.

73

"Poem of adherence to the good old cause—the 'good old cause' is that in all its diversities, in all lands, at all times, under all circumstances,—which promulges liberty, justice, the cause of the people as against infidels and tyrants.

"All through writings preserve the equilibrium of the truth that the material world, and all its laws, are as grand and superb as the spiritual world and all its laws. Most writers have disclaimed the physical world and they have not over-estimated the other, or soul, but have under-estimated the corporeal. How shall my eye separate the beauty of the blossoming buckwheat field from the stalks and heads of tangible matter? How shall I know what the life is except as I see it in the flesh? I will not praise one without the other or any more than the other.

"*Tell the American people their faults*—the departments of their character where they are most liable to break down—speak to them with unsparing tongue—carefully systematize beforehand *their faults.*

"Lessons—Clear, alive, luminous,—full of facts, full of physi-ology—acknowledging the democracy, the people—must have an alert character, even in the reading of them. The enclosing theory of 'Lessons' to permeate All The States, answering for all (no foreign imported models), *full of hints, laws and informations,* to make a superb American Intellect and Char-acter in any or all The States. Also the Strength, Command and Luxuriance of Oratory.

"Poet! beware lest your poems are made in the spirit that comes from the study of pictures of things—and not from the spirit that comes from the contact with real things them-selves.

"America (I to myself have said) demands at any rate one modern, native, all-surrounding song with face like hers turned to the future rather than the present or the past. It should nourish with joy the pride and completion of man in himself. What the mother, our continent, in reference to humanity, finally means (where it centres around the prairies, Missouri, Ohio, the great lakes, and branches away toward the Eastern and Western Seas) is *Individuality* strong and superb, for broadest average use, for man and woman: and that most should such a poem in its own form express. Of such a Poem (I have had that dream) let me initiate the attempt; and bravas to him or to her who, coming after me, triumphs.

"The same thoughts and themes—unfulfilled aspirations, the enthusiasms of youth, ideal dreams, the mysteries and failures and broken hopes of life, and then death the common fate of all, and the impenetrable uncertainty of the Afterwards —which Wordsworth treats (in) his *Intimations of Immortality*, Bryant in his *Thanatopsis* and in the *Flood of Years*, and Whittier often in his pieces, W. W. also treats in *Leaves of Grass*. But how different the treatment! Instead of the gloom and hopelessness and spirit of wailing and reproach, or bowed down submission as to some grim destiny, which is the basis and background of those fine poems. Instead of Life and Nature growing stale—instead of Death coming like a blight and end-all" (this was written probably in 1876), "Mine are not the songs of a story teller, or of a voluptuous person, or of an ennuyéed person,—but of an American constructor, looking with friendly eyes upon the earth and men and beholding the vista of the great mission of The States."

And then, much later, he wrote: "In future *Leaves of Grass,* be more severe with the final revision of the poem, nothing will do, not one word or sentence, that is not *perfectly clear*—with positive purpose—harmony with the name, nature, drift of the poem. Also no *ornaments,* especially no *ornamental adjectives,* unless they have come molten hot, and imperiously prove themselves. *No ornamental similes at all—not one: perfect transparent clearness, sanity and health are wanted— that is the divine style*—O if it can be attained."

The greatness of Whitman lies in the fact that in 1855 when he was about thirty-six years old, America having grown after its wonderful boyhood into an amorphous creature, he came into his prophetical power of this country and the prospect before his eyes of what American poetry could and should be. A poet of great vision, never realized in words or poems, may be a poet no less of greater achievement than one who fully expresses the content of his imagination. Whether Whitman by this test is higher in the realm of poetry than Tennyson, than Wordsworth, than Emerson, is something to think about, and if possible to decide—every one for himself. That he is more important to the world than Swinburne or Matthew Arnold is not hard to resolve. To see what was in Whitman's thinking when he wrote *Leaves of Grass* reference may be made to the preface to the edition of that book in 1855. Let us take some sentences from it:

"America does not repel the past, or what the past has produced under its forms, or amid other politics, or the idea of castes, or the old religions—accepts the lesson with calmness —is not impatient because the slough still sticks to opinions and manners and literature, while the life which served its requirements has passed into the new life of forms—perceives that the corpse is slowly borne from the eating and sleeping rooms of the house. . . . The American of all nations at any time upon the earth have probably the fullest poetical nature. The United States themselves are essentially the greatest poem. In the history of the earth hitherto, the largest and most stirring appear tame and orderly to their ampler largeness and stir. Here at last is something in the doings of man that corresponds with the broadcast doings of the day and night. Here is action untied from strings, necessarily blind to particulars and details, magnificently moving in masses. Here the performance disdaining the trivial, unapproached in the tremendous audacity of its crowds and groupings, and the push of its perspective, spreads with crampless and flowing breadth, and showers its prolific and splendid extravagance. . . . Other states indicate themselves in their deputies—but the genius of

the United States is not best or most in its executives or legislatures, not in its ambassadors or authors or colleges or
churches or parlors, nor even in its newspapers or inventors
—but always most in the common people, south, north, west,
east, in all its States, through all its mighty amplitude. The
largeness of the nation, however, were monstrous without a
corresponding largeness and generosity of the spirit of the citi-
zen. Not swarming states, nor streets and steamships, nor prosperous business, nor farms, nor capital, nor learning may
suffice for the ideal man—nor suffice the poet. No reminiscences
may suffice either. A live nation can always cut a deep mark,
and can have the best authority the cheapest—namely from its
soul . . . (As if it were necessary to trot back generation after
generation to the eastern records! As if the beauty and sacred-
ness of the demonstrable must fall behind that of the mythical!
. . . As if the opening of the western continent by discovery,
and what has transpired in North and South America were
less than the small theatre of the antique, or the aimless sleep-
walking of the middle ages!) . . . The American poets are to
enclose old and new, for America is the race of races. The
expression of the American poet is to be transcendent and
new. It is to be indirect and not direct or descriptive or epic.
Its quality goes through these to much more. Let the age
and wars of other nations be chanted, and their eras and
characters be illustrated, and that finish the verse. Not so the
great psalm of the republic. Here the theme is creative, and
has vista.

"The land and sea, the animals, fishes and birds, the sky
of heaven and the orbs, the forests, mountains and rivers are
not small themes—but folks expect of the poet to indicate more
than the beauty and dignity which always attach to dumb real
objects—they expect him to indicate the path between reality
and their souls. . . . The passionate tenacity of hunters,
woodmen, early risers, cultivators of gardens and orchards and
fields, the love of healthy women for the manly form, seafar-

ing persons, drivers of horses, the passion for light and the open air, all is an old varied sign of a residence of the poetic in out-door people. . . . The poetic quality is not marshaled in rhyme or uniformity, or abstract addresses to things, nor in melancholy complaints or good precepts, but is the life of these and much else, and is in the soul. . . . Who troubles himself about his ornaments or fluency is lost. This is what you shall do: Love the earth and sun and the animals, despise riches, give alms to everyone that asks, stand up for the stupid and crazy, devote your income and labor to others, hate tyrants, argue not concerning God, have patience and indulgence toward the people, take off your hat to nothing known or unknown, or to any man or number of men—go freely with powerful uneducated persons, and with the young, and with the mothers of families—re-examine all that you have been told in school or church or any book, and dismiss whatever insults your own soul; and your very flesh shall be a great poem, etc. . . . The known universe has one complete lover, and that is the greatest poet. . . . Without effort, and without exposing in the least how it is done, the greatest poet brings the spirit of any or all events and passions and scenes and persons, some more, some less, to bear on your individual character as you hear or read. . . . The greatest poet does not only dazzle his rays over character and scenes and passions— he finally ascends, and finishes all—he exhibits the pinnacles that no man can tell what they are for. . . . The greatest poet does not moralize or make application of morals—he knows the soul. . . . The art of art, the glory of expression and the sunshine of the light of letters is simplicity. . . . But to speak in literature with the perfect rectitude and insouciance of the movements of animals and the unimpeachableness of the sentiment of trees in the woods and grass by the roadside, is the flawless triumph of art. . . . The great poet has less a marked style, and is more the channel of thoughts and things without increase or diminution, and is the free channel of himself. He swears to his art, I will not be meddlesome, I will not have in my writing any elegance, or effect, or originality, to hang in the way between me and the rest like curtains. . . . The old red blood and stainless gentility of great poets will be proved by their unconstraint. . . . The American bards shall be marked for generosity and affection, and for encouraging competitors. . . . The American bard shall delineate no class of persons, nor one or two out of the strata of interests, nor love most nor trust most, nor the soul most, nor the body most—and not be for the Eastern states more than the Western, or the Northern states more than the Southern. . . . Exact science and its practical movements are no checks on the greatest poet, but always his encouragement and support. . . . In the make of the great masters the idea of political liberty is indispensable. . . . As the attributes of the poets of the kosmos concenter in the real body, and in the pleasure of things, they possess the superiority over all fiction and romance. . . . Of the human form especially, it is so great it must never be made ridiculous. . . . Clean and vigorous children are jetted only in those communites where the models of natural forms are public every day. . . . The great poets are to be known by the absence in them of tricks, and by the justification of perfect personal candor. . . . A great poem is for ages and ages in common, and for all degrees and complexions and all departments and sects, and for a woman as much as a man, and a man as much as a woman. . . . There will soon be no more priests. Their work is done. A new order shall arise, and they shall be the priest of man, and every man shall be his own priest. They shall find their inspiration in real objects today, symptoms of the past and future. They shall not deign to defend immortality or God, or the perfection of things, or liberty, or the exquisite beauty and reality of the soul. They shall arise in America, and be responded to from the remainder of the earth."

There is a good deal of Emerson in this challenging preface, and the tone and the interplexus of Emerson's words and their arrangement seem in it. It may have been that Emerson was as much delighted with it as he was with the poems themselves, and was moved by these fresh inspiring blasts to send Whitman the letter of congratulation which has become a part of the famous notes of the first edition of *Leaves of Grass*.

H. L. Mencken and Emory Holloway have seen the influence of Carlyle in Whitman's prose. It has some of Carlyle's sprawl and ellipsis and inversion and strange effects of brevity, and roughness of the soil of things. Yet it is Whitman's own style after all; and no one in America has written better criticism. Lowell was learned and scholarly, but how he drags with remote allusions and with tedious approaches compared to Whitman! Here is a good place to bring in a sample of Emerson's prose in order to place it side by side with Whitman's, and not only that but to quote him on the subject of the poet; the title of his famous essay:

"Here is the difference betwixt the poet and the mystic, that the last nails a symbol to one sense, which has a true sense for a moment, but soon becomes old and false. For all symbols are fluxional; all language is vehicular and transitive, and is good, as ferries and horses, for conveyance, not as farms and houses are, for homestead. Mysticism consists in the mistake of an accidental and individual symbol for a universal one. The morning-redness happens to be the favourite meteor to the eyes of Jacob Behmen, and comes to stand to him for truth and faith; and, he believes, it should stand for the same realities to every reader. But the first reader prefers as naturally the symbol of a mother and child, or a gardener and his bulb, or a jeweller polishing a gem. Either of these, or of a myriad more, are equally good to the person to whom they are significant. Only they must be held lightly, and be very willingly translated into the equivalent terms which others use. And the mystic must be steadily told,—All that you say is just as true without the tedious use of that symbol as with it. Let us have a little algebra, instead of this trite rhetoric,—universal signs, instead of these village symbols,—and we shall both be gainers."

There remains something to be said about Whitman's verse form for *Leaves of Grass*. Some poets, notably Swinburne, after he had turned against Whitman, scored him for his loose and irregular measures. In point of fact Whitman invented no form. He put into his long lines the rise and fall of his own spiritual diaphragm, just as a poet writing iambic pentameter will be Shakespeare or be Milton or Wordsworth or Browning. So Whitman did with a long free line in his own way what Ossian had done, and the Bible as well, Job, and the Psalms. The dactylic hexameters of Homer differ from each other in music and in the places of stress, yet all are hexameters. Whitman's lines differ from each other in meter and rhythm, yet all are stamped with his spiritual tone. It may be that Whitman knew what Aristotle said about poetry, and how it did not differ from prose and how it did.

But Coleridge, whose work was done, whose life was ended when Whitman was a boy in Brooklyn, wrote about the art of poetry in words which may well be quoted here for their bearing upon the prosody of Whitman. "The writings of Plato and Bishop Taylor," he said, "and the *Theoria Sacra* of Burnet, furnish undeniable proofs that poetry of the highest kind may exist without metre and even without the contradistinguishing objects of a poem. The first chapter of Isaiah (indeed a very large proportion of the whole book) is poetry in the most emphatic sense; yet it would be no less irrational than strange to assert that pleasure and not truth was the immediate object of the prophet, in short, whatever specific import we attach to the word poetry, there will be found involved in it, as a necessary consequence, that a poem of any length neither can be, nor ought to be all poetry. Yet if a harmonious whole is produced, the remaining parts must be preserved in keeping with the poetry; and this can be no other wise effected than by such a studied selection and artificial arrangement as will partake of one, though not a peculiar, property of poetry. And this again can be no other than the property of exciting a more continuous and equal attention than the language of prose aims at, whether colloquial or written. The poet, described in ideal perfection, brings the whole soul of man into activity, with the subordination of its faculties to each other, according to their relative worth and dignity. He diffuses a tone and spirit of unity, that blends, and (as it were) fuses, each into each, and by that synthetic and magical power, to which we have exclusively appropriated the name of imagination. This power first put in action by the will and understanding, and retained under their irremissive, though gentle and unnoticed, control (*laxis effertur habenis*) reveals itself in the balance or reconciliation of opposite or discordant qualities: of sameness with difference; of the general with the concrete; the idea with the image; the individual with the representative; the sense of novelty and freshness with old and familiar objects; a more than usual state of emotion, with more than usual order; judgment ever awake and steady self-possession, with enthusiasm and feeling profound or vehement; and while it blends and harmonizes the natural with the artificial, still subordinates art to nature; the manner to the matter; and our admiration of the poet to our sympathy with the poetry."

As already said a definite spiritual change came over Whitman in his early thirties. His friend, Doctor Richard Maurice Bucke, asserted that Whitman achieved cosmic consciousness at about that time. Bucke was a medical superintendent of the asylum for the insane at London, Canada; and becoming interested in Whitman went to Camden to see him in 1877. From that time to the last he was one of Whitman's devoted friends and champions. In 1901 Bucke published his book entitled *Cosmic Consciousness, A Study in the Evolution of the Human Mind*. This book ran through three editions by 1912, and was published in a corrected edition and entirely reset in 1923; there was a fifth edition in 1926. As Bucke studied Whitman at first hand and with reference to this matter of a rebirth his words have weight and interest.

CHAPTER SIX

It is common enough for men of genius to feel an almost sudden accession of power and understanding at some definite time of life. Shelley described the experience in his "Hymn to Intellectual Beauty," when the awful shadow of some unseen power was cast upon him. He wrote this poem when he was twenty-four years old; but he declared that he was a boy when the shadow fell upon him. Then he "shrieked and clasped his hands in ecstasy." Wordsworth was thirty-two when he wrote his ode on the intimations of immortality; though the strophe beginning, "our birth is but a sleep and a forgetting" was composed later at thirty-six or thirty-eight. In this poem we have the lines:

> Not for these I raise
> The song of thanks and praise;
> But for those obstinate questionings
> Of sense and outward things,
> Falling from us, vanishings;
> Blank misgivings of a creature
> Moving about us in worlds not realized,
> High instincts before which our mortal nature
> Did tremble like a guilty thing surprised.

Now Whitman was about thirty-four when he went through a similar psychical stage, call it a new vision, the full exuberant feeling of mature power, or cosmic consciousness, as one may please. Bucke in his strange book thus described cosmic consciousness: "Cosmic consciousness is a third form which is as far above self-consciousness as that is above simple consciousness. With this form, of course, both simple and self-consciousness persist (as simple consciousness persists when self-consciousness is acquired) but added to them is the new faculty so often named and to be named in this volume. The prime characteristic of the cosmic consciousness is, as its name implies, a consciousness of the cosmos, that is, of the life and order of the universe."

Edward Carpenter, who saw Whitman in 1877, and again in 1884, and who studied him, and entered into his heart, even so much that he wrote *Towards Democracy*—poems in the Whitman manner, and of the Whitman spirituality—accepted Bucke's theory of cosmic consciousness and detailed the evidence that he saw that Whitman reached that state. He affirmed that the subjective light appeared strongly to Whitman; that Whitman's moral elevation and intellectual illumination were clear and extreme, and stood out clearly to those who knew Whitman before and after the coming on of the cosmic sense. He said that in no other man who ever lived was the sense of eternal life so absolute, and the fear of death so absent, something that in both sickness and health were perfectly evident.

He further affirmed that Whitman had no sense of sin, though he realized that he was immeasurably below the ideal which he set before himself, toward which to work to reach the perfection morally and intellectually for which he strove. Whitman realized quite suddenly his own greatness through the change which came over him. Carpenter averred that the change from the self-conscious man into the man of cosmic consciousness was instantaneous, and came at a certain hour of a certain day; and that it occurred at the characteristic age and at the characteristic time of the year. Having looked upon Whitman, Carpenter declared that the cosmic conscious state was seen and noted by himself as it was by others, by those who testified to Whitman's serenity, his philosophical peace, his conviction of the good order of the world. This state of mind or evolution in the development of human vision may also be called that out of which comes a philosophical conception of nature, a subject treated with great scholarship and richness by Joseph Warren Beach in his *The Concept of Nature in Nineteenth Century English Poetry.*

In this book Beach discusses such illuminants as Wordsworth, Shelley, Goethe, Coleridge, Emerson; and of Whitman he wrote, "in his interpretation of nature he stands at the peak of transcendentalism." He referred to the influence which Emerson exercised on Whitman by such essays as "Self-Reliance" and said, "Behind all of Whitman's poetic enthusiasm lies the implicit faith in immortality." As others have noted, Beach mentioned Whitman's unfailing confidence in human nature, in men, and his calm optimism about the course of the world and man's life upon it.

Bucke's book on *Cosmic Consciousness* is a fascinating performance, whatever stock may be taken in its mysticism. It shows scholarship, too. There are 208 items of books and authors quoted to buttress his thesis. Poetry, science, history, psychology, sociology, theology, religion, and the makers of religion, are all marshalled to the aid of his exposition. About Whitman he is quite definite as to the age at which Whitman achieved illumination. He said that Whitman was thirty-four and, that his much later "Prayer of Columbus" is an expression of the experience. His list of men who reached cosmic consciousness, and those who were of lesser illumination, imperfect or doubtful, will challenge the analysis of many. Those who really reached this state, according to Bucke's list, were Buddha, Jesus, Paul, Plotinus, Mohammed, Dante, Bartolmé Las Casas, John Yepes, Francis Bacon, Jacob Behmen, William Blake, Honore de Balzac, Walt Whitman and Edward Carpenter. Among the lesser, doubtful or imperfect instances were Socrates, Pascal, Spinoza, Swedenborg, Wordsworth, Emerson, Tennyson, Thoreau and Traubel.

Whitman's walks along the shore and through the woods of

Long Island have already been recorded, and his reading of Homer and Shakespeare under the full pour of the sun and within sound of the sea. Later Whitman as a poet of nature will be treated. Whitman was about fifty-eight years of age when Bucke first saw him, and he wrote of him as follows on the subject of Whitman's love of nature:

"His favorite occupation seemed to be strolling or sauntering about outdoors by himself, looking at the grass, the trees, the flowers, the vistas of light, the varying aspects of the sky, and listening to the birds, the crickets, the tree-frogs, the wind in the trees, and all the hundreds of natural sounds. It was evident that these things gave him a feeling of pleasure far beyond what they give to ordinary people. Until I knew the man it had not occurred to me that any one could derive so much absolute happiness and ample fulfilment from these things as he evidently did. He himself never spoke of all this pleasure. I dare say he hardly thought of it, but any one who watched him could see plainly that in his case it was real and deep."

Along the way reference has been made to certain poems written and published by Whitman before he began to produce *Leaves of Grass.* There was "Blood Money" which appeared in *The New York Tribune* on March 22, 1850. Soon after this Greeley spoke in a lecture of "Walt Whitman's rare poetic genius." Also there was "Wounded in the House of His Friends," which has been quoted. On June 21, 1850, Whitman published "Resurgemus" in *The New York Tribune,* and signed it *Walter Whitman.* This poem now appears in Whitman's works as "Europe, the 72nd and 73d Year of these States." "New Year's Day 1848" was written that year in an album and was not in print until 1892, when it appeared in *The New York Home Journal.* "Isle of La Belle Riviere" was written on Blennerhasset Island in 1848, but was not published until it appeared in *The Cincinnati Post* in April of 1892. When Whitman was twenty he wrote a love poem which will be considered in relation to Whitman's love life. It may be said here that this poem has no merit, and gave no promise of what he became at last. Moreover, none of these poems has any distinction whatever, though they show that when Whitman was under thirty he had taken up with free measures.

It is said that Whitman wrote *Leaves of Grass* several times, destroying his first drafts. However this be it can be asserted that he revised and rewrote the book before he published it in 1855. How slow he was toward measurably finding himself may be determined by looking at the state of American literature at this time. Longfellow was forty-eight and had published the "Psalm of Life," "Excelsior," *Hiawatha, Evangeline,* and other works. Whittier was Longfellow's age and had published *Voices of Freedom* and *Songs of Labor.* Lowell was the same age as Whitman and had published *A Fable for Critics, The Biglow Papers,* and the "Vision of Sir Launfal." Emerson was fifty-two and had given the world his priceless essays and many poems. Hawthorne was fifty-one and had practically done his work. Thoreau was forty and had become something of a name for his *A Week on the Concord and Merrimack Rivers,* and *Walden.* Poe had been dead six years. Bryant was sixty-one and was running out—soon to embark upon the translation of Homer, an occupation that often engages poets who can no longer create. In England Tennyson, Browning and Arnold had done much of their best work.

The first edition of *Leaves of Grass* was a thin quarto paged I–XII for the preface already considered, and 13–95 for the poems. It was bound in leather ornamented with flowers and with the title *Leaves of Grass,* Brooklyn, New York. No name of the author was given except in the copyright certificate, and in a line in the body of the work, where the words occur, "Walt Whitman, an American, one of the roughs, a kosmos." There was a steel engraving of Whitman at thirty-six for a frontispiece. Eight hundred copies of this book were printed.

The book contained the following twelve poems: "Poem of Walt Whitman, an American," which later appeared under the

88

title of "Song of Myself"; "Poem of the Daily Work of the Workmen and Workwomen of These States," later entitled "A Song For Occupations"; "Burial Poem," later entitled "To Think of Time"; "Night Poem," afterwards called "The Sleepers"; "Poem of the Body" ("I Sing the Body Electric"); "Poem of Faces" ("Faces"); "Poem of the Poet" ("Song of the Answerer"); "Poem of the Dead Young Men of Europe, The 72nd and 73d Year of These States" ("Europe"); "Poem of Apparitions in Boston the 73d Year of These States" ("A Boston Ballad"); "Poem of the Child that Went Forth and Always Goes Forth, Forever and Forever" ("There was a Child Went Forth"); "Lesson Poem" ("Who Learns My Lesson Complete"); "Poem of a Few Greatnesses," called later "Great Are the Myths."

It is not wonderful that the America of that time was shocked to stupefaction by these revolutionary poems so full of strange and forthright words. In "Poem of Walt Whitman, an American," he came out with such celebrations as this:

I mind how once we lay such a transparent summer morning,
How you settled your head athwart my hips and gently turn'd
    over upon me,
And parted the shirt of my bosom, and plunged your tongue to my
    bare stript heart.

What was the gentle Whittier to think of that, and cynical New York? Or what of the egotism that could spread forth as interesting to the world:

    What is commonest, cheapest, nearest, easiest is me?

Or the revelation:

The old husband sleeps by his wife, and the young husband sleeps
    by his wife?

And the modesty of:

These are really the thoughts of men in all ages and lands, they
    are not original with me.

Here was a Browningesque declaration taken out of the Mesmerism, reforms, radicalisms and stir of the times:

I also say it is good to fall, battles are lost in the same spirit in
which they are won.

But then there was the great beauty of the strophe:

Smile O voluptuous cool-breath'd earth!
Earth of the slumbering and liquid trees!
Earth of departed sunset — earth of the mountains misty-topt!
Earth of the vitreous pour of the full moon, just tinged with blue.

And the bravado, "Hurrah for Positive Science," and this manifesto about himself:

Walt Whitman, a kosmos of Manhattan the son,
Turbulent, fleshy, sensual, eating, drinking and breeding.

. . . .

I speak the pass-word primeval, I give the sign of democracy,
By God! I will accept nothing which all cannot have their counterpart of on the same terms.

Imagine Longfellow reading these words:

Copulation is no more rank to me than death is.
I believe in the flesh and the appetites,

Side by side with this:

Divine I am inside and out, and I make holy whatever I touch or
am touch'd from,
The scent of these arm-pits aroma finer than prayer
This head more than churches, bibles, and all the creeds,

A sort of summation of the Unitarian, Emersonian protests and enlargements of the day; while this is scarcely so:

Unbuttoning my clothes, holding me by the bare waist,

Which is pure vulgarity and shows neither courage nor genius to utter.

Then there are the Emersonian lines in which a blade of

grass is made as important as the journey of the stars, and the apostrophe to animals which do not "sweat and whine about their condition . . . not one is respectable or unhappy over the whole earth." The poem delves into nature with such descriptions as the rattlesnake lying with its "flabby length on a rock," and the "tough pimples" of the alligator, the fin of the shark like a "black chip out of the water." Geese "nip their food with short jerks," there is the "crawling spread of buffaloes" and the swan "curving and winding" its neck. His eyes wander over the field of living things,

I turn the bridegroom out of bed and stay with the bride myself,
I tighten her all night to my thighs and hips.

Whitman's genius for entering into every human fate is exhibited in this poem. He sees the crushed fireman, and suffers with him all night. And in this poem he referred to Old Cassabone, his distant relative, who fared the sea,

Not a cholera patient lies at the last gasp but I also lie at the last
    gasp.

He is stunned by all that his imagination sees. "Enough! Enough! Enough! Somehow I have been stunn'd, Stand back."

On women fit for conception I start bigger and nimbler babes,
This day I am jetting the stuff of far more arrogant republics.

He takes the exact dimensions of Jehovah, and all the gods, for what they are worth "and not a cent more. . . . Not objecting to special revelations, considering a curl of smoke or a hair on the back of my hand just as curious as any revelation. . . . What is reason? and what is love? and what is life?" He could not fail the "young man who died and was buried . . . nor him in the poor house tubercled by rum and the bad disorder. My lovers suffocate me. . . . I tramp a perpetual journey. . . . I have no chair, no church, no philosophy. . . . He most honours my style who learns under it to destroy the teacher. . . . I have said that the soul is not more than the body, and nothing, not God is greater to one than one's self is.

And I say to mankind 'Be not curious about God . . . I hear and behold God in every object, yet understand God not in the least.' . . . And as to you, Life, I reckon you are the leavings of many deaths, no doubt I have died myself ten thousand times before."

So, as Emerson said of the book, we have the "Bhagavad Gita and the *New York Herald* combined," and all the solipsism, errant spirituality, transcendentalism, Emersonism, socialism, and the stir of America of that day of 1855.

In the "Poem of the Daily Work of the Workmen and Workwomen of These States," later called "A Song for Occupations," Whitman sang of the labor of engines, the trades and the labor of the fields. Therein, he declared, he found the eternal meanings:

If you stand at work in a shop, I stand as nigh as the highest in
    the same shop.

On the subject of soul equality:

(Because you are greasy or pimpled, or were once drunk, or a thief,
Or that you are diseas'd, or rheumatic, or a prostitute,
Or from frivolity or impotence, or that you are no scholar and never
    saw your name in print,
Do you give in that you are any less immortal?

As to the soul:

You may read the President's message and read nothing about it
    there,

or in prices current, or stock accounts. The purport of us here is not in a "bon mot or reconnaisance." Whitman's French was a delirious joke. Amid so much fierce Americanism and championship of a new order and a new poetry, with no backward glances to Europe, he kept larding his lines with French words, and such as were shopworn and to be found in any list of foreign words and phrases. Yes, we are reminded in this poem that the President is in "the White House for you, you are not here for him." The people exurge doctrines, sculptures, and the "sweet romanza" of the baritone singer. In this poem we have a catalogue of forty-three lines which runs from oil-works, through stone-cutting, cotton-baling, calking, leather-dressing, butchering, raising hogs, making flour to railroading. These are the occupations of America "the hourly routine of your own or any man's life." Why not for brevity's sake merely say "the routine of all." This "any man's life," as well as "or anywhere" after enumerating all places runs the line into a kind of laughable weakness and flatness. There is another but briefer catalogue in this poem. It utters the profound doctrines that when the psalm sings instead of the singer, and the minted gold smiles like the watchman's daughter and so on, "I intend to reach them my hand, and make as much of them as I do of men and women like you."

"Poem of the Body" in this edition appeared later as "I Sing the Body Electric." "The love of the body of man or woman balks account," he writes, and then resorts to long catalogues again, minute descriptions of laborers, wrestlers, firemen and swimmers. He enters into their bodies and participates in their activities. Such multiform dramatizations! "To be surrounded by beautiful, curious, breathing, laughing flesh is enough. . . . There is something in staying close to men and women and looking on them, and in the contact and odour of them that pleases the soul well." The female form exhales a divine nimbus. He is drawn by its breath as if he were a helpless vapour:

Hair, bosom, hips, bend of legs, negligent falling hands all diffused, mine too diffused,
Ebb stung by the flow and flow stung by the ebb, love-flesh swelling and deliciously aching,
Limitless limpid jets of love hot and enormous, quivering jelly of love, white blow and delirious juice,
Bridegroom night of love working surely and softly into the prostrate dawn,
Undulating into the willing and yielding day,
Lost in the cleave of the clasping sweet-flesh'd day.

93

Then he describes the body of a man and a woman at auction:

> Have you ever loved the body of a woman?
> Have you ever loved the body of a man?

In stanza nine he goes into human anatomy naming every part of the body. As to man, there are "hips, hip-sockets, hip-strength, inward and outward round, man-balls, man-root." As to the woman there are the "womb, the teats, nipples, breast milk, tears, laughter, weeping, love-looks, love-perturbations and risings.

> O I say these are not the parts and poems of the body only, but of
>   the soul,
> O I say now these are the soul.

It is not a matter of lawful right to use such coarse and ugly words as Whitman did in this poem; it is a matter of taste and æsthetics. Even today with a much more liberal attitude toward frankness in writing Whitman would have difficulties in his way; but they would be rather those of laughter than of censorship.

The "Poem of the Poet" in this edition of *Leaves of Grass* appeared in the 1856 edition as "Poem of the Singers and of the Words of Poems." In the Everyman edition of *Leaves of Grass,* for which Traubel wrote the preface, published in 1912, the poem appears under the title of "Song of the Answerer." Again we encounter the word *romanza,* and Whitman's invention *philosophs,* which never became current. The answerer is the poet,

> The singers are welcom'd, understood, appear often enough, but
>   rare has the day been, likewise the spot of the birth of the
>   maker of poems, the Answerer.

If the quality of a poem can be tested by turning it into prose, as Goethe said, the quality of much of this poem can be manifested by changing its formal appearance in type from poetry to prose. The bathos and the absurdity of line upon line stir the wells of laughter. "The Answerer" meets the President and upon that impressive occasion is not abashed.

He says indifferently and alike, "How are you friend?"

Not only does he walk into the halls of Congress, all in perfect ease, but speaks to congressmen, who nudge each other and say "here is our equal appearing."

The names of the singers from century to century are "eye singer, ear singer, head singer, sweet singer, night singer, parlour singer, love singer, weird singer, or something else"— like "or anyone" already noted. Whitman may never have read Rabelais, but this listing of singers sounds very much like Rabelais' pages on pages of adjectives for the cod-piece.

"Poem of Apparitions in Boston in the 73d Year of These States" finally became "A Boston Ballad" (1854). It celebrated the imagined escapade of digging up the body of George III, and bringing it to America in a clipper ship, with the royal crown on top of the skull. The crown is thus come to its own.

Stick your hands in your pockets, Jonathan — you are a made man
    from this day,
You are mighty cute — and here is one of your bargains.

Whitman had not read Juvenal to much advantage.

This was the first book, produced at thirty-six years of age, of Whitman who had been silent and the better for being so, during the years when his contemporaries were doing important work. Longfellow sang "Life is real, life is earnest." Whitman very emphatically made it real and realistic by these poems. The critical reception given them was by no means encouraging to the author. *The New York Criterion* called these poems "muck." The London critics said, "Walter Whitman is as unacquainted with art as a hog with mathematics." *The Boston Intelligencer* shouted "bombast, vulgarity and nonsense." *The Christian Examiner* accused Whitman of "impious libidinousness." Reverend Rufus W. Griswold, who had dealt

unfortunately with Poe, wrote a savage attack on Whitman. In
The Momus, a comic paper in America, appeared these lines:

> Walt Whitman well names his obscene productions
> Where he riots in filth, on indecency feasts,
> For 'tis plainly the simplest of simple deductions
> That such "Leaves of Grass" can but satisfy beasts.
> Humanity shrinks from such pestilent reekings
> As rise, rotten and foul, from each word, line and page,
> Of the foulness within him the nastiest leakings,
> Which stamp him the dirtiest beast of the age.

Wendell Phillips said that *Leaves of Grass* contained every
leaf except the fig leaf. Bryant was cold and distant, according to Whitman, after this book appeared. And Emerson, who
had hailed the book and its author as being upon the thresh-
old of a great career, spoke of its inventories and later drew
away from Whitman. In 1874 when he brought out his
Parnassus, an anthology of poetry, he left Whitman out completely, though including such poets as H. H. Willis, Timrod,
George Lunt, Julia C. R. Dorr, Channing, Jones Very, Charles
Sprague, Stedman, Lucy Larcom; and of course, the popular
poets of the day like Longfellow, Bryant, Whittier and Lowell.
Burroughs and the devoted coterie around Whitman buzzed
about this. Burroughs said that Whitman could afford to
ignore Emerson but that Emerson could not afford to ignore
Whitman. Emerson had tried to persuade Whitman to cut
out some of his ugly words; but Whitman stood fast. His
colossal egotism, his active narcism, not only held him to his
original course, but one feels that Whitman rather enjoyed the
publicity which his scandalous stuff brought to him.

Meanwhile Whitman won the regard of young men like
Stedman and Taylor; the former remained critically faithful
to the end—not so Taylor. Thus had phrenology, mesmerism,
table-rapping, religious revivals, skepticism, invention, steam,
telegraphs, the science of life, free love, and all that characterized those times, produced a book. The charge that could

most effectively be made against Whitman in 1855 was that he was sexual. Today he would be criticised for vulgarity and needless vulgarity. Breasts is a more beautiful word than teats. The smell of armpits could possibly have a more beautiful rendering. As to the catalogues, they are too frequently strung upon no significant idea. Once Whitman was after the names of all the insects intending to interweave them upon some thread of thought. His mind seemed to work restlessly to get the whole content of a given subject into a list, and to miss nothing. Whitman's catalogues run riotously and much of the time come to little when set down.

Whitman was not feazed, but rather encouraged to go on, by the reception given this, his first book. He went on writing. In 1856 he brought out the second edition of *Leaves of Grass,* a book of 380 pages. It was a sixteen duodecimo with the title printed in gilt on the back: *Leaves of Grass,* and a quotation from Emerson's letter, "I greet you at the beginning of a great career." Figures of leaves adorned the cover. A picture of Whitman, the same one that appeared in the 1855 book, was the frontispiece. The copyright was printed as being in the name of *Walt Whitman.* The place of publication was given as Brooklyn, New York. There was an index and the poems were numbered. There were twenty new poems. In an appendix, called "Leaves-Droppings," Emerson's letter with its date of July 21, 1855, was included. Also Whitman's letter to Emerson dated in August, 1856. This appendix contained further the opinions on the first book (favorable) of the American and English Press. The publisher was named as Fowler and Wells.

The twenty new poems were as follows: "Poems of Women" ("Unfolded out of the Folds"), "Poems of Salutation" ("Salut au Monde"), "Broad-Axe Poem" ("Song of the Broad-Axe"), "Poem of Many in One" ("By Blue Ontario's Shore"), "Poem of Wonder at the Resurrection of the Wheat" ("This Compost"), "Poem of You Whoever You Are" ("To You"), "Sun-down

Poem" ("Crossing Brooklyn Ferry"), "Poem of the Road" ("Song of the Open Road"), "Poem of Procreation" ("A Woman Waits for Me"), "Clef Poem" ("On the Beach at Night Alone"), "Poem of the Heart of the Son of Manhattan Island" ("Excelsior"), "Poem of the Singers and of the World's Poems" (being the second strophe of "The Answerer"), "Faith Poem" ("Assurances"), "Liberty Poem for Asia, Africa, Europe, America, Australia, Cuba, and the Archipelagoes of the Sea" ("To a Foiled European Revolutionaire"), "Poem of Remembrances for a Girl or Boy of these States" (not in the last editions of *Leaves of Grass*), "Poem of Perfect Miracles" ("Miracles"), "Bunch Poem" ("Spontaneous Me"), "Poem of the Propositions of Nakedness" ("Respondez," also not in the last editions), "Poem of the Sayers of the Words of the Earth" ("Song of the Rolling Earth").

Whitman was not always happy in his invention of titles, in fact, was more often awkward than otherwise. In this edition the preface of the 1855 book was omitted, though some sentences from it were used in certain of the poems.

Whitman was not affrighted from his original course by the critics. Some of these new poems contain outlandish lines of swelling lust and turgescence by which he probably relieved himself by a kind of autogamous imagination.

A sample is as follows, from "A Woman Waits for Me":

It is I, you women, I make my way,
I am stern, acrid, large undissuadable, but I love you,
I do not hurt you any more than is necessary for you,
I pour the stuff to start sons and daughters for these States,
I press with slow rude muscles,
I brace myself effectually, I listen to no entreaties,
I dare not withdraw till I deposit what has so long accumulated
    within me.

This from a man who never to this date had been in love with a woman. And these lines from "Spontaneous Me":

Love thoughts, love-juice, love-odour, love-yielding, love-climbers,
  and the climbing sap,
Arms and hands of love, lips of love, phallic thumb of love, breasts
  of love, bellies press'd and glued together with love.

Surely Whittier could now take his fill of grossness if he
wanted to do so. However, this book contained some of the
greatest poetry that Whitman ever wrote, and outside of the
threnody on Lincoln he never did anything better. Here are
such poems as "Song of the Open Road," and "By Blue Ontario's Shore," which are packed with thought and beauty, and
which opened the way for fresh singing and interpretation in
America for America, whether that way was to be followed or
not.

In 1888, during the days of Traubel's Boswellian comradeship, Whitman thought back to the days of antagonism to
Leaves of Grass, and thus expressed himself:

" 'The world now can have no idea of the bitterness of the
feeling against me in those early days. I was a tough—obscene:
indeed, it was my obscenity, libidinousness, all that, upon which
they made up their charges.' He repeated the story of the
nobleman whom Lowell turned back. 'He came over here
with a letter of introduction from some man of high standing
in England—Rossetti, William Rossetti, I guess'—but correcting
himself after a pause: 'No—not Rossetti: it could not have been
Rossetti: some other. There was the Cambridge dinner: there
were many of the swell fellows present: the man I speak of
was the principal guest. In the course of their dinner he mentioned his letter to me. Lowell, who had had a couple of glasses
of wine—was flushed—called out: 'What! a letter for Walt
Whitman! For God Almighty's sake don't deliver it! Walt
Whitman! Do you know who Walt Whitman is? Why—Walt
Whitman is a rowdy, a New York tough, a loafer, a frequenter
of low places—friend of cab drivers!—and all that.' "

Reflecting upon Emerson's criticisms he delivered himself
as follows in the same year, also in a talk with Traubel:

" 'Emerson's objections to the outcast passages in *Leaves of Grass*,' said W. tonight, 'were neither moral nor literary, but were given with an eye to my worldly success. He believed the book would sell—said that the American people should know the book: yes, would know it but for its sex handicap: and he thought he saw the way by which to accomplish what he called "the desirable end." He did not say I should drop a single line—he did not put it that way at all: he asked whether I could consent to eliminate certain popularly objectionable poems and passages. Emerson's position has been misunderstood: he offered absolutely no spiritual argument against the book exactly as it stood. Give it a chance to be seen, give the people a chance to want to see it—that was the gist of his contention. If there was any weakness in his position it was in his idea that the particular poems could be dropped and the *Leaves* remain the *Leaves* still: he did not see the significance of the sex element as I had put it into the book and resolutely there stuck to it—he did not see that if I had cut sex out I might just as well have cut everything out—the full scheme would no longer exist—it would have been violated in its most sensitive spot!' "

In the same book (*With Walt Whitman in Camden*) Traubel makes this entry, dated in 1889:

"W. asked me about my sister. How was she? 'The mother of Herbert Spencer Harned.' He said: 'She went through that business of having a babe like the sun comes up in the morning: no cross, no shock, no shame, no apology: she was normal, sweet, whole—a perfect mother. Oh! how gloriously beautiful motherhood is when it comes normally in this way! We have got so in our civilization, so-called (which is no civilization at all) that we are afraid to face the body and its issues—when we shrink from the realities of our bodily life: when we refer the functions of the man and the woman, their sex, their passion, their normal necessary desires, to something which is to be kept in the dark and lied about instead of being avowed and gloried in. Your sister has done the proudest of proud things: she has been a mother—she is a mother: she submitted her woman's body to its noblest office. I look at the girls—at the childless women—at the old maids, as you speak of them: they lack something: they are not completed: something yet remains undone. They are not quite full—not quite entire: the woman who has denied the best of herself—the woman who has discredited the animal want, the eager physical hunger, the wish of that which though we will not allow it to be freely spoken of is still the basis of all that makes life worth while and advances the horizon of discovery. Sex; sex; sex; whether you sing or make a machine, or go to the North Pole, or love your mother, or build a house, or black shoes, or anything—anything at all—it's sex, sex, sex: sex is the root of it all: sex—the coming together of men and women: sex: sex.'

"He stopped at this point. I cried: 'I wish you had kept on, Walt!' He said: 'Why should I? I have got it all said: sex, sex: always immanent: here with us discredited—not suffered: rejected from our art: yet still sex, sex: the root of roots: the life below the life!' I said: 'You grow eloquent on that subject.' W. answered: 'I have a right to: it is the thing in my work which has been most misunderstood—that has excited the roundest opposition, the sharpest venom, the unintermitted slander, of the people who regard themselves as the custodians of the morals of the world. Horace, you are too young to know the fierceness, the bitterness, the vile quality, of this antagonism—how it threw aside all reserves and simply tore me to pieces metaphorically without giving me half a chance to make my meanings clear. You have only heard the echoes of that uproar: it's bad enough, still, to be sure—bad enough even in its echoes: but we have to some extent worn the enemy out—have in some part won our contention.'

" 'When you debated "Children of Adam" with Emerson did he show any sympathy whatever with this outcry?' 'None whatever: he in fact expressly disclaimed it: he said "Always understand, Mr. Whitman, that my idea is not that there is evil in the book: my idea is that by taking certain things out of the book you are likely to be instrumental in removing some evil out of people": that, in about such words: that was what Emerson said.' 'Was it your impression that Emerson was less physical than yourself?' W. was quiet a minute. Then he said: 'Yes, he was less physical: but he did not hesitate to say he regretted that as a defect in himself.' 'Did he use the word *defect*?' 'Yes —that word: I remember it clearly.' 'Would you describe it as a defect in Emerson?' 'It was surely a defect: and yet, Horace, somehow, I don't think I could honestly describe anything as a defect in Emerson: He seems surely so far beyond defect: is not perfect, either: yet is beyond defect—beyond it.' "

And again in 1889 Traubel records:

"Talking about *marriage forms* W. said tonight: 'Some time they will have to yield—give way.' I asked: 'To what?' W. said: 'I don't know to what—to something bigger than themselves.' 'Then you don't consider the present laws on the subject ideal?' He laughed heartily: 'Ideal? Far from it: far, far from it.' Was it to go utterly—the system? Were we to have free love? He asked me: 'What do you call free love? There's no other kind of love, is there? As to the next step—who knows what it means? I only feel sure of one thing; that we won't go back; that the women will take care of sex things—make them what they choose: man has very little to do with it except to conform.' I laughed as I asked him: 'What will become of the foundations of society if our mothers are mothers for love rather than for some other reason?' 'You are cute—that is well said: yes: what will become of them? Why, the mothers *are* the foundations of society: mothers need no law.' I asked W.: 'When you and Emerson had that talk on Boston Common about the "Children of Adam" poems did the free-love matter so-called come up?' 'O yes! it did: Emerson said: "for one thing you are in danger of being tangled up with the unfortunate heresy." I told him that it had already occurred: that worse heresies than that were charged to me: that nothing I could do now would mend matters.' 'Did Emerson appear to be shocked at the poems, or at free love, or at your defense of the books?' 'Not at all: he was calm, equable, agreeable: he was as he himself said only putting up a worldly argument: he wanted my book to sell—thought I had given it no chance to be popularly seen, apprehended: thought that if I cut out the bits here and there that offended the censors I might leave a book that would go through editions—perhaps many editions. He did not urge this for my sake but for the sake of the people: he seemed to be arguing that I didn't need the people so much as the people needed me.' "

Over and over again Whitman declared that what he purposed to do was to sing the story and the theretofore unexpressed nature of a man, in particular an American, himself, in short. In "physiology from top to toe," not "brain alone is worthy of the Muse," but "life immense in passion, pulse and power, cheerful for freest action form'd under the laws divine, the Modern Man I sing." To some extent he did this, but his genius was not of a cast to do it in all, or even in many of the main particulars which he set before his ambition. And as for singing the soul, which was to have been his second part of *Faust,* or his *Paradiso,* he didn't do it at all. The War of the States helped him to the writing of great poems, but not to the accomplishment of his original plan. In truth he did not have the power to write of the soul according to his primal vision and purpose.

Whitman had much less capacity than Goethe had to make the second part of *Faust* an exposition of the great world. Goethe had achieved one of the world's great poems when creating Margaret and her tragedy, when depicting the soul weariness of Faust and his extrication from that by a rejuvenation. When he sent Faust to courts where matters of finance were considered, and when he had to invent that superb hour in which Faust would say, "Delay, thou art so fair," he had already risen to heights where it was difficult to breathe and difficult to conceive what was fairest and best. Something in the quality and limitation of the human mind compels it to stick to men and the earth. Homer and Shakespeare did this. Only Æschylus soared to the heights where earth is lost, and heaven is not found. Milton with all his gorgeous rhetoric failed of both. Whitman's acute opinion of Milton will be presented in its place. It substantially agrees with what is here expressed. There is another purpose in *Leaves of Grass* which Whitman announced to his critics. It is in these words:

"Something more may be added—for, while I am about it, I would make a full confession. I also sent out *Leaves of Grass* to arouse and set flowing in men's and women's hearts, young and old, endless streams of living, pulsating love and friendship, directly from them to myself, now and ever. To this terrible, irrepressible yearning (surely more or less down underneath in most human souls)—this never-satisfied appetite for sympathy, and this boundless offering of sympathy—this universal democratic comradeship—this old, eternal, yet ever-new interchange of adhesiveness, so fitly emblematic of America—I have given in that book, undisguisedly, declaredly, the openest expression. Besides, important as they are in my purpose as emotional expressions for humanity, the special meaning of the "Calamus" cluster of *Leaves of Grass* (and more or less running through the book, and cropping out in "Drum-Taps") mainly resides in its political significance. In my opinion, it is by a fervent, accepted development of comradeship, the beautiful and sane affection of man for man, latent in all the young fellows, north and south, east and west—it is by this, I say, and by what goes directly and indirectly along with it, that the United States of the future (I cannot too often repeat) are to be most effectually welded together, intercalated, anneal'd into a living union."

The *irrepressible yearning* with which Whitman credited the human soul is nothing less than that lacuna at its center which sex, by some trick of nature, fills. It lifts human beings out of their soul loneliness while it stays, if only for a moment, the desolate gap of eternity which tortures the soul all through its earth pilgrimage. But it does not allay the pain of separation from eternal things.

Whitman's words are to be remembered for their bearing upon his intentions: "It is said," he wrote, "perhaps rather quizzically, by my friends, that I bring civilization, politics, the topography of the country, and even hydrography, to one final test—the capacity of producing, favoring and maintaining a fine crop of children—a magnificent race of men and women. I must confess I look with comparative indifference on all lauded triumphs of the greatest manufacturing, exporting, gold-and-silver-producing nation in comparison with a race of really fine physical perfectionists."

So he felt and so he wrought. He would have Americans the finest breed in the world past or present. He described the new woman who knew how to swim, to row, to run, to engage in athletic contests, and to bear strong children. He had the Spartan idea. He saw, too, that the power to create a new race of mind and brawn lay with such women, and that a new world could not be brought into being without them.

These noble dreams and labors were out of a man who was egotistical and vain, who was an exhibitionist and who published puffs about himself written by himself, who was secretive about little things, such as his bank account, and who could on occasion be guilty of *whoppers*—as when he wrote to Emerson in August, 1856, saying that *Leaves of Grass* had sold a thousand copies, which was very far from the truth.

CHAPTER SEVEN

As WHITMAN tried to sing America, thereby to create it, so America did much for Whitman in these exciting days of the middle 1850's. Whitman was America's rightful son. The Communist Manifesto of 1848 was spreading its influence over the Western World. The Compromise of 1850 was breaking down. A federal court in Wisconsin had declared the Fugitive Slave Law unconstitutional. A Free State Convention was held in Kansas in August 15, 1855, and another one was held there in October to draw a free constitution. In Philadelphia difficulty arose over some slaves owned by a man named Wheeler of North Carolina. In New England Whittier, Garrison, Phillips and others kept the agitation going concerning slavery. The air was vocal with a hundred reforms and remedies.

On the quack side of American life the Fox sisters of Hydeville, New York, were founding spiritualism, and Cooper, Bryant and Bancroft sat in the spirit circle and tried to communicate with the dead. Elizabeth Cady Stanton, Mrs. Bloomer, and other women appeared in bifurcated costume and addressed a meeting of Hydropathists at Skaneateles Lake. On the material side of life the Panama Railroad was completed, cables were being laid to Europe, and a great Southern Commercial Convention was held in New Orleans. Amid this Whitman was busy with other poems, and projections for poems as America drifted toward war. He was thinking of taking to the lecture platform, and wrote the *Primer* already considered, intending to use it as a lecture.

He was jotting down such suggestions as these: "make a poem including a list of what poems yet wanted. As of walking along a street, in this house lives—I wonder who lives in these houses. . . . The time and lands are devoted to the real. Make a demand for the ideal (or rather of the ideal of the real). Whether I shall make the Poem of the New World, transcending all others—depends, rich persons, upon you. . . . Be happy. Going forth seeing all beautiful things—in Ohio, Indiana, Illinois, on companions, on the ancient earth to the ancient heaven, on names, on American boys, on fables, signal bells, on happiness, ecstatic life, serene calm, old age, love, friendship, on the democracy of the future, on women, young men, on pictures, on the drum." These were his meditations before and after he wrote the "Calamus" poems of the 1860 and 1861 edition of *Leaves of Grass*.

Whitman's father, the carpenter, had died in July of 1855, but there was still his dear mother. She continued to marvel about his poems though she did not understand them, and the brother, George, did not. Whitman had become a notable in New York and was going about the city taking in the ever-fascinating sights of crowds, buses, ferries, ships and the Battery. He had no love affairs. He may have been living the jolly, full life which he desired his friends later to believe he had lived in those days before he was forty—for his sex life became a subject of curiosity. As in earlier days he went to the theatre, to the museums, and the cafés.

In 1860 William Dean Howells was a man of twenty-three. He came to New York from Boston where he was domiciled at the time, and on this visit he met Whitman at Pfaff's. In the *Harper's Magazine* for June, 1895, he published an article in which he described this meeting with Whitman. "He had a fine head," wrote Howells, "with a cloud of Jovian hair upon it, and a branching beard, and gentle eyes that looked most kindly into mine, and seemed to wish the liking which I instantly gave him, though we hardly passed a word. . . . I didn't see him again for twenty years. . . . Some years later I saw him for the last time, one day after his lecture on Lincoln. Then and always he gave me the sense of a sweet and true soul, and I felt in him a spiritual dignity. . . . As to his work itself I suppose that I do not think it so valuable in effect as in intention. He was a liberating force, a very 'imperial anarch' in literature; but liberty is never anything but a means, and what Whitman achieved was a means and not an end. . . . I like his prose much better. His verse seems to me not poetry, but the material of poetry, like emotion."

Whitman matured early—in his late thirties and before, he was gray and grizzled, giving one the impression that he was much older. His beard, his flowing hair, his heavy-lidded, sleepy eyes, his patriarchal and prophetical figure and dress, made him a conspicuous face at Pfaff's, or anywhere that he appeared. The story circulated by Thomas Wentworth Higginson that Whitman was dissipated was quite untrue. Whitman loved to sip a glass of beer; later in life he took a whiskey on occasions, but he was studiously temperate. His erotic life, if he had any of any moment at any time, remains to this day obscure and without details.

A few years after Howells met Whitman, John Burroughs became acquainted with him. It was at the close of the War between the States. Whitman was on a street car in Washington, wearing a broad-brimmed white hat. The car was crowded, and a woman with a baby in her arms was standing in a stifling place in the car. The baby was crying. Whitman took the baby in his arms and held it so gently that it fell asleep.

In the December, 1866, number of *The Galaxy* Burroughs gave this description of Whitman: "Lethargic during an interview, passive and receptive, an admirable listener, never in a hurry, with the air of one who has plenty of leisure, always in perfect repose, simple and direct in manners, if lover of plain, common people, 'meeter of savage and gentlemen on equal terms,' temperate, chaste, sweet-breathed, tender and affection-ate, of copious friendship, preferring always to meet as flesh and blood, and with a large, summery, motherly soul that shines in all his ways and looks, he is by no means the 'rough' people have been so willing to believe. Fastidious as a high-caste Brahman in his food and personal neatness and clean-liness, well dressed with a gray, open throat, a deep sympathetic voice, a kind, genial look, the impression he makes upon you is that of the best blood and breeding. He reminds me of the first men, the beginners; has a primitive out-door look—not so much from being in the open air as from texture and quality of his make—a look as of the earth, the sea or the mountains, and is 'usually taken' says a late champion of his cause for 'some great mechanic, or stevedore, or seaman, or grand laborer of one kind or another.' His physiognomy presents very marked features—features of the true antique patterns, almost obsolete in modern faces—seen in the strong, square bridge of his nose, his high arching brows, and the absence of all bulging of the forehead, a face approximating in type to the statued Greek. He does not mean intellect merely, but life: and one feels that he must arrive at his results rather by sympathy and absorption than by hard intellectual processes; by the effluence of power rather than by direct and total application of it. In keeping with this his poems do not have the character of carefully elaborated specimens—of gems cut and polished by the intellect, but are warm and vascular like living organisms. In the matter of health he is an exception to most known instances. He presents the rare phenomenon of a man giving himself to in-tellectual labor without suffering the slightest detriment to his physical powers: never knowing dyspepsia, nervousness, ennui, and an entire stranger to headache, until his presence in the army hospitals, and his stopping too long consecutively after the battles of the Wilderness with a collection of gangrened wounds had inoculated his system with malignant virus."

The fiery William Douglas O'Connor joined the Whitman adorers in the early sixties; and in 1892 published a book entitled *Three Tales* from which this description of Whitman as he was in 1866 is taken:

"He was tall and stalwart: a brow not large but full, and seamed with kindly wrinkles: a complexion of rosy clearness: heavy-lidded, fine, blue eyes which had a steadfast and draining regard: a short, thick, gray beard, almost white, and thinly flowing dark gray hair. His countenance expressed a rude sweetness. He was dressed in a long dark overcoat, much worn, and of such uncertain fashion that it almost seemed a gaberdine. As he stood there in the gracious darkling light, he looked an image of long and loving experience with men, of immovable composure and character, of serene wisdom, of immortal rosy youth in reverend age. A faint perfume exhaled from his garments. In the lapel of his coat he wore a sprig of holly. In his aspect were singularly blended the prophet and the child. The child in his inspired love: the prophet awe. He drew and he repelled. In a way quite in keeping with his unconventional aspect and manner he moved with a sort of measured alertness among the group, paying, paying his ample and affectionate address to each person, with the air of being already on familiar terms with them: thus establishing himself in close rapport with every one, as only a man with powerful intuitions, vivid impressions, and great, magnetic force and dignity could have done, and leaving them with a sense as of something electric, and very sweet had swept them."

Whitman made no money out of these two editions of *Leaves of Grass,* and in the nature of things could not do so. But his expenses were slight, and he managed to get along, living with his mother in Brooklyn, where his brother George also lived. George Whitman has left us a report of Whitman's self-absorbed and irregular ways of life, about his eating, resting and writing.

By 1860 Whitman had ready the third edition of *Leaves of*

Grass. It was a duodecimo of 456 pages, bound in imitation leather with the title stamped in gilt on the face of the cover and the name *Walt Whitman* together with various emblems: a sunrise, a globe in space, a butterfly poised upon a hand. It was brought out by Thayer and Eldridge of Boston in the "year 85 of the States, 1860–'61." The frontispiece was a steel engraving of Whitman at the age of forty, reproduced from a painting of him by Charles Hine made in 1859. There were 124 new poems in this book. "Starting from Paumanok" was one. There were fifteen "Chants Democratic," and such well-known poems as "Out of the Cradle Endlessly Rocking," and "As I Ebb'd with the Ocean of Life." There were twelve poems under the general title of "Enfans d'Adam," and 45 poems belonging to the "Calamus" series, including "Once I Pass'd through a Populous City," "Scented Herbage of My Breast," "I am He that Aches with Love," "Of Him I Love Day and Night," "We Two Boys Together Clinging," "To a Western Boy," "To a Common Prostitute," "To the States," and "To Old Age."

He was still writing brief lines, of no poetical quality and of little significance as philosophy, which he called *Thoughts.* There were seven of these. The poems of the former editions were revised, and many rewritten, sometimes fundamentally. He had now dropped the words of the Julian calendar and was speaking in Quaker fashion, calling the Fourth of July the Fourth of the Seventh Month. He employed "Chants Democratic" and "Leaves of Grass" and "Messenger Leaves" as group titles. The important additions to his previous poems in this book were "Enfans d'Adam" and the "Calamus" poems.

The war came on when Whitman was forty-two. Whitman once wrote that "but for the war the *Leaves* would not have been complete." It is admitted that but for the war they would not have been what they were, for we could not have had "When Lilacs Last in the Dooryard Bloom'd," and some of the other poems of moving beauty, if that terrible strife had been spared America.

There were thousands of men in their twenties and early thirties eager to take up arms for the North and eligible by law to service. Whitman was too old to be pressed into soldiership, but there was something mysterious about his conduct. Between April, 1861, and December 21, 1862, his life is submerged in silence. In *Specimen Days* he wrote of two days that he could never forget: that of the first battle of Bull Run, and that of Lincoln's assassination. The text of *Specimen Days* then passes to Falmouth, Virginia, opposite Fredericksburg, December 21, 1862. This entry reads: "Begin my visits among the camp hospitals in the Army of the Potomac."

What was Whitman doing during the preceding twenty months? He has been accused of unpatriotic conduct, and indifference to national problems. William E. Barton in his book *Abraham Lincoln and Walt Whitman* said, "He [Whitman] loved to loaf and invite his soul. He had been doing this for nearly two years since the war broke out, and he might have continued to do it if George had not been wounded."

Harvey O'Higgins, the author of a book of acute analysis, *The American Mind in Action,* wrote an article which was published in *Harper's Monthly Magazine* in May, 1929, in which he said, "but when the Civil War broke out on April 12, 1861, he [Whitman] disappeared for eighteen months from the sight of his biographers, and the only entry in his notebook for that period is the following, dated April 16, 1861, four days after the beginning of hostilities: 'I have this day, this hour, resolved to inaugurate for myself a pure, perfect, sweet, clean-blooded robust body, by ignoring all drinks but water and pure milk, and all fat meats, late suppers—a great body, a purged, cleansed, spiritualized, invigorated body.'"

What does this mean? What was Whitman getting ready for? For war service, or for more poetry? And exactly what kind of life was he leaving for this new program?

Whitman was also attacked by Thomas Wentworth Higginson, who called him a slacker, idly staying at home during the first two years of the war, while the destiny of the nation was at stake.

In 1933 a book was published by the University Press of Pennsylvania entitled *Walt Whitman and the Civil War* which is concerned with showing what Whitman was doing, and where he was between April, 1861, and December, 1862. The argument of the book is that Whitman during this period was visiting the New York hospitals, and writing articles about them for the newspapers. This being true an explanation is still lacking as to why he was not in the army.

There is evidence in abundance that the war stunned Whitman. Those who experienced the nervous shock of the World War can easily imagine what the firing on Fort Sumter did to Whitman, followed as it was by the swift gathering of troops and the disaster of Bull Run. The republic of Jefferson, the republic which Whitman had envisaged and sung in *Leaves of Grass,* still struggling for maturity, was in peril, or about to be erased from the page of literature. Whitman's own career as a poet was threatened with eclipse by the clouds of war, and the republic he loved was for the time being divided. In *Specimen Days* he wrote, "The dream of humanity, the vaunted Union we thought so strong, so impregnable—lo, it seems already smashed like a china plate." This after Bull Run. And again, "one of our returning colonels expressed in public that night [the night after Bull Run] amid a swarm of officers and gentlemen in a crowded room, the opinion that it was useless to fight, that the Southerners had made their title clear, and that the best course for the national government to pursue was to desist from any further attempt at stopping them, and admit them again to lead, on the best terms they were willing to grant. Not a voice was raised against this judgment, amid the large crowd of officers and gentlemen. (The fact is the hour was one of three or four of those crises we had then and afterward, during the fluctuations of four years, when human eyes appeared at least just as likely to see the last breath of the Union as to see it continue.)"

Was Whitman's mind, however, clearly made up about the war? He was a child of Jefferson, of Jefferson's republic, and of the Declaration of Independence. When the South was invoking the doctrine that all governments derive their just powers from the consent of the governed, when Greeley was saying "let the erring sisters go"; when many of the ablest and most high-minded men in the North were against the war, against the coercion of the South, it would be interesting indeed to know Whitman's feelings, nurtured as they were on the revolutionary spirit that had brought America into being. He was nonplussed, to say the least, and naturally inclined toward silence and hiding until he could gather his thoughts clearly together. In *Specimen Days* he characterizes these days as being "overcome by stupors," and in *Drum Taps and Sequel to Drum Taps* he writes these lines under the title "Year that Trembled and Reel'd Beneath Me":

Year that trembled and reel'd beneath me!
. Your summer wind was warm enough, yet the air I breathed froze me,
A thick gloom fell through the sunshine and darkened me,
Must I change my triumphant songs? said I to myself,
Must I indeed learn to chant the cold dirges of the baffled?
And sullen hymns of defeat?

Whitman was not the rugged man that his poems might lead one to believe. He had not the tough physique that Carlyle and Tennyson boasted—nor the wiry and enduring organization of Emerson. He had no such labors and exhaustions as Grant had, and many other men in the armies of that day. Rapid growth does not make for strength or longevity, and fifty-four found Whitman an invalid. Others of that day suffered malaria and recovered. But Whitman was highly sensitive and one can read through the lines he wrote about the war and his hospital experiences and see that his sufferings were excruciating. Before volunteering his service in the army hospitals, before he went South to the hospitals, before he took any step which would indicate to us now what his activity and cleavage should be exactly, he must have gone through great torture of mind.

Let us turn back to the articles contributed to *The New York Leader* in 1862, which are exploited in *Walt Whitman and the Civil War* and attributed to Whitman. The clue for finding them was furnished by a letter written by John Burroughs in October, 1862, in which Burroughs stated, "He wrote a number of articles for *The Leader* some time ago, on the hospitals. Do you remember them?" When this clue was followed up research showed that there were no articles signed by Whitman but that there were seven articles signed by *Velsor Brush*. The theory is that this was Whitman's pseudonym, made up from Velsor, his mother's maiden name, and Brush, his grandmother's maiden name. But why would Whitman use a pseudonym for such articles? Was that a part of his attempt to remain under cover while mulling over the questions of the war, and the right of revolution which Lincoln had advocated as a congressman only thirteen years before 1861?*

These articles may be advanced as evidence to show what Whitman was doing between April, 1861, and December, 1862, but they fall short of proving that his heart was in the war, or that he had intellectually aligned himself. Let us examine them with more care.

The first article was published March 15, 1862, and was on the subject of the Broadway Hospital. It described the building, the entrance and the rooms, the offices and the wards, the arrangement of the beds, and the cards tacked above the beds with the name of the patient and his injury or malady. He

---

*In *New York Dissected* published by Rufus Rockwell Wilson, Inc., in 1936, a number of articles attributed to Whitman were reproduced from *Life Illustrated*, a publication of the 1850's. One was "Christmas at Grace," another was on the Egyptian Museum at 659 Broadway, another was "Advice for Strangers." These were published anonymously but evidence was brought forward to indicate that they were Whitman's.

wrote in particular of several patients: one had a broken leg incurred while driving a stage on Broadway, another was a fireman on a steamer who was knocked down while driving to a fire, another had had his hand nipped in a steam engine, another was a foundry worker who had been struck on the head by a hammer and another had been thrown from a railroad car at Jersey City. Finally of the hospital wards he wrote, "After I have passed through them of late, especially in the South Building, which is now filled with soldiers, I have many hours afterwards, in far different scenes, had the pale faces, the look of death, the appealing eyes come curiously of a sudden, plainly before me." This is all. No word whatever of giving attention to wounded soldiers.

The next article or letter was published March 22, 1862, and it also was on the Broadway Hospital. This contained statistics of diseases and patients, remarks on the medical staff, a report of an operation for calculus, a description of the pathological museum, remarks upon elephantiasis, the price of board, and the manner in which the hospital was sustained. There are descriptions of the nurses and of a colored nurse in particular named Aunty Robinson. That is all.

The next was published March 29, 1862, and began by giving a list of the boards of governors of the Broadway Hospital. It told of the surgeons, who they were and what their accomplishments were, some by name, others in general. It told of the ventilation in the rooms, of the surgical instruments used, of the bequests made to the hospital, and of the painted portraits that filled the governor's room of the hospital. The article is without any merit even as straight reporting. Any one could have written it.

Another was published April 12, 1862. This was the month in which the bloody battle of Shiloh was fought, with 24,000 men killed, wounded or missing. The month before, just six days before the letter of March 15 was published, the dramatic duel of the *Monitor* and *Merrimac* had been fought in Hampton Roads. In this April letter the writer, Velsor Brush, gave his parting bow to the Broadway Hospital. He noted changes in the hospital staff. He wrote of the case of a young man who had a broken back from skylarking, from standing on his head on a table in a spirit of fun. A case of delirium tremens was next described. And now there were references to wounded soldiers. The article as to this reads, "I have spent two or three Sunday afternoons of late in going around among the sick soldiers, just to help cheer and change a little the monotony of their sickness and confinement—and indeed, just as much too, for the melancholy entertainment and friendly interest and sympathy I found aroused in myself toward and among men. Many of them have no relatives or acquaintances at all in New York, and time moves on slowly and dully enough to them. . . . One Sunday night in a ward in the South Building I spent one of the most agreeable evenings of my life amid such a group of seven convalescent soldiers of a Maine regiment. We drew around together, on our chairs, in the dimly lighted room, and after interchanging the few magnetic remarks that show people it is well for them to be together, they told me stories of country life and adventures &c., away up there in the Northeast. They were to leave the next day in a vessel for the Gulf, where their regiment was. I shook hands with them all around at parting."

Was Whitman possibly gathering material, and that alone, for poems? Certainly he was doing no war service. In this article the writer went on about other soldiers who were coming, of different cases of sickness, of an amputation, of death from city casualties, of a case of a dislocated jaw from gaping, of the most numerous kinds of diseases, of the nativity of patients, and their grand total, of the Bloomingdale Insane Asylum.

These are all the articles by Velsor on hospitals. The other three by the same writer published in *The Leader* related to entirely different subjects, subjects having nothing to do with hospital patients. The one of April 19, 1862, treated of the Bowery, its sights and sounds, its hotels, sports, circus men, and its reception to Tom Hyer the pugilist. The next article, bearing the date May 3, 1862, described the old theatre in the Bowery, and the melodramas produced there in the writer's recollection. It had comments on the elder Booth and the parts he played, and referred to other actors of those days.

An article published May 17, 1862, was also about the Bowery. The first paragraph related to lager beer and the Germans; the next to a popular lager beer hall in the Bowery. There is a long paragraph on Lindmüller's dance hall. Such was the work and interest of Velsor Brush, or Walt Whitman, at a time when the world was being stirred by Farragut's capture of New Orleans—an event of Homeric size and drama. The reverberations of Shiloh were still in the air, and the thunder of guns at Hampton Roads, and the second Bull Run Campaign was near at hand. In the latter, Walt's brother, Lieutenant George Whitman, participated.

Remembering that Æschylus fought at Marathon, Salamis and Plataea, and that Sir Philip Sidney died as a soldier at Zutphen; that Sidney Lanier, as sensitive a soul as Whitman and nothing like so robust physically, took up arms for the South, one wonders that Whitman could hide under a pseudonym and write these articles about hospitals, theatres, dance halls, beer and actors while his country was gripped in death war. They are articles of no moment, without distinction of any sort. They are the product of a slack hand, a lazy and inert mind; or they are the product of a mind half paralyzed by fear and counter-thinking. Would that we had vivid, rich, well-written articles about New York in those days—and by Whitman.

George Whitman joined the Thirteenth Regiment of Brooklyn in April, 1861, as a hundred-day man, impelled to do so by the assault of the Baltimore mob on Massachusetts troops passing through that city. He had gone on until he had become a sergeant-major and then a liteutenant, doing valiant service until wounded at Fredericksburg on December 13, 1862. A week later in that year Walt Whitman was himself at Fredericksburg, and thus his work as an army nurse began.

The editor of these *Leader* articles, Mr. Charles I. Glicksberg, presented in his book, *Walt Whitman and the Civil War,* many argumentive matters in justification of the claim that these were the work of Whitman. For example items set down in Whitman's notebook published May 17, 1862, embodied material which can be found in a notebook stamped "Walt Whitman—1862," and so on. But that these articles show that Whitman made an active study of hospital cases before he took up his duties in Washington and on the field, is a claim that stretches the size of the material. His articles on the theatre and acting may be evidence that Whitman was striving for a native theatre and drama, so that America would no longer play second fiddle to Europe. They are not evidence that he was interested in the war, but in the theatre in spite of the war.

There has been some contention over Whitman's connection with what was called the *Christian Commission.* A book has come down to us stamped in gold letters *Christian Commission;* on the inside of this was written "Walt Whitman—Soldier's Missionary to Hospital, Camp and Battlefield." A good authority has denied that Whitman was ever connected with the *Christian Commission.* Traubel declared that Whitman gave him a large yellow envelope on which was written "From office Christian Commission 343 Pennsylvania Av., Washington, D.C. Commission of Walt Whitman of Brooklyn N. Y., Jan. 20, 1863." On the other hand Whitman spoke of himself as "a regular self-appointed missionary to these thousands and tens of thousands of wounded and sick young men here, left upon Government hands, many of them languishing, many of them dying. I am not connected with any society, but go on my own individual account, and to the work that appears called for." Just as Whitman's relation to Lincoln turns out to be nebulous and trivial when examined, just as his conduct for the twenty months of the war is mysterious, so his exact position as a nurse is as irregular and informal as his verse. But that he contributed most beautiful and moving pages to the book of human service by what he did in the war is beyond any dispute.

Whitman found his wounded brother, George, at Fredericksburg where he looked over the battlefield. First and last he visited several battlefields, observing the horrors and the butcheries that had been done. In the hospitals, on the field, and at Washington he went about from cot to cot speaking words of comfort, writing letters home for wounded men, bringing tobacco, fruit, stamps, stationery, and sometimes money, to those who were sick or disabled. He stood by while terrible operations were performed. He held the hands of the dying, and talked religion to those who wanted to hear about it. Weininger in his book on *Sex and Character* held to the theory that men make better nurses than women. However, it was Whitman in his feminine nature, as that nature is commonly accepted for tenderness, that predominated in his actions as a war nurse. All his services were given without pay. He was earning something at the time by doing correspondence for *The New York Times*. Also he accepted subscriptions of money from his friends.

In *Specimen Days* Whitman gives us many pages on what he did and who it was that he served in those ghastly days. The doctors were wont to say, "He is a hopeless case, turn him over to Whitman, Whitman will save him." Sample items of Whitman's work at Fort Corcora may be given here: "John Watson, 49, get some apples. . . . Llewellyn Woodin (bed 14) sore throat, wants some candy. . . . Bed 15 wants an orange. . . . Bed 59 (James) wants some liquorice. . . . April 7th, 1863. John Armstrong, quiet Pennsylvania boy, very low with dysentery—I write this sitting by his bed—tells me he can't help thinking of the time when his mother died—both of us are crying and very ashamed & mad about it afterward. . . . Wm. VonVliet—shell wounded in arm. . . . Gave 20 cents. . . . Wants some smoking tobacco & pipe—arm amp.—turn out bad—died poor boy. . . . To Clinton Minzey Ward E. parcel of cakes and crackers."

What infinite pity there is written in these loose scrawls none can miss who reads them in *Specimen Days*. By January, 1863, Whitman was back in Washington visiting the hospitals and doing any service that came to him at the Campbell Hospital, the Armory Square Hospital and others. Pleurisy and typhoid were prevalent, and operations were almost countless. Whitman went through all this. He was living in one little room at 394 L Street when in Washington at this time. He writes of strolling about town observing the White House by moonlight, sometimes seeing Lincoln at a distance. He witnessed the arrivals from Chancellorsville of men with bloody rags bound around their brows, legs or arms. He saw the battlefield of Chancellorsville, exclaiming, "O heavens what scene is this?—is this indeed humanity—these butchers' shambles?— There they lie in the largest, in an open space in the woods, from 200 to 300 poor fellows. . . . One man is shot by a shell, both in the arm and leg—both are amputated—there lie the rejected members. . . . Amid the woods that scene of flitting souls—amid the crack and crash and yelling sounds . . . the radiance of the moon, looking from heaven at intervals so placid—the sky so heavenly—a few large placid stars beyond, coming silently and languidly out and then disappearing—the melancholy, draperied night above, around. . . . What history, I say can ever give—for who can know—the mad, determin'd tussle of the armies . . . who knows the conflict, hand to hand —the many conflicts in the dark, those shadowy-tangled, flashing moon-beam'd woods—the writhing groups and squads, the cries, the din, the crack of guns and pistols . . . the distant cannon . . . the devils fully rous'd in human heart . . . the strong shout, Charge men, charge."

He calls the soldiers of the North "our hardy darlings." There is Tom Haley the Irish boy who is dying, "Little he knew, poor death stricken boy, the heart of the stranger that hover'd near." There is the New Jersey soldier gaunt and gray haired with pneumonia, and J. G. to whom Whitman gave tobacco and twenty-five cents; and the New Jersey youth who has gangrene of the foot, and so on. Whitman cared for 600 cases in all through the battle of Gettysburg and through the dreadful heat of the summer of 1863. He went over the Long Bridge to the convalescent camp at Alexandria. He rambled at night from hospital to hospital. At first he was in magnificent health and stood the strain of his trying life. He journeyed to Culpeper in February, 1864, and back to Washington that summer. Whitman made notes about one John Glover who kept a diary. "Today the doctor says I must die—all is over with me—ah so young to die—dear brother Thomas I have been brave but wicked—pray for me." Whitman was getting money from people in Boston, Salem, Providence, Brooklyn and New York to give to the destitute soldiers.

A sample of one of Whitman's letters to the relative of a dead soldier written as Whitman phrased it by "a casual friend that sat by his death-bed," follows. This soldier had suffered the amputation of a leg.

"For a couple of weeks afterward he was doing pretty well. I visited and sat by him frequently, as he was fond of having me. . . . I was in the habit of coming in afternoons and sitting by him . . . and he liked to have me—liked to put his arm out and lay his hand on my knee. . . . And now like many other noble and good men, after serving his country as a soldier, he has yielded up his young life at the very outset of his service. . . . I am merely a friend visiting the hospitals occasionally to cheer the wounded and sick."

This letter was dated May 1, 1865. By this time Whitman had been sick himself. In the 600 visits which he had made to the hospitals he had passed among "eighty thousand to one hundred thousand of the wounded and sick, as sustainer of spirit and body in some slight degree, in their time of need." Such were his own words. Whether Whitman had hospital malaria, or a form of blood poisoning contracted while assisting at an operation on a gangrened soldier, it is true that the labors he performed and the suffering he endured in seeing these tragedies about him were enough to wear down his sensitive nature.

In June of 1864 Whitman had an illness concerning which he wrote to his mother as follows:

"Washington, June 7, 1864. Dearest Mother—

. . . Mother, I have not felt well at all the last week. I had spells of deathly faintness and bad trouble in my head too, and sore throat (quite a little budget, ain't they?). My head was the worst, though I don't know, the faint spells were not very pleasant—but I feel so much better this afternoon I believe it has passed over.

"Washington, June 10, 1864. Dearest Mother—

. . . Mother, I have not felt well again the last two days as I was Tuesday, but I feel a good deal better this morning. I go round, but most of the time feel very little like it. The doctor tells me I have continued too long in the hospitals, especially in a bad place, Armory building, where the worst wounds were, and have absorbed too much of the virus in my system— but I know it is nothing but what a little relief and sustenance of (the) right sort will set right.

"Washington, June 14, 1864. Dearest Mother—

I am not feeling very well these days—the doctors have told me not to come inside the hospitals for the present. I send there by a friend every day; I send things and aid to some cases I know, and hear from there also, but I do not go myself at present. It is probably that the hospital poison has affected my system, and I find it worse than I calculated. I have spells of faintness and very bad feeling in my head, fullness and pain—and besides sore throat. My boarding place, 502 Pennsylvania Av., is a miserable place, very bad air."

Whitman's service as a war nurse stands out immortally among those who have shown self-sacrifice and tenderness to the wounded and dying in war. What he suffered is recorded in such poems as "A March in the Ranks Hard-Prest," "Come up from the Fields, Father," "Vigil Strange" and "Wound Dresser." Imagination may easily dwell upon this lonely man, this poet with the great vision wandering about from hospital to hospital, from bed to bed, or strolling the streets of Washington looking at the capital by gas-light, watching the returning soldiers when the war ended, and standing among the crowds while Lincoln again took the oath of office. Whitman writes of this, "The President very quietly rode down to the capitol in his own carriage, by himself on a sharp trot about noon. . . . I saw him on his return at three o'clock, after the performance was over . . . he look'd very much worn and tired; the lines, indeed, of vast responsibilities, intricate questions, and demands of life and death cut deeper than ever upon his dark brown face; yet all the old goodness, tenderness, sadness and canny shrewdness underneath the furrows."

Then there was the reception at the White House. Whitman was there. What was to hinder this poet from approaching Lincoln and making himself known? It didn't happen. Whitman never passed a word with Lincoln beyond a salutation in the street. William E. Barton in his book on Lincoln and Whitman makes this clear. There stood Whitman, grizzled and prematurely old, and really a sick man, looking at Lincoln. "I saw Mr. Lincoln, drest all in black, with white kid gloves and a claw-hammer coat, receiving, as in duty bound, shaking hands, looking very disconsolate, and as if he would give anything to be somewhere else."

Whitman also went to the inaugural ball at the Patent Office, and remarked what a different scene was presented from that a little while before of the "crowded mass of the worst wounded in the war, brought in from Bull Run, Antietam and Fredericksburg. Tonight beautiful women, perfumes, the violin's sweetness, the polka and the waltz; then the amputation, the blue face, the groan, the glassy eye of the dying, the clotted rag, the odour of wounds and blood, and many a mother's son amid strangers passing away untended there, (for the crowd of the badly hurt was great, and much for nurse to do, and much for surgeon)."

There were the grand reviews of the returning troops. There was the assassination of Lincoln. The spiritual kinship between Lincoln and Whitman was founded upon their Americanism, their essential Westernism. Whitman had grown up without much formal education; Lincoln had had scarcely any education. One had become the notable poet of the day; one the orator of the Gettysburg Address. It was inevitable that Whitman as a poet should turn with a feeling of kinship to Lincoln, and even without any association or contact feel that Lincoln was his.

In *Specimen Days* Whitman wrote under date of April 16, 1865, "the tragic splendor of his death, purging, illuminating all, throws round his form, his head, an aureole that will remain and grow brighter through time while history lives and love of country lasts. . . . Honesty, goodness, shrewdness, conscience, and (a new virtue unknown to other lands, and hardly yet really known here, but the foundation and tie of all, as the future will grandly develop), Unionism, in its truest and amplest sense, form'd the hard pan of his character." Yes, Whitman saw in Lincoln and his work the hope of that "dear love of comrades" all over these states which had become the preoccupation of his imagination.

Whitman reached the age of forty-six with his superb health somewhat altered, without money, without any profession save that of the newspaper business in which he had failed to shine in stronger days, and with his heart surging with poems. He had gathered tremendous spiritual strength from the war. What was there to do but write poems? Could he now produce the second part of *Leaves of Grass?*

CHAPTER EIGHT

IN A COUNTRY having higher regard for literary achievement, not to mention gratitude for hard labor in behalf of the wounded in a time of national peril, Whitman would have received some more fitting recognition from the government than came to him. Whitman as the war was closing needed something to do by which means he could earn a living, since he was not given a pension. No one, no soldier in the field and no captain, deserved an honorarium more than he. He was a treasure to America that should have been carefully prized and sustained. But he was compelled to make his way as best he could, and fortunately he had some ability to look after himself.

In early January of 1865, he received an appointment to a clerkship of the second class in the Department of the Interior at $1200 a year. In May of the same year he was promoted to a clerkship of the second class in the same department. But on June 30 following he was dismissed by James Harlan, Secretary of the Interior, for the scandalous indecency, as Harlan viewed it, of *Leaves of Grass.* The next day a man named Ashton, acting in Whitman's behalf, had an interview with Harlan touching Whitman's dismissal. It transpired that Harlan had got into Whitman's desk and found a copy of *Leaves of Grass,* in which Whitman had marked passages for correction and elision in future editions. Harlan told Ashton that Whitman was a free lover, and unfit, in consequence, to be in the service of the United States Government. Therefore, the poet who had given his time and his money, and as it turned out his good health, to his country in time of war, had to shift again for himself. Pretty soon Whitman settled his economic life by getting a clerkship in the Department of Justice, and there he stayed until June 30, 1874, on duty or on pay. On that date as one of the clerkships in that department had been abolished he was selected to be the sacrifice. Meantime, in February of 1873 he had been stricken with paralysis.

Among Whitman's "Small Memoranda" will be found a note about Harlan. According to Whitman, Harlan's appointment as Secretary of the Interior was brought about by the pressure of the Methodists upon Lincoln, led by Bishop Simpson. Lincoln preferred to name a Colonel Dubois to the post, but as a part of Whitman's fate one of the sponsors for Dubois failed to appear at a critical meeting held for discussion of the subject. Then, according to Whitman, Lincoln said, "I have thought the matter all over, and under the circumstances think the Methodists too good and too great a body to be slighted. They have stood by the government and help'd us their very best. I have had no better friends; and as the case stands I have decided to appoint Mr. Harlan." Thus Harlan got in and Whitman soon went out. The poet who admired Lincoln extravagantly, and immortalized him in verse, had no influence, it seems, none at least to compare to that of the Methodists.

While Whitman was still in the Department of the Interior Lincoln was assassinated, and the poet wrote his great threnody and the poem definitively entitled "O Captain, My Captain." These were included in the book *Drum Taps and Sequel to Drum Taps of 1865-6*. The book *Drum Taps* had come from the press before Whitman had written the two poems in question. From Traubel's second volume of talks with Whitman is reprinted here a stanza of the first draft of "O Captain, My Captain" called then "My Captain":

The mortal voyage over, the gales and tempests done,
The ship that bears me nears her home the prize I sought is won,

The port is close, the bells I hear, the people all exulting,
While (As) steady sails and enters straight my wondrous veteran
    vessel;
But O heart! heart! heart! leave you not the little spot,
Where on the deck my Captain lies — sleeping pale and dead.

Traubel recorded his conversation about the poem as follows: "When I spoke to W. about this manuscript he said:
'You don't like the poem anyway.' I explained: 'I don't say
that. I think it clumsy: you tried too hard to make it what you
shouldn't have tried to make it at all—and what you didn't
succeed in making it in the end.' W. laughed and responded:
'You're more than half right.' 'Technically it conforms neither
to the old nor the new: it is hybrid.' W. laughed and said: 'If
you keep on talking you'll convince me you're the other half
right also! The thing that tantalizes me most is not its rhythmic
imperfection or its imperfection as a ballad or rhymed poem
(it is damned bad in all that, I do believe) but the fact that my
enemies and some of my friends who half doubt me, look upon
it as a concession made to the Philistines—that makes me mad.
I come back to the conviction that it had certain emotional,
immediate reasons for being: that's the best I can say for it myself.' "
    On the reverse sides of the two sheets of paper containing the
draft of "My Captain" was this stanza:

And by one great pitchy torch, stationary, with a wild flame, and
    much smoke,
Crowds, groups of forms, I see, on the floor, and some in the pews
    laid down;
At my very feet a soldier, a mere lad, in danger of bleeding to
    death — (he is shot in the abdomen,)
I staunch the blood temporarily, (the youngster's face is white as
    a lily;)
Then before I depart I sweep my eyes o'er the scene around, — I
    am fain to absorb it all,
Faces, varieties, postures beyond description, some in obscurity,
    some of the dead.

Traubel writes, "W. quizzed me: 'I guess you like this better than "My Captain." ' I asked him: 'Shall I lie to you or shall I tell you the truth?' 'You needn't do either: I know anyhow: you do like it better.' He stopped as if for me to say something. I didn't. Then he smiled and added: 'I like it better, too—but you mustn't tell on me.' "

"O Captain, My Captain" is Whitman's best poem in formal verse and rhyme. It has technical blemishes but its deep tenderness and moving passion and sorrow fuse these defects into the harmony of a lyric never to be forgotten. "When Lilacs Last in the Dooryard Bloom'd" may better be considered in connection with Whitman's poems in general.

Drum Taps and Sequel to Drum Taps contained in all 96 pages, the first division 72 pages and the second 24. It was in pamphlet form with this title page: *"Walt Whitman's Drum Taps 1865; Sequel to Drum Taps* (Since the preceding came from the press) 'When Lilacs Last in the Dooryard Bloom'd' and other pieces, Washington 1865-6." The very notable poems in this book were: "Pioneers! O Pioneers!" "Rise O Day from your Fathomless Deeps," "Come up from the Fields, Father," "A March in the Ranks Hard Press'd," "Year that Trembled and Reel'd Beneath Me," "Out of the Rolling Ocean the Crowd," the threnody, and "O Captain, My Captain." In all there were 41 poems. They formed the first and second annexes of the fourth edition of *Leaves of Grass* published in 1867. In 1871 the greater number of them were placed in the body of that book appearing under the title *Drum Taps*. No one can read these poems understandingly without seeing that they are charged with intense emotion, and were written under a spiritual stress which must have sapped Whitman's vitality. They were not subsequently revised to any extent.

Whitman was now approaching greater recognition. There in Washington in these years was John Burroughs, who was twenty-six when he first met Whitman. They became fast friends for life. Burroughs fairly lived in Whitman's being.

In 1867 he published in *The Galaxy* an article entitled "Walt Whitman and His Drum Taps," and in 1867 his book *Walt Whitman as Poet and Person*. Before this Whitman had received favorable attention from Charles Eliot Norton in *Putnam's Monthly* for September, 1855, from Edward Everett Hale in *The North American Review* for January, 1856, and from Moncure D. Conway in *The Dial* for August, 1860. Norton called *Leaves of Grass* excited prose, gross but elevated, superficial yet profound, preposterous yet fascinating. In 1865 William Douglas O'Connor had come to the defense of Whitman on the occasion when he was dismissed from the Department of the Interior, calling Whitman "The Good Gray Poet," and seeking to vindicate his character. But he paid little attention to the æsthetics and philosophy of Whitman's poems.

In 1868 William Rossetti brought out in England selections from Whitman's poems, and thus his English recognition started, which led to the extravagant enthusiasm of Swinburne, and the composition of his poem, "To Walt Whitman in America," included in *Songs Before Sunrise* in 1868. There were other English friends to follow, such as Dowden, Edward Carpenter, Tennyson, and Anne Gilchrist, who became Whitman's memorable friend, and one of his most devoted literary champions.

In these sixties, while Whitman was a clerk in the Department of Justice, he formed a friendship which has few parallels in literary annals, and to which adequate attention must be paid. The devotion of Michelangelo to Tomasso Cavalieri may be compared to Whitman's masculine love. At this time there was in Washington a street car driver named Peter Doyle. The manner of their meeting will presently be disclosed. First it is in order to say that Doctor Bucke brought out a book entitled *Calamus—A series of Letters written during the years 1868–1880 by Walt Whitman to a young Friend*. Bucke in this book presented other letters written by Whitman to young men. One of October, 1868, to Harry Hurt commenced "Dear Friend

Harry Hurt" and contained Whitman's love sent to "Ben Thompson, conductor" and to "John Trovers, conductor." There was another letter to "Dear Lewy" which spoke about various bus drivers on Broadway. All this was by way of pointing out that Whitman had many young men friends and that Peter Doyle was not the only one.

In this book Bucke made the following prefatory comment: "That the friendship existing between Walt Whitman and Peter Doyle was as compared with the average sentiment that passes under that name, exceptional and remarkable, there can be no doubt, but it does not seem at all clear that there was anything about it which was not of the regular and ordinary course when considered as a fact in the life of Whitman. The present editor possesses a series of letters by the poet to other young men evincing nearly as great, if not as great affection on his part, and that section of the *Leaves* named "Calamus" (written long before he knew Doyle) proves the existence of previous friendships at least equally warm and tender."

In May of 1895, two years after Whitman had died, Bucke and Traubel went to see Peter Doyle to request the letters that Whitman had written him. Whether they got all of the letters, or if they did whether Bucke published all of them or not, history and psychology can speculate as they please. In the case of Michelangelo and Cavalieri the sonnets of the artist were edited by his nephew out of respect to an altered social feeling upon Platonic masculine love.

Considering how profound and beautiful Whitman's conception of love was, and by that fact to be grossly misunderstood by America which is notably matter of fact and materialistic on that subject, it would be natural that these two friends of Whitman would not expose him to any vulgar gaze or comment. Foreigners have remarked that men in America are not really friends, and that love is not so passionate, so tender, among Americans as among the Latin races, or the Germans. The fact that no American has produced a genuine love story, intimate, shameless and unreserved proves these things. Returning to the letters written by Whitman to Doyle as published in Bucke's book, there were nine in 1868, three in 1869, twelve in 1870, five in 1871, fourteen in 1872, twenty-seven in 1873, twenty-three in 1874, seven in 1875 and nine from 1876 to 1880. By this is meant these are the numbers and the dates of the letters selected by Bucke. It should be repeated here in this connection that Whitman became an invalid in February of 1873.

In October of 1868 Whitman went to Providence to visit Thomas Davis, formerly a member of Congress. From there Whitman wrote Doyle as follows: "Providence, October 18 '68 —Dear boy and comrade, In the evening I went by invitation to a party of ladies and gentlemen—mostly ladies. We had a warm animated talk, among other things about spiritualism. I talked too, indeed went in like a house afire. . . . I also made love to the women, and flatter myself that I created at least one impression—wretch and gay deceiver that I am. The truth is, Peter, that I am here at the present time mainly in the midst of female women, some of them young and jolly, and meet them most every evening in company, and the way in which this aged party comes up to the scratch and cuts out youthful parties and fills their hearts with envy is absolutely a caution. You would be astonished, my son, to see the brass and coolness and the capacity of flirtation and carrying on with the girls—I would never have believed it of myself. My going in amounts to just talking and joking and having a devil of a jolly time carrying on—that's all."

It is fair to the reader to say that I have cut out of this letter some sentences of mere trivial stuff, that has no bearing whatever on Whitman's attitude toward Doyle, and the same course will be followed with the other letters. Whitman was in Brooklyn by October 22nd in the year of 1868 and from there he wrote to Doyle, "Take care of yourself, Dear Pete, we will soon be together again."

In August of 1869 Whitman wrote Doyle from Brooklyn as follows:

"I have thought of you, my darling boy, very much of the time. How is it with you? Dear Pete, you must forgive me for being so cold the last day and evening. I was unspeakably shocked and repelled from you by that talk and proposition of yours—you know what—there by the fountain. It seemed indeed to me (for I will talk it out plain to you, dearest comrade) that the one I loved, and who had always been so manly and sensible was gone and a fool and intentional suicide stood in his place. I spoke so sternly and cutting. (Though I see now that my words might have appeared to have a certain other meaning, which I didn't dream of—insulting to you, never for one moment in my thoughts.) But I will say no more of this—for I know such thoughts must have come when you was not yourself, but in a moment of derangement—and have passed away like a bad dream. Pete, I send you some money by Adams' Express—you use it, dearest son, and when it is gone you shall have some more, for I have plenty. I will write again before long—give my love to Johnny Lee, my dear darling boy. I love him truly—(let him read these three last lines)—Dear Pete, *remember*—Walt."

From Brooklyn on July 30, 1870, Whitman wrote to Doyle again:

"Dear Pete, dear son, I received your second letter today, Dear Son I can almost see you drowsing and nodding since last Sunday, going home late—especially as we wait there at 7th st. and I am telling you something deep about the heavenly bodies —and in the midst of it I look around and find you fast asleep, and your head on my shoulder like a chunk of wood—an awful compliment to my lecturing powers. Good night, Pete, Good night, my darling son—here is a kiss for you, dear boy—on the paper here—a good long one."

In August of 1870 Whitman wrote to Doyle that he had not

heard from him for nine days. "I hope all is well with you—but why have you not written? Dear Son if not to work I wish to send you a little money."

In February of 1872 there is this letter: "Dear Pete, dear, dear son. I will write only this very short letter to you this time, but send you my love, my darling son—I think about you every day, dear son—will write soon—here is a kiss for you, dear loving son. Good bye today, my loving boy—Your true Father and comrade always."

Whitman went to Dartmouth in June of 1872 there to read his poem "As a Strong Bird on Pinions Free." From there he wrote Doyle telling about delivering the poem, about receiving a recent letter from him, and it is signed "Your loving Walt." In a letter of August 1873 Whitman sent Doyle $20. From this time forward there are many letters with the address "Dear Son" and the ending "good bye dear loving boy" signed "Walt." In a letter of January 1874 Whitman called Doyle "my darling boy," and in April of that year, "Pete, darling, shant I send you a little money?" In May, 1874, "Dear Peter. I hope you will be able to come as you said in your last. Dear Son I shall look for you."

There are other brief notes acknowledging receipt of Doyle's letters. Parenthetically Doyle was not cordially welcomed by the housekeeper and others who surrounded Whitman after he became domiciled on Mickle Street in Camden, after 1884 that is. In November, 1875, Whitman sent Doyle $10. In June, 1877, Whitman wrote Doyle as follows: "Dear, dear boy Pete I spend most of my time down at an old farm in Jersey where I have a fine secluded wood and creek and springs, where I pass my time alone, and yet not lonesome at all (often think of you, Pete, and put my arm around you and hug you up close, and give you a good bus—Often)."

In July, 1877, Whitman wrote from Kirkwood, New Jersey, "Dear Boy Pete (in better health still making headquarters in Camden). Love, love, love. Your old Walt." In September,

1877, he wrote, "Love to you, my darling son, and here is a kiss for you."

In November, 1879, Whitman was in St. Louis with his brother Jeff, who was a prosperous bridge-builder there. He wrote Doyle about his trip to the Rocky Mountains, giving descriptions of the country of Colorado and the cities. This letter ended, "I often think of you and no doubt you often do of me—God bless you, my darling friend—from your Old Walt." Later in 1880 from London, Ontario, where Whitman was visiting Bucke, he wrote Doyle acknowledging receipt of some papers.

When Bucke and Traubel interviewed Doyle in May, 1895, Traubel took notes of what Doyle said, and reported Doyle as follows: Doyle said that he was born in Ireland in 1847, which made him around twenty when he first met Whitman. He was brought to America when two years old. His father was a blacksmith, who took up his residence in Alexandria, Virginia. Afterwards the family moved to Richmond. When the War broke out Doyle enlisted in the Confederate army, but being paroled went to Washington to live and became a horse-car conductor. Here I quote Doyle's own words as Traubel set them down:

"How different Walt was then in Washington from the Walt you knew in the later years. You would not believe it. He was an athlete—great, great! You ask where I first met him. It is a curious story. We felt to each other at once. I was a conductor. The night was very stormy—he had been over to see Burroughs before he came down to take the car—the storm was awful. Walt had his blanket—it was thrown over his shoulders—he seemed like an old sea captain. He was the only passenger, it was a lonely night, so I thought I would go in and talk with him. Something in me made me do it, and something in him drew me that way. He used to say there was something in me had the same effect on him. Anyway I went into the car. We were familiar at once—I put my hand on his knee—we understood. He did not get out at the end of the trip—in fact went all the way back with me. I think the year of this was 1866. From that time on we were the biggest sort of friends. I stayed in Washington until 1872, when I went on the Pennsylvania Railroad. Walt was then in the Attorney General's office. I would go out to the treasury to see Walt; Hubley Ashton was coming there—he would be leaning familiarly on the desk where Walt would be writing. They were fast friends—talked a good deal together. Walt rode with me often—often at noon —always at night. He rode with me on the last trip—sometimes rode for several trips. Everybody knew him. In his habits he was very temperate. He did not smoke. People seemed to think it odd that he didn't, for everybody in Washington smoked. But he seemed to have a positive dislike for tobacco. He was a very moderate drinker. You might have thought something different, to see the ruddiness of his complexion—but his complexion had no whiskey in it. We might take a drink or two together occasionally—nothing more. It was our practice to go to a hotel on Washington Avenue after I was done with my car. Like as not I would go to sleep—lay my head on my hands on the table. Walt would stay there, wait, watch, keep me undisturbed—would wake me up when the hour of closing came. In his eating he was vigorous, had a big appetite, but was simple in his tastes, not caring for any great dishes.

"I never knew a case of Walt being bothered up by a woman. In fact he had nothing special to do with any woman except Mrs. O'Connor and Mrs. Burroughs. His disposition was different. Woman in that sense never came into his head. Walt was too clean. He hated anything which was not clean. No trace of any kind of dissipation in him. I ought to know about him those years—we were awful close together. In the afternoon I would go up to the Treasury Building and wait for him to get through if he was busy. Then we'd stroll out together, often without any plan. This occurred days in and days out, months running. Towards women generally Walt had a good way—he very easily attracted them. But he did that with men too. And it was an irresistible attraction. I've had many tell me —men and women. He had an easy, gentle way the same for all —no matter who they were or what their sex.

"Towards the end I saw very little of Walt, but he continued to write me. He never altered his manner toward me; here are a few more recent postal-cards. You will see that they show the same old love. I knew he wondered why I saw so little of him the three or four years before he died, but when I explained it to him he understood. Nevertheless I am sorry for it now. The obstacles were too small, it was only this: in the old days I had always open door to Walt—going, coming, staying, as I chose. Now I had to run the gauntlet of Mrs. Davis [Whitman's housekeeper] and a nurse and what not. Then I had a mad impulse to go over and nurse him. I was his proper nurse—he understood me—I understood him. We loved each other deeply. But there were things preventing that too. I saw them. I should have gone to see him, at least, in spite of everything. I have talked a long while. Let us drink up this beer together. Now here's to the dear old man, and the dear old times too and every one that's to come."

Thus the street car conductor was written and wrote himself into the life and story of America's national poet. The "dear love of comrades" found its highest exemplification in Whitman's association and correspondence with this simple heart who never tired of talking of his great friend. He lived to be toward sixty years of age, separated from Whitman in those days of his invalidism in Camden. He died some fifteen years after Whitman did; and at a fellowship dinner in 1907 at which there were gathered devotees of the poet, a toast was proposed to "dear brother Pete Doyle now passed beyond."

CHAPTER NINE

WHITMAN'S compassion, his tenderness and devotion to democracy, his love of mankind, and his celebration of the "dear love of comrades" lead to subtle analysis if the roots of those things are to be found. Once discovered and laid out his ministrations as war nurse, and his "Calamus" and other poems become more understandable. That precocious delver into secrets such as these, Otto Weininger, wrote that "there are transitional forms between the metals and non-metals, between chemical combinations and simple mixtures, between animals and plants, between phanerogams and cryptogams, and between animals and birds. . . . The improbability may be henceforth taken for granted of finding in Nature a sharp cleavage between all that is masculine on the one side and all that is feminine on the other; or that any living being is so simple in this respect that it can be put wholly on one side, or wholly on the other, of the line."

The same writer in his book *Sex and Character,* speaking of womanly compassion and sympathy maintains that "it is especially from womanly kindness, womanly sympathy, that the beautiful descriptions of the soul of woman have gained most support, and the final argument of all belief in the superior morality of woman is the conception of her as the hospital nurse, the tender sister. . . . It is very short sighted of any one to consider the nurse as proof of the sympathy of women, because it really implies the opposite. For a man could never stand the sight of the suffering of the sick; he would suffer so intensely that he would be completely upset and incapable of lengthy attendance upon them. Any one who has watched nursing sisters is astounded at their equanimity and 'sweetness' even in the presence of most terrible death throes; and it is well that it is so, for man, who cannot stand suffering and death, would make a very bad nurse. A man would want to assuage the pain and ward off death, in a word he would want to help; where there is nothing to be done he is better away; it is only then that nursing is justified and that woman offers herself for it."

There are a number of things to be said in objection to this doctrine of Weininger. It may be granted that nurses are hard, but so are surgeons. By that fact the feminine side of Whitman would have been hard; the masculine side of him would have been the sympathetic side. Perhaps it would be nearer the truth to say that his ambivalent nature made him the compassionate ministrant that he was in the war hospitals. His spiritual composition was of that rare quality that often distinguishes geniuses, such as Goethe, Shakespeare, Michelangelo, Marlowe, Alexander the Great, and Julius Cæsar. Examples of the same thing may be found in the relationship between Jesus and John the beloved, between David and Jonathan, Virgil and the youth Alexander, Sappho and her friends. It is written in many stories of antiquity such as those of Achilles and Patroclus, Harmodius, and Aristogiton. The sonnets of Shakespeare are expressions of the love of a man for a man, familiar to all. Sonnet fifty-four of Michelangelo, translated by J. A. Symonds, eloquently describes this passion:

> From thy fair face I learn, O my loved lord,
> That which no mortal tongue can rightly say:
> The soul, imprisoned in her house of clay,
> Holpen by thee to God hath often soared:
> And though the vulgar, vain, malignant horde
> Attribute what their grosser wills obey,
> Yet shall this fervent homage that I pay,
> This love, this faith, pure joys for us afford.

We are concerned here with what this emotional attitude leads to in respect to art and poetry, what its spiritual significance is. The rest of the matter may be left as one would leave the love relations of a man and woman in that reticence where intimate things belong. Whitman's letters to Pete Doyle, his "Calamus" poems, and some in which the words are too gross, may be passed over for an undivided consideration of Whitman's genius and his works which were the product of the Uranian nature.

Edward Carpenter, who knew Whitman, wrote in his book *The Intermediate Sex,* of Uranians, "It would be a great mistake to suppose that their attachments are necessarily sexual, or connected with sexual acts. On the contrary (as abundant evidence shows), they are often purely emotional in their character; and to confuse Uranians (as is often done) with libertines having no law but curiosity in self-indulgence is to do them a great wrong. At the same time, it is evident that their special temperaments may sometimes cause them difficulty in regard to their sexual relations."

Whitman's writings are destitute of love poems to a woman, all except brief lines to the woman, if it was a woman, whom he met in New Orleans. His declaration, that he was the father of several children, cannot be accepted. It is impossible that he could have been the father of several children without the secret coming forth in time in various and abundant proof. Bliss Perry wrote in his *Walt Whitman: His Life and Work,* published in 1906, that "there is also abundant evidence that from 1862 onward his life was stainless so far as sexual relations were concerned." If true, that may have sprung from the resolve entered in his notebook on April 16, 1861, to achieve "a great body, a purged, cleansed, spiritualized, invigorated body." The evidence for Perry's statement, however, lies more in the fact of Whitman's Uranian nature, and the interests in poetry which that nature cultivated and sublimated, than it does in any other kind of proof.

141

The Uranian is described by Carpenter in the book already mentioned, as "a man who while possessing thoroughly masculine powers of mind and body combines with them the tenderer and more emotional soul-nature of the woman—and sometimes to a remarkable degree. Such men, as said, are often muscular and well-built, and not distinguishable in exterior structure and the carriage of body from others of their own sex; but emotionally they are extremely complex, tender, sensitive, pitiful and loving, 'full of storm and stress, of ferment and fluctuation' of the heart; the logical faculty may or may not in their cases he well developed, but intuition is always strong; like women they read characters at a glance, and know without knowing how, what is passing in the minds of others; for nursing and waiting on the needs of others they have often a peculiar gift; at the bottom lies the artist nature, with the artist's sensibility and perception. Such an one is often a dreamer, of brooding, reserved habits, often a musician, or a man of culture, courted in society, which nevertheless does not understand him—though sometimes a child of the people, without any culture, but almost always with peculiar inborn refinement."

De Joux, the author of *Die Enterbten des Liebes-glückes,* wrote of Uranians, "They are enthusiastic for poetry and music, are often eminently skilful in the fine arts, and are overcome with emotion and sympathy at the least sad occurrence. Their sensitiveness, their endless tenderness for children, their love of flowers, their great pity for beggars and crippled folk are truly womanly. . . . The nerve system of many an Urning is the finest and most complicated instrument in the service of the interior personality that can be imagined."

Havelock Ellis called Uranians "sports" or variations, such as can be seen throughout living nature in plants and animals. And to quote De Joux again, "As nature and social law are so cruel as to impose a severe celibacy on him his whole being is consequently of astonishing freshness and superb purity, and his manners of life modest as those of a saint—a thing which in the case of a man in blooming health and moving about in the world, is certainly very unusual. . . . If the soul of woman in its usual form represents a secret closed with seven seals, it is when prisoned in the sturdy body of a man and fused with some of the motives of manhood, a far more enigmatic scripture of whose sybilline meaning one can never be really sure."

For many years authority has grown in volume and strength on the subject of the Uranian to the point that variations from the physical and spiritual norm are to be considered in the light of biological truth, in the same manner as such things are considered in the realm of botany. No one has done more to reach this rational conclusion than Havelock Ellis who in his *Psychology of Sex,* Volume II went into this subject with masterly analysis. In a book bearing the same title published in 1935, which is however a redaction of his great work, he recapitulates these conclusions. In the Symposium, Socrates in discoursing on love said:

"But souls which are pregnant—for there certainly are men who are more creative in their souls than in their bodies—conceive that which is proper for the soul to conceive or contain. And what are these conceptions?—wisdom and virtue in general. And such creators are poets and all artists who are deserving of the name inventor. But the greatest and fairest sort of wisdom by far is that which is concerned with the ordering of states and families, and which is called temperance and justice. And he who in youth has the seed of these implanted in him and is himself inspired, when he comes to maturity desires to beget and generate. . . . Who when he thinks of Homer and Hesiod and other great poets would not rather have their children than ordinary human ones? . . . Or who would not have such children as Lycurgus left behind him to be the saviors, not only of Lacedæmon, but of Hellas, as one may say. There is Solon, too, who is the revered father of Athenian laws; and many others there are in many other places, both among the Hellenes and barbarians, who have given to the world many noble works, and have been parents of virtue of every kind; and many temples have been raised in their honor for the sake of children such as theirs; which were never raised in honor of any one for the sake of his mortal children."

In like manner Carpenter pointed out in the book referred to that while marriage provides the workshop for the breeding and rearing of children, a union with an ideal is often indispensable to supply the basis for social and artistic activities; and that this kind of love is a great leveler which passes the bounds of class and caste, just as Whitman devoted himself to the laborer Pete Doyle. Carpenter's strong belief on this subject led him to forecast that the Uranian people may form an advance guard of civilization which may transform the common life by substituting the bond of personal affection and compassion for the monetary, legal and other external ties which for so long have controlled society.

"If the day is coming, as we have suggested," wrote Carpenter, "when Love is at last to take its rightful place as the binding and directing force of society (instead of the Cashnexus), and society is to be transmuted in consequence to a higher form, then undoubtedly the superior types of Uranians—prepared for this service by long experience and devotion, as well as by much suffering, will have an important part to play in the transformation. For that the Urnings in their own lives put Love before everything else, postponing it to the other motives like money making, business success, fame, which occupy so much space in most people's careers—is a fact which is patent to everyone who knows them."

The work of Shelley inevitably comes to mind in connection with words like these. The wonderful choruses of *Prometheus Unbound* with their prophecies of a happier world based on love; a new day of earth happiness created by social love, are things which Shelley looked forward to and sang in many poems and fragments. In his *Epipsychidion* he transmuted into verse the words of Diotima and Agathon. Of himself he spoke as "A love in desolation." In a fragment he wrote,

> But love, though misdirected, is among
> The things which are immortal, and surpass
> All that frail stuff which will be — or which was.

In "Marenghi" he showed how superior is the love of comrades to that supposedly greatest test of virtue to love one's enemies,

> I am a spirit who has dwelt
> Within his heart of hearts, and I have felt
> His feelings, and have thought his thoughts and known
> The inmost converse of his soul ——

This concerning wedded souls. Browning, too, is full of this philosophy, beginning with love of men for women and emerging into general love, into ethical passion and social ideals.

In his preface to the first edition of *Leaves of Grass* Whitman declared his faith as follows: "No great literature, nor any style of behaviour or oratory, or social intercourse of household arrangements, or public institutions, or the treatment by bosses of employed people, nor executive detail, or detail of the army and navy, nor spirit of legislation or courts, or police or tuition or architecture, or songs or amusements, can long elude the jealous and passionate instinct of American standards. Whether or no the sign appears from the mouths of people, it throbs a live interrogation in every freeman's and freewoman's heart, after that which passes by, or this built to remain. Is it uniform with my country? Are its disposals without ignominious distinctions? Is it for the ever growing communes of brothers and lovers, large, well-united, proud beyond the old models, generous beyond all models? Is it something grown fresh out of the fields, or drawn from the sea for use to me today here? . . . I know that what answers for me, an American, in Texas, Ohio, Canada, must answer for any individual or nation that serves for a part my materials. Does this answer? Is it for the nursing of the young of the republic? Does it solve readily with the sweet milk of the nipples of the breasts of the Mother of Many Children?"

So he would make the "most splendid race the sun ever shone upon, I will make divine, magnetic lands. . . . I will make inseparable cities with their arms about each others' necks by the love of comrades." And in *Democratic Vistas* Whitman declared, "It is to the development, identification, and general prevalence of that fervid comradeship (the adhesive love at least rivaling the amative love hitherto possessing imaginative Literature, if not going beyond it), that I look for the counterbalance and offset of materialistic and vulgar American Democracy, and for the spiritualization thereof. . . . I say Democracy infers such loving comradeship, as its most inevitable twin or counterpart, without which it will be incomplete, in vain, and incapable of perpetuating itself."

Upon consideration of these things the poems in "Calamus" take on a clear significance. In an afternoon in his forty-first year Whitman sang "In Paths Untrodden":

Escaped from the life that exhibits itself,
From all the standards hitherto publish'd, from the pleasures, profits, conformities,
Which I too long was offering to feed my soul,
Clear to me now standards not yet publish'd, clear to me that my soul,
That the soul of the man I speak for rejoices in comrades,
Here by myself away from the clank of the world,
Tallying and talk'd to here by tongues aromatic,
No longer abash'd (for in this secluded spot I can respond as I would not dare elsewhere),
Strong upon me the life that does not exhibit itself, yet contains all the rest,
Resolv'd to sing no songs today but those of manly attachment,
Projecting them along the substantial life,
Bequeathing hence types of athletic love.

And again in "Scented Herbage of My Breast":

O slender leaves! O blossoms of my blood! I permit vou to tell in
   your own way of the heart that is under you,
Or I do not know what you mean there underneath yourselves,
   you are not happiness,
You are often more bitter than I can bear, you burn and sting me,
Yet you are beautiful to me, you faint-tinged roots, you make me
   think of death,
Death is beautiful from you (what is finally beautiful except death
   and love?)
Or I think it is not for life that I am chanting here my chant of
   lovers, I think it must be for death,
For how calm, how solemn it grows to ascend to the atmosphere
   of lovers,
Death or life I am then indifferent, my soul declines to prefer,
(I am not sure but the high soul of lovers welcomes death most).

And again in "Whoever You Are Holding Me Now in Hand":

Or else in stealth in some wood for trial,
Or back of a rock in the open air,
(For in any roof'd room of a house I emerge not, nor in company,
And in libraries I lie as one dumb, a gawk, or unborn, or dead)
But just possibly with you on a high hill, first watching lest any
   person for miles around approaches unawares,
Or possibly with you sailing at sea, or on the beach of the sea, or
   some quiet island,
Here to put your lips upon mine I permit you,
With the comrade's long-dwelling kiss, or the new husband's kiss,
For I am the new husband and I am the comrade.
Or if you will, thrusting me under your clothing,
Where I may feel the throbs of your heart, or rest upon your hip,
Carry me when you go forth over land or sea;
For thus merely touching you is enough, is best
And thus touching you would I silently sleep and be carried eter-
   nally.

And again in "Of the Terrible Doubt of Appearances":

When he whom I love travels with me or sits a long while holding
   me by the hand,

When the subtle air, the impalpable, the sense that words and rea-
son hold not, surround us and pervade us,
Then I am charged with untold and untellable wisdom, I am
silent, I require nothing further
I cannot answer the question of appearances or that of identity
beyond the grave,
But I walk or sit indifferent, I am satisfied,
He ahold of mv hand has completely satisfied me.

Whitman here is hinting at those profound intimations of
nature, of man and of love, which visit all deeply imaginative
souls. He is catching the flashing lights of realms afar and
around us, and doing it, as only it can be done by the experience of love which is union, merging with the infinite through
the finite. It is the very opposite of coldness, indifference, and
of hate in its hostile separateness from love—for hate is sterility.
It is death and ignorance. Whitman asked in "Recorders Ages
Hence" that his name be published "as that of the tenderest
lover. . . . Who was not proud of his songs, but of the meas-
ureless ocean of love within him, and freely Pour'd it forth."
Scarcely has such a soul been seen in the world before. He
seems more articulate, more definite, and more forth standing
than Leonardo, Michelangelo; and so much more powerful and
ample than Shelley. This vision is to be had through the "one
I love most," who lies "sleeping by me under the same cover
in the cool night," as the poet sings:

In the stillness in the autumn moonbeams his face was inclined
toward me,
And his arm lay lightly around by breast — all that night I was
happy,

As he sang "When I Heard at the Close of the Day," who shall
impugn the experience and deny this vision?
Never has a man so fully expressed his cosmic longing as
Whitman did, flinging to the winds all reticences, and daring
to use words and images which shadow it forth. He incurred
the risk of being mocked, of being grossly interpreted by the

vulgarity of the world. He kisses the Manhattanese as an observation of American comrades, and as natural and nonchalant
persons. He looks longingly upon the passing stranger chanting, "O I know we should be brethren and lovers." He does
not envy the conquered fame of heroes and victors:

But when I hear of the brotherhood of lovers, how it was with
them,
How together through life, through dangers, odium, unchanging
and long,
Through youth, and through middle and old age, how unfalter-
ingly, how affectionate and faithful they were,
Then I am pensive—I hastily walk away fill'd with the bitterest
envy.

We may say here with Shelley:

My Song, I fear that thou wilt find but few
Who fitly shall conceive thy reasoning.

This is the love which divines the **recapitulation** of the urge
of the life essences, blindly and powerfully, inevitably and
swiftly seeking to be merged and to be one. Man as a lover
repeats this passion and this process and finds in them, when
he finds it, the secret of the mystery of life.
Whitman epitomizes this:

An athlete is enamoured of me and I of him,
But toward him there is something fierce and terrible in me eligible
to burst forth,
I dare not tell it in words, not even in these songs.

When he saw the live oak growing in Louisiana it made him
think of "manly love." He rose from the individual to America with this love, writing, "I believe the main purport of these
states is to found a superb friendship, exalté, previously unknown." Women, too, are included in this passion:

Fast-anchor'd O love, O woman I love,
O bride, O wife, more resistless than I can tell, the thought of you!

149

> The separate, as disembodied or another born,
> Etherial, the last athletic reality, my consolation,
> I ascend, I float in the regions of your love, O man,
> O sharer of my roving life.

This is a spiritual metaphysic not to be touched by what Whitman called "infidels," by unbelievers in the shadows of unseen powers that haunt the high imagination and call it to the duty of love on earth. When he applied it to Democracy it was to annihilate strife and hate and to bring in peace and union, it was to substitute life and life-giving ministrations for death and destruction.

In Whitman's day people went behind closed doors to talk of the simple facts of life. Perhaps Whitman wanted to a degree to shock his countrymen out of their false modesty, and to cleanse the land by fresh and even violent air. In any case he was not a sonneteer with perfumed lines. He belonged to the great like Homer who use any word they choose and speak of any experience with forthright naturalness. Hence it was that he used gross words at times, and employed gross imagery. These will betray the unlearned and uninitiated. They will fasten their eyes upon these expressions exclusively, and fail to see the meaning beneath them, ignoring the intentions which govern their use. I do not, myself, like the sound and appearance of such words as "man root," "man nuts," and "teats"; but my objection to them is purely æsthetic. I think Whitman could have used other words to convey his meaning, and that these coarse words take him no further in the expression of himself than more delicate words would have taken him.

But let us see what Whitman was about. In a conversation with the faithful Traubel in 1888 the following came forth: "I spoke of 'Calamus' as 'supreme among love-poems in the English language.' He said: 'There seem to be various ideas on that subject. The South has produced love poems, songs, sweet, delicate, true; Paul H. Hayne was one of its poets

—Cooke (was it Pendleton?): men of that stamp. It is a fact, of course, that they were piano tunes: still, they were good in their range. But there is a more rugged—a universal—sentiment which has most largely and primarily to be recognized in the basic big chants of the affections.'"

Finally on this subject we find in Whitman's notes the following: "Mothers precede all. Put in a poem the sentiment of women (mothers) as preceding all the rest."

CHAPTER TEN

A MONG Whitman's pieces in early youth, 1834-'42, there is a story called *The Boy Lover,* and very well told, though a simple narrative. Some youths happen upon a girl named Ninon at a tavern in the country. She is the daughter of a widow. All these youths then fall in love with her. They return to drink beer and to see Ninon again. She has died. They look upon her grave, somewhat in the manner of Poe's tragic loves. One of the young men is so deeply hurt that he dies soon too. The unfortunate youth is not Whitman, one gathers—but the passion of love is comprehendingly, even if somewhat conventionally told. The story is in the melodramatic style of that period.

Emory Holloway found a poem by Whitman written in his twentieth year; two stanzas of which may be quoted:

> O mighty power of Destiny
> When from this coil of flesh I'm free,
> When through my second life I rove
> Let me but find one heart to love,
>   As I would wish to love.
>
> For vainly through this world below
> We seek affection, naught but woe
> Is with our earthly journey wove,
> And so the heart must look above,
>   Or die in dull despair.

Whitman strikes me as a poet who realized the preoccupations of his calling and did not want to burden himself with

152

a wife and domesticity. According to Mrs. William D. O'Connor, Whitman once said that he did not think it would have been well for him to have formed that closest of ties, marriage. He did not envy men their wives, but their children. To this day in Camden people who knew Whitman and saw him about the streets or on the way to the ferry to Philadelphia, speak of his fondness for children and their affection for him. He never passed a child without putting his hand upon its head and speaking some gentle word to it.

At the same time there were the pent up rivers of his being, his aching passion. In Whitman's unpublished diary, kept when he was forty-nine, there is this entry following a page that has been torn out: *"Remember where I am most weak & most lacking.* Yet always preserve a kind spirit & demeanor to 16. *But pursue her no more.* A cool, gentle (less demonstrative) *more* uniform demeanor—give to poor, help any—be indulgent to the criminal & silly and low person generally & the ignorant —but say little—make no explanations—*give no confidences."*

In an 1870 notebook when Whitman was fifty-one there is this entry: "It is imperative that I obviate and remove myself (& my orbit) at all hazards (away from) from this incessant enormous & (enormous) perturbation." The word perturbation is emphasized by two crudely drawn fists with the forefinger pointing to it.

On the same page he writes: *"To give up absolutely* & for good, from this present hour (all) the *feverish, fluctuating,* useless undignified pursuit of 164—too long (much too long), persevered in—so humiliating—It must come at last & had better come now. (It cannot possibly be a success.) *Let there from this hour be no faltering* (or) no *getting* [word erased] at all henceforth. (*Not once* under any circumstances)—avoid seeing her, or meeting her, or any talk or explanation—or *Any meeting whatever from this hour forth for Life."*

It is clear that "164" was not a beloved woman, but a woman of convenience. Whitman would not have referred to a woman he loved as "164." And it may be that he was beginning to feel senescent, if not quite so, and that his humiliation lay in the fact that the woman all too charitably made allowance for his decreased power as a man.

In 1890 Whitman wrote to John Addington Symonds a letter, later printed by Edward Carpenter, about his children, in these words: "My life, young manhood, my mid age, times South etc., have been jolly bodily, and doubtless open to criticism. Though unmarried I have had six children. Two are dead —one living . . . circumstances connected with their fortune and benefit have separated me from intimate relations with them."

Is this true? Traubel recorded that he could get from Whitman no concrete allusion to any woman by whom he had had children. Traubel was with Whitman day by day for several years in intimate conversation about every subject, and yet Whitman withheld the names of the women by whom he had had six children, or any child. He was sending money and writing letters to Pete Doyle. Why no money to his children or their mothers? The conclusion is inevitable, that the children were the product of casual relationships and not very creditable ones, or that he had no children. Whitman was not above telling "whoppers," and he may have thought it well to invent a parenthood in order to repel the whispers of homosexuality which were buzzing around him, not realizing that fecundity and homosexuality may well be harmonious conditions.

John Addington Symonds (1840–1893), who wrote on Dante and Greek culture, became greatly interested in Whitman and the "Calamus" poems and from the standpoint of an intelligence which comprehended the psychology of the Uranian, asked Whitman the direct question about the homosexual basis of the "Calamus" poems. Whitman was much annoyed and dodged away. But as to children, Clara Barrus in her book *Whitman and Burroughs Comrades* said that Burroughs told her that Whitman was not himself at times toward the last, and that this declaration of being a father was one of his senile dreams. Eldridge, Kennedy, and Moncure D. Conway all held to the belief that Whitman had never had any children. These men were all close to him for years.

By way of being generous about accepting this statement, however, it would have been possible for Whitman to have been told by women of fugitive contacts that they had had a child by him. He then, not having been sure of the truth of what they said, might have indulged himself in carelessness concerning them, and indifference to their happiness and comfort. But if he had any respect for the mothers (and he repeatedly sang motherhood in his poems) he presents a marked contrast to Franklin who was fatherly, and openly so, toward his natural son.

Some of Whitman's friends and champions have said that it was the tragedy of his life that he could not or did not marry some one of these women, or some woman, if it was only one by whom he claimed the six children. There is no evidence, however, that there was any tragedy so far as Whitman was concerned. No woman has risen up to say that she loved Walt Whitman and that it was her tragedy not to have won him for a husband. No human being has come forward publicly with any proof worth noticing, that Whitman was his father. According to the course of human events it is only barely possible that there could be such a situation as this, for things of this kind can hardly be hidden as completely as Whitman's supposed children are lost to the knowledge of the world, existing only unnamed and in vague generalizations and rumor.

But at last a woman did come into Whitman's life and with unreserved fervor and dedication. This was when Whitman reached the age of fifty and the woman was Anne Gilchrist of England, then just beyond forty and a widow.

In June of 1869 she came across *Leaves of Grass* through

Madox Brown and took fire. In May of 1870 she published in *The Boston Radical* an "Estimate of Walt Whitman" which Harned called the "finest as it was the first public tribute ever paid the poet by a woman." Later Whitman called it, "The proudest word that ever came to me from a woman—if not the proudest from any source." When she died in November, 1885, Whitman said, "She was a wonderful woman—a sort of human miracle to me. . . . Her taking off . . . was a great shock to me. I have never quite got over it: she was near to me: she was subtle: her grasp on my work was tremendous—so sure, so all around, so adequate."

Herbert Harlakenden Gilchrist, son of Anne Gilchrist, described her thus: "A little above the average height, she walked with an even light step. Brown hair concealed a full and finely chiseled brow, and her hazel eyes bent upon you a bright and penetrating gaze. Whilst conversing her face became radiant as with an experience of golden years; humor was present in her conversation—flecks of sunshine, such as sometimes play about the minds of deeply religious natures. Her animated manner seldom flagged, and charmed the taciturn to talking in his best humor. Once when speaking to Walt Whitman of the beauty of the human speaking voice he replied: 'The voice indicates the soul. Hers with its varied modulation and blended tone was the tenderest, most musical voice ever to bless our ears.' "

In September of 1871 Mrs. Gilchrist wrote Whitman her first letter, and thus began her wooing of him. Many letters followed from her but not so steady a stream from Whitman, who acted as though he were cautiously studying what had come to him. When she died her son wrote to ask Whitman for the letters his mother had written him and Whitman replied: "I do not know that I can furnish any good reason, but I feel to keep these utterances exclusively to myself. But I cannot let you go to press without at least saying—and wishing it put on record—that among the perfect women I have met (and it has been my unspeakable good fortune to have had the very best for mother, sister & friends) I have known none more perfect in every relation than my dear, dear friend Anne Gilchrist."

The son seems not to have got the letters. When Harned, Bucke, and Traubel, Whitman's literary executors, put together his complete works they passed over the Gilchrist matter by saying: "While we do not regard the present as the time, nor this page as the place to go into the details of such an episode, it may be said that the correspondence . . . reveals on both sides the existence of a superterrestrial confidence and respect." But in 1918 Harned gave the letters to the world in a book entitled *Letters of Anne Gilchrist and Whitman;* and thus what Anne Gilchrist felt and what Whitman did not feel in that crisis of a woman's life are open to the world.

Mrs. Gilchrist's first letter is dated September 3, 1871. By way of showing that her love for Whitman was really the first love of her life she said that she didn't want to marry Gilchrist. This is contradicted by her letter to her friend Julia Newton announcing her engagement to Gilchrist, a letter brought to light by her son. But last love is best love according to the psychology of such things, so that this protestation may be passed.

She wrote to Whitman: "The time will come when man will understand that a woman's soul is as dear and needful to his, and as different from his as her body to his body. This is what happened to me when I had read for a few days, nay hours, in your books. It was the divine soul embracing mine. I never before dreamed what love meant: not what life meant. Never was alive before—no words but those of new birth can hint the meaning of what happened to me. In May, 1869, came the voice over the Atlantic—to me—O the voice of my mate; it must be so—my love rises up out of the depths of the grief and tramples upon despair, I can wait—any time, a lifetime, nay life times—I can suffer, I can dare, I can learn, grow, toil, but nothing in life or death can tear out of my heart the passionate belief that one day I shall hear that voice say to me, 'My mate.' The one I so much want. Bride, wife, indissoluble, eternal.

"And my darling above all because I love thee so tenderly that if hateful words had been spoken against me I could have taken joy in it for thy dear sake. There never yet was the woman who loved that would not joyfully bare her breast to wrest the blows aimed at her beloved. . . . O come, come, my darling, look into these eyes and see the long ardent aspiring soul in them. Easily, easily you will learn to love all the rest of me for the sake of that and take me to your breast forever."

On October 23, 1871, Mrs. Gilchrist wrote to Whitman again: "I know that a woman may without hurt to her pride—without stain or blame—tell her love to thee. I feel for a certainty that she may. Try me for this life, my darling—see if I cannot so live, so grow, so learn, so love, that when I die you will say, 'This woman has grown to be a very part of me. My soul must have her long companionship everywhere & in all things. I alone and she alone are not complete identities—it is I and she together in a new, divine, perfect union that form the one complete identity."

Mrs. Gilchrist's letter of November 27, 1871, may be taken to mean that she had heard from Whitman, but not in answer to her letter of September 3. She writes:

"I gather from it [Whitman's letter] that a long letter in which I opened all my heart to you never reached your hands." It had, however, for Harned included it in this book of correspondence. She went on: "Do you know, dear friend, what it means for a woman, what it means for me to understand these poems?—It means for her whole nature to be kindled . . . that thenceforth she cannot choose but live & die striving to be worthy to share this divine man's life . . . her soul to mate with his forever & ever . . . But I could face, I could joyfully accept the fiercest anguish, the hardest toil, the long-est, sternest probation to make me fit to be your mate, so at the last you would say, 'This is the woman I have waited for, the woman prepared for me: this is my dear eternal comrade, wife—the one I so much want.'"

Then followed letters from her to Whitman on January 24 and February 8, 1872. On April 12, 1872 she wrote as follows: "My love, flowing ever fresh & fresh out of my heart, will go with you day and night, soul & body, with tenderness that tries vainly to utter itself in these poor, helpless words, that clings closer than any woman's love can cling—O I could not live if I did not believe that sooner or later you will not be able to help stretching out your arms toward me & saying, 'Come, my darling.'"

On June 3, 1872 she wrote: "How can I be content to live wholly isolated from you? I am sure it is not possible for any one—man or woman, it does not matter which, to receive these books not merely with the intellect critically admiring their power & beauty, but with an understanding, responsive heart, without feeling it drawn out of their breasts, so that they must leave all & come to be with you sometimes without a resistless yearning for personal intercourse that will take no denial."

She wrote him again in July and in November, 1872. Evidently Whitman did not answer her. Then on January 31, 1873, about a month before he had the first paralytic stroke which rendered him thenceforth an invalid, she wrote as follows:

"Dearest Friend: Shall you never find it in your heart to say a kind word to me again? or a word of some sort? Surely I must have written what displeased you very much that you should turn away from me as the tone of your last letter & the ten months silence which have followed seem to express to me with such emphasis. But if so tell me of it, tell me how—with perfect candor, I am worthy of that—a willing learner & striver; not afraid of the pain of looking my own faults & shortcomings steadily in the face. . . . But I can wait long, wait patiently, know well, realize more dearly indeed that this wingless, clouded, half-developed soul of me has a long, long initiate to live through before it can meet & answer yours on equal terms so as fully to satisfy you, to be in very truth & deed a dear Friend, a chosen companion, a source of joy to you as you of light & life to me. But that is what I will live & die hoping and striving for. That covers & encloses all the aspiration, all the high hopes I am capable of. And were I to fall away from this belief it would be a fall into utter blackness & despair, as one for whom the Sun in Heaven is blotted out."

By August Mrs. Gilchrist had heard of Whitman's illness. She wrote on the 12th of that month in 1873: "The paper has just been forwarded here which tells me you are still suffering and not, as I was fondly believing, already quite emerged from the cloud of sickness. My Darling, let me use that tender, caressing word once more—for how can I help it, with heart so full & no outlet but words? My darling—I say it over & over to myself with voice, with eyes so full of love, of tender yearning, sorrowful, longing love. I would give all the world if I might come (but am held here yet awhile by a duty nothing supersedes) & soothe & tend & wait on you & with such cheerful, loving companionship lift off some of the wait of the long hours & days & perhaps months that must still go over while nature slowly, imperceptibly, but still so surely repairs the mischief within: result of the tremendous ordeal to your frame of those great over-brimming years of life spent in the Army Hospitals."

Some time in the summer of 1873 Whitman wrote Mrs. Gilchrist as follows: "On the night of 3d January last I was paralyzed, left side, and have remained so since. Feb. 19 I lost a dear, dear sister, who died in St. Louis leaving two young daughters. May 23d my dear, inexpressibly beloved mother died in Camden, N. J. I was just able to get from Washington to her dying bed and sit there. . . . (Your letters of Jan. 24, June 3 & July 14 of last years and January 31 and May 20 of this year, with certainly one other, maybe two) all came safe. Do not think hard of me for not writing in reply. If you could look into my spirit and emotion you would certainly be entirely satisfied and at peace. . . . You must not be unhappy about me, as I am as comfortably situated as can be—& many things—indeed everything—in my case might be much worse."

On September 4, 1873, Mrs. Gilchrist wrote Whitman: "I am entirely satisfied and at peace, my Beloved—not words can say how divine a peace. . . . My Darling Take comfort & strength & joy from me that you have made so rich and strong. Perhaps it will yet be given us to see each other, to travel the last stage of this journey side by side, hand in hand."

On December 18, 1873, she wrote him again: "Perhaps if my hand were in yours, dear Walt, you would get along faster. Dearer and sweeter that lot than even to have been your bride in the full flush of strength and glory of your youth. I turn my face to the westward sky before I lie down to sleep, deep and steadfast within me the silent aspiration that every year, every month & week may help something to prepare and make fitter me and mine to be your comfort and joy." Later in February she wrote: "In discouraged moods . . . I say to my-self, 'what sort of bird with unfledged wings are you that you would mate with an eagle? . . . Is your heart like his, a great glowing sun of Love?'"

In March of 1874 she received *Harper's Magazine* containing Whitman's "The Prayer of Columbus"; two months later she wrote about her busy days. In July she pleaded: "Oh it makes me long with passionate longing, with yearnings I know not how to bear, to come, to be your loving, cheerful compan-ion, the one to take such care, to do all for you—to beguile the time, to give you of my health as you have done to thousands.

... I believe if I could only make you conscious of the love, the enfolding love my heart breathes out toward you it would do you physical good." And again a little later, "O sorrowing, helpless love that waits, and must wait, useless afar off, while you suffer. But trying every day of my life to grow fitter, more capable of being your comfort and joy and true comrade—never to cease trying this side of death or the other."

Mrs. Gilchrist wrote to Whitman December 9 and 30, 1874, and February 21, 1875—this is mentioned only to show the frequency of her letters. They need not be quoted. There was nothing in them of much moment. On August 28, 1875, she made mention of a letter which she had received from Whitman on the occasion of the death of her mother who died August 15, 1875.

In November, 1875, she wrote as follows: "I have been wanting the comfort of a talk with you, dearest Friend, for weeks & weeks, without being able to get leisure and tranquility enough to do it to my heart's content—indeed heart's content is not for me at present—but restless, eager longing to come—& the struggle to do patiently & completely & wisely what remains for me here before I am free to obey the deep faith and love which govern me—so let me sit close by you, my Darling & feel your presence & take comfort and strength & security from it as I do, as I can when with all my heart & soul I draw close to you, realizing your living presence with all my might."

On December 4, 1875, she wrote: "O cling close to life with a resolute hold, my beloved, to bless us with your presence unspeakably dear, beneficent presence—me to taste of it before so long now, thirsting, pining, loving me. Take through these poor words of mine some breath of the tender, tender, ineffable love that fills my heart and soul and body: take it to strengthen the very springs of your life: it is capable of that; O it's cherishing warmth and joy, if it could only get to you, only fold you round close enough, would help you, I know. Soon, soon as ever my boy has one to love and care for him all his own, I will come."

On January 18, 1876, Whitman received in a letter from her the startling announcement: "Do not think me too wilful or headstrong, but I have taken our tickets & we shall sail August 30th for Philadelphia." She wrote him again on February 25: and on March 11: "Oh may I be full of sweet comfort for my Beloved's soul and body through life, through and after death."

Then in March, 1876, Whitman sent from Camden the following message to Mrs. Gilchrist: "Dearest Friend: To your good and comforting letter of February 25 I at once answer, at least with a few lines. . . . My dearest friend, *I do not approve of your American trans-settlement. I see so many things here you have no idea of—the social and almost every other kind of crudeness, meagreness, here (at least in appearance). Don't do anything towards it, nor resolve in it nor make any move at all in it without further advice from me. If I should get well enough to voyage we will talk about it yet in London.*"

To this Mrs. Gilchrist replied: "I will not act without further advice from you; but as to not resolving on it, dear friend, I can't exactly obey that, for it has been my settled, steady purpose (resting on a deep strong faith) ever since 1869. Nor do I feel discouraged or suppressed at what you say of American 'crudeness'."

Then again in late April of 1876 she wrote: "Do not dissuade me from coming this autumn, my dearest Friend. I have waited patiently—7 years—patiently yet often, especially since your illness, with such painful yearning, your heart would yearn towards me if you realized it—I cannot wait any longer."

On May 18, 1876, she wrote thus explicitly: "If I do not hear from you to the contrary am to take our passage by one of the 'State' Line of Steamers that come straight to Philadelphia—sailing about the 1st Sept."

And so Mrs. Gilchrist and her children arrived in due course in Philadelphia. Emory Holloway is authority for saying that there is no record of the first meeting between Mrs. Gilchrist and Whitman. He had been more or less prostrated with paralysis from 1873 to this year of 1876; and whether he was reconciled to her visit, or what they said to each other must remain unexpressed. She took a place in 22d Street in Philadelphia where she remained for more than a year.

Mrs. Gilchrist set aside a room for Whitman and he went to see her frequently. On one occasion he took her and her children to see Joaquin Miller's "The Danites." Finally she wandered to Boston, Concord and New York, writing him from these places constantly, addressing him sometimes "My dearest Friend," sometimes "Dear Darling Walt," sometimes "Dear Walt." In New York she sojourned at 112 Madison Avenue. On March 26, 1879, she wrote from Madison Avenue: "It seems quite a long while since I wrote & a *very long* while since you wrote. I am beginning to turn my thoughts Philadelphia-ward that we may have some weeks near you before we set out on fresh wanderings across the sea; and though I feel quite cheery about them I look eagerly forward to the time beyond that when we have a fixed, final nest of our own again, where we can welcome you just when and where you please."

By this time Whitman was improved in health. In September he started for the Rocky Mountains and remained away from Camden until December. By June of this year Mrs. Gilchrist had set foot on land at Glasgow after a good passage from America. She wrote Whitman soon about Durham Cathedral and Whitman replied saying that he wished he could see it. Now her letters began to lag as if the fire which had flamed in her at first was dying away for lack of fuel. A month would elapse between her letters, then five months; then she would flare again into a semblance of the old persisting thought. She wrote him in December, 1881, and again in January, 1882, then in May of that year, then in November.

In January, 1883, she addressed him without an inscription and said, "It is not for want of thinking of you, dear Walt, that I write but seldom." By May of that year she had evidently received a letter from Whitman, as she remarked, "you cannot think, dear friend, what a pleasure it was to have a whole big letter from you (not that I despise postcards—they are good stop-gaps, but not the real thing)." Whitman wrote to Silas Baxter and others on these postcards; but he was more than usually indifferent to good taste so to address Mrs. Gilchrist.

In July she wrote Whitman about Bucke's life of Whitman. In October she complained, "long & long does it seem since I have had any word from you." Her next letter was in April, 1884. In May she wrote, "your card (your very voice and touch drawing me across the Atlantic close beside you) was put into my hand just as I was busy copying out 'With Husky, Haughty Lips O Sea.' " Then she mentioned that Edward Dowden of the University of Dublin had recently come to see her. Her letters now skipped to August, to October, then in December she wrote, "At last I have extracted a little bit of news about you from friend Carpenter." She then referred to Froude's life of Carlyle, and of Carlyle's remorse for the way he had treated his wife Jane Welsh.

The next letter from her was in February of 1885, and the next in May—finally on July 20, 1885, she wrote, "My Dearest Friend: A kind of anxiety has for some time weighed upon me and upon others, I find, who love and admire you, that you do not have all the comforts you ought to have; that you are sometimes straitened for means." Mrs. Gilchrist's fears were unfounded, for Whitman was never in the deep poverty that some people have imagined him to have been in. By 1885 he was occupying a house of his own in Camden, while his brother George who had lived in Stevens Street in that town, about two blocks from Whitman's Mickle Street home, was in comfortable circumstances. Though George had by this time removed from Camden he was in convenient touch with the poet.

Four months after Mrs. Gilchrist's letter to Whitman of July 20 she died, being in her fifty-eighth year and Whitman in his sixty-sixth. Her eager, almost frantic love came to whatever she was able to take from it in the way of spiritual sustenance, which could scarcely have been more than she derived from his poems—read afar in England at that. What did Whitman get from her love? He was human enough to love adoration and her unreserved worship must have given him deep, satisfaction. However, he wrote her into no poem, just as he never sang a woman. He did not do for her even so much as he had done for the woman in New Orleans—if it was a woman. There he had passed through a populous city and touched transiently another human life. Here was a cultivated woman, who had given him great critical aid, who had crossed the ocean to be near him, to comfort him and even to nurse him, if permitted, to devote her life to him; and he wrote no poem to her. *Once a divine woman crossed the ocean to help me,* might have been his title for such a poem. The "dear love of comrades" might have fastened upon Mrs. Gilchrist as the medium of a concrete celebration. But such was not the case.

There are intimations, even assertions, that Whitman would have married Mrs. Gilchrist except for the fact that he was in love with another woman—a married woman whom he could not take to wife. Always a mysterious woman! Emory Holloway in his book *Whitman: an Interpretation,* published in 1926, said that Mrs. O'Connor declared that Whitman during his life in Washington fell in love with this unnamed married woman, that one of Whitman's letters to her fell into her husband's hands and that he flew into a rage, confronting Whitman with abusive reproof. It was also said that Whitman wrote to this woman the poem "Out of the Rolling Ocean the Crowd Came a Drop Gently to Me." For my part I do not believe a word of this. If the husband intercepted such a letter why did he not give it out at last? What became of it? If Whitman loved this woman why only one letter? Would not any woman save the letter of such a celebrity? Why would Whitman, in love, act so differently from all other poets in love, save that by his nature he did not love women romantically? Women to him were as men were, human beings, and except in the rôle of mothers, by his own statement, did not interest him so much as men did. With this history of Whitman's life thus set down, these conclusions seem beyond controversy.

The death of Whitman's mother during the time that Mrs. Gilchrist was addressing him most ardently was not without its influence upon Whitman's attitude in this affair. In *Parenthood and the Newer Psychology,* by Frank Howard Richardson, published in 1926, these words have application to all cases of mother love preemption: "Such an individual will never be able to consummate a happy marriage, the biological end for which we agreed that every individual was foreordained, and the emotional acme of human experience. For such a one has never learned to love, he is absolutely lacking in the ability to love—in the self-forgetting and self-sacrificing way in which nature functions."

So much may be said without going into the somewhat doubtful ramifications of the overworked Œdipus complex. Viewing Whitman in the present particular with the average eyes, practised in observing human nature and the working of the literary mind, one must pay attention to Whitman's passion for America into which he sublimated his powers. Moreover, one must take into account Whitman's moral determination to aid the rights of women, and to place sex where it normally belongs in a rational scheme of life. To do these things it was necessary for him to range with philosophical eyes over the points involved. It would have been a detriment to him in this high work as a prophet and a philosopher to have been deeply involved in amorous preoccupations, and he never was in his life.

In looking through the list of Whitman's rejected lines and passages one comes across this: "That only when sex is properly treated, talked, avowed, accepted will the woman be equal with the man, and pass where the man passes, and meet his words with her words, and his rights with her rights." No one has done more than Whitman to advance these consummations. Again he wrote, "I know that amativeness is just as divine as spirituality—and this which I know I put in my poems." And again, "I admire a beautiful woman. . . . I am easy about who paints her portrait."

Look at the poems of Verlaine and Villon on the prostitute, at Swinburne's febrile verses about the erotic woman, at Rossetti's almost revolting picture of "Jenny," and then turn to Whitman's poem "To a Common Prostitute," and see how his all comprehending compassion, his deep understanding of life and of a woman, addressed the figure that has always been hunted and cursed,

Be composed—be at ease with me—I am Walt Whitman, liberal
    and lusty as nature,
Not till the sun excludes you do I exclude you.

CHAPTER ELEVEN

To RESUME now the history of Whitman's literary productiveness: In 1867 Whitman issued the fourth edition of *Leaves of Grass,* a book of 470 pages by this time, which contained eight new poems, among them "Tears, Tears, Tears." In 1871 Whitman published *Democratic Vistas,* a prose retrospect upon the country, and a castigation of post-war corruption and political and spiritual degradation in the land. It was and still is one of the great pieces of prose, of more than Miltonic warning and reproof, that America can call altogether its own. Also in 1871 Whitman published *Passage to India,* a volume which contained seventy-three poems in all, twenty-three of which were new. Among these was "Proud Music of the Storm," a truly magnificent poem; and "Passage to India," which gave the book its title.

In 1888 Whitman had this to say concerning this poem: "There's more of me, the essential ultimate me, in that poem than in any of the poems. There is no philosophy, consistent or inconsistent, in that poem—there Brinton would be right —but the burden of its evolution—the one thing escaping the other—the unfolding of cosmic purposes." Whitman as the poet of *Passage to India* had reached the purest heights of his art. He had become pure flame out of suffering through the war, by long meditation. Even his mannerisms of an earlier time, which rather lowered the tone of his work, his use of coarse words, his incongruous grabbing at French phrases, had passed away in the fire of a solemn purpose and inspiration.

To call Whitman an idler is to overlook his tremendous activity of mind. In September of 1871 he recited before the American Institute in New York his poem "After All Not to Create Only." This he published that year in a pamphlet of twenty-four pages. Also in 1871 he brought out the fifth edition of *Leaves of Grass,* which contained the *Passage to India* poems, and thirteen new poems. Among them was "In Cabin'd Ships at Sea," and "Ethiopia Saluting the Colors." In 1872 Whitman published at Washington *As a Strong Bird on Pinions Free* and other poems, which contained "O Star of France" and "By Broad Potomac's Shore." The latter he recited at Dartmouth College on June 26, 1872. It was included in the 1876 edition of *Leaves of Grass.*

Never to be overlooked, but always to be read with close attention are Whitman's various prefaces. They contain much wise direction to America both for that time and for today. The preface to *As a Strong Bird on Pinions Free* may at this point be quoted from to show his state of mind in this his fifty-third year.

"When I commenced years ago," he wrote, "elaborating the plans of my poems, and continued turning over that plan, and shifting it in my mind through many years (from the age of twenty-eight to thirty-five), experimenting much, and writing and abandoning much, one deep purpose underlay the others, and has underlain it and its execution ever since— and that has been the religious purpose. . . . Not of course to exhibit itself in the old ways, as in writing hymns or psalms with an eye to the church-pew, or to express conventional pietism, or the sickly yearnings of devotees, but in new ways, and aiming at the widest sub-bases and inclusions of humanity, and tallying the fresh air of the sea and land. I will see (said I to myself) whether there is not, for my purposes as poet, a religion, and a sound religious germenancy in the average human race, at least in their modern development in the United States, and in the hardy common fibre and native yearnings and elements, deeper and larger, and affording more profitable returns, than all mere sects and churches—as boundless, joyous and vital as Nature itself—a germenancy that has too long been unencouraged, unsung, unknown. With science, the old theology of the East, long in its dotage, begins evidently to die and disappear. . . . It is, indeed too important to the power and perpetuity of the New World to be consign'd any longer to the churches, old or new, Catholic or Protestant—Saint this or Saint that. It must enter into the poems of the nation. It must make the nation."

What profound, salutary and American words these, looking to a new day, a higher beauty, spoken too at a time when "infidel" and "infidelity" was the word of reproach to free minds, and when they could be smudged by being arrayed under the banner of Thomas Paine—who was, as Theodore Roosevelt said, "a filthy, little atheist." No poet but Whitman in America had sent forth these emancipating words—not Whittier, not Lowell, not Longfellow. Only Robert G. Ingersoll was then calling to his countrymen in prose poems to shake off the degrading chains of superstition.

All these labors of writing poems and prefaces with the intense nervous and spiritual drain that they involved, all that Whitman had endured during the war, so terribly portrayed in poems of amputations, death and horror, in poems about the camps where the dead lay under blankets as he passed from form to form, and lifted up the covering to gaze into old and young faces covered with blood and bled white—all this had told upon Whitman.

He was of giant frame, and if some of his friends are to be believed he was of giant strength in muscle and brawn. He was all that as a mind and an intellectual power. But if he was an athlete and a man of great muscular fibre he might conceivably have endured all that he did and still have escaped the fate of invalidism which befell him. I am constrained to think that the theory of hospital malaria does not account clearly for his cerebral hemorrhage in 1873, and as for a blood poisoning contracted in a hospital while assisting at an operation on a soldier with gangrene, I have not found the facts clear. A septicæmia is a serious thing, and would have put Whitman to bed for some time; it would have gravely threatened his life. However, malaria can result in paralysis. There are cases of luetic infection taking place in youth and resulting twenty years later in locomotor ataxia, with no secondary or tertiary stages of the infection having manifested themselves in the interval. Whitman's "jolly, bodily life" was thrown up to him by literary enemies when he became paralyzed. But I have talked to Doctor MacAlister who attended Whitman for several years, and who helped perform the autopsy on Whitman's body. Doctor MacAlister told me that Whitman's brain and organs were normal and sound, quite in keeping with his age, and that after an attack of pneumonia Whitman developed miliary tuberculosis, as evidenced by countless small tubercles on the brain.

Let us then turn to the facts as we find them. All through 1864–65–66 Whitman was complaining of pain in his head. In 1867 he had some relief from it and was in fair health intermittently. In 1869 he suffered from pain in the head and great dizziness. During the evening of February 23, 1873, he had been reading Bulwer's novel *What Will He Do With It,* and read at the book until very late. This was in his office in the Department of Justice. When he went home that night he felt and looked ill. His white face was noticed by the doorman and some friends whom he met as he left. At three that morning he woke up and found that he could not move his left arm and leg. Still he fell asleep again and slept till daylight. In the morning he found that he could not get up. He was paralyzed.

Thus in his fifty-fourth year he was compelled to give up his bread-earning employment. George Whitman was then living in Camden and Whitman went there to regain his health, if possible. Twelve miles east from Camden is Timber Creek, a stream that enters the Delaware River some miles farther down. Near this creek was the home of the Staffords, where Whitman was welcomed when he went to the woods of that countryside to rest, or to sit in the sun on its banks. It is a charming spot where the branches of great trees over-reach the water, and where an old water mill, then in operation as it was in June of 1936, may still be viewed from a bridge and seen in all its age-worn picturesqueness. How wise Whitman was! He sat in the sun, he bathed in Timber Creek, he had happy hours with the Staffords, he got close to the heart of nature after the days of city life in Washington, after the hospitals and the horrors of war. So he went frequently to visit the Staffords, sometimes catching a ride on hay wagons, and then he would repair to their farm house or sit in their cool yard where one giant oak tree threw its shadows upon the grass.

America was at this time in its foulest period. The South had been crushed and was being devoured by political buzzards. Liberty was dead in the land. A riot of crooked finance had crazed and demoralized the people. The Credit Mobilier sent forth its stink. The banks got what legislation they wanted in order to pick the pockets of the nation. Monopolies began to rise like giant poisonous weeds in the soil enriched by the blood of the youths whom Whitman had nursed. Whitman, unremembered, unrewarded for his priceless service in the war, poor and aging and dishonored, wandered away to Camden to die or to creep back to some kind of health. In England Tennyson had been poet laureate for twenty years, and in a debtless competence was living in a house that he had built at Aldworth. In America honors, degrees and prosperity were falling in autumnal richness upon Longfellow and Lowell. Whitman, America's greatest poet at the time, had nothing from his country, and was compelled to shift for himself, as he limped from the city of Washington to the solitude of Timber Creek. Well for him that he was rich in spirit and knew what to do for himself and for his country as well in these desperate days.

173

He knew nature, and to the breast of nature he betook himself.

Some of the simplest and most beautiful prose that Whitman ever wrote went into the record he made of his hours of meditation and observation of nature, when he ambled from the Stafford house down a cow-path to the bank of the creek, there to sit in the sun and ponder the secrets of life and creation. In June of 1936 I went over this ground at Timber Creek and for a distance trod the path that Whitman followed for more than three years. Here he fought the paralysis that had smitten him and administered self-healing to his shattered body and his grieving heart. For America was thrown and roped and no one knew that so well as Whitman. He had hated the war and he hated it now. He rejoiced that the Union was saved but now it seemed a ruin. In *Democratic Vistas* he had written in 1871, "Never was there, perhaps, more hollowness of heart than at present and here in the United States. Genuine belief seems to have left us. The underlying principles of the states are not honestly believed in (for all this hectic glow, and these melodramatic screamings), nor is humanity itself believed in. What penetrating eye does not everywhere see through the mask? The spectacle is appalling. We live in an atmosphere of hypocrisy throughout. The men believe not in the women, nor the women in the men. A scornful superciliousness rules in literature. The aim of all literature is to find something to make fun of."

Democratic Vistas must be read in its entirety for the immense sweep of its spiritual appraisement of the people and politics and culture of the United States in the seventies. The satires of Juvenal did not cut through the quick of things or pare off the gangrene of national flesh with such realistic and remorseless sharpness. This was the flowering of Whitman's earnestness and unfaltering sincerity in his truly wonderful prose of *Democratic Vistas*. Here at last after young manhood's faith and after great belief in Lincoln he saw his country come to the control of gamblers and careerists as the result of an unnecessary war in which one of Jefferson's great principles was trampled into the bloody mire of Gettysburg, namely, that governments derive their just powers from the consent of the governed. All that Whitman had done for an American language, an American culture and poetry, seemed lost in this internal decay, while foreign influences were creeping in to complete the collapse of American character. For himself there was nothing left but solitary hours by Timber Creek.

Let us enter Whitman's meditations: "After you have exhausted what there is in business, politics, conviviality, love, and so on—have found that none of these finally satisfy, or permanently wear—what remains? Nature remains; to bring out from their torpid recesses the affinities of a man or woman with the open air, the trees, the fields, the changes of seasons —the sun by day and the stars of heaven by night. . . . Dear, soothing, healthy, restoration hours—after the long strain of war, and its wounds and death."

With what loving words he mentioned the cow-path, the lane, fenced by old chestnut rails, gray-green with dabs of moss, lined with weeds and briers scented according to the season with apple blossoms or mint, or with August buckwheat, amid sounds of pigs and poultry and birds. All this down the lane to the creek, to the spring, which gurgled ceaselessly, saying something. Here Whitman found his choice of sun or shade, for his July sun-baths, and for water baths in the creek, while he listened to the ripple of water and exclaimed, "Babble on, O Brook, with that utterance of thine." And, "Away from curtain, carpet, sofa, book—from 'society'—from city houses, street and modern improvements and luxuries—away to the primitive winding, aforementioned wooded creek, with its untrimm'd bushes and turfy banks—away from ligatures, tight boots, buttons and the whole cast iron civilized life—from tailordom and fashion's clothes—from any clothes, perhaps for the nonce, the summer heats advancing, there in those watery, shaded solitudes."

He watched the migration and the swarming and singing of birds in the mating season, and heard the sound of chanticleer at the farm-houses afar, as he looked upon the bright green of the grass. "How the sun silently mounts in the broad clear sky, on his day's journey! How the warm beams bathe all, and come streaming kissingly and almost hot on my face." The frogs croaked in the nearby ponds. "Now the golden dandelions in endless profusion, spotting the ground everywhere. The white cherry and pearblows—the wild violets with their blue eyes looking up and saluting my feet, as I saunter the wood-edge—the rosy blush of budding apple trees—the light clear emerald hue of the wheat fields—the darker green of the rye—a warm elasticity pervading the air, and the wild bees and bumble bees, all as I walk, or hobble, from the farm-house down to the creek, I traverse the before-mentioned lane, fenced by old rails, with many splints, splinters breaks, holes, &c., the choice habitat of those crooning, hairy insects"—the bumble bees.

Sometimes he sat under a big wild cherry tree enveloped in the deep musical drone of the bumble bees. "Is there not a hint in it for a musical composition, of which it should be the back-ground? Some bumble bee symphony? . . . How it all nourishes, lulls me, in the way most needed; the open air, the rye fields, the apple orchards." No sanitarium for Whitman, no expensive therapy, nor electric appliances which after all must take their power from the sun—but the sun itself, nature! Then there were the russet-backed thrushes, those marvellous singers of America; and the summer nights by the creek when the American nightingale, the whippoorwill, poured forth plaintive notes under the full moon.

By day there was the "flageolet" note of the quail, and the "fretting" of the hylas; and Whitman even took delight in a drove of hogs that rooted in the soft ground around the oak tree and sniffed near him, then grunted and scampered away. The shadows of leaves quivered over the page as he wrote these notes, while the sky aloft was white with clouds, and the sand swallows darted out of their holes in the bank of the creek. In the evening the hermit-thrush sang an epilogue to the enchanted day. In the afternoons he watched for hours the dragon flies with their wings of "lace," and the water snakes slipping about—and listened to the grasshoppers and the crickets. By night there were katydids, "But the katydid—how shall I describe its piquant utterance? One sings from a willow tree just outside my bedroom window, twenty yards distant; every clear night for a fortnight past he has sooth'd me to sleep." No hospital opiate for Whitman! "I rode through a piece of woods for a hundred rods the other evening, and heard the katydids by myriads—very curious for once; but I like better my single neighbor on the tree."

A yellow poplar ninety feet high! How strong, how dumbly eloquent! "What suggestions of imperturbability and being as against the human trait of seeming. It is, yet says nothing. How it rebukes by its tough and equable serenity all weathers, this gusty-temper'd little whiffet man, that runs indoors at a mite of rain or snow."

In these notes Whitman listed twenty-four trees with which he was familiar, the names of which he knew, also thirty-eight different kinds of birds or fowl.

As to flowers he writes, "Let me give the names of some of these perennial blossoms and friendly weeds I have made acquaintance with here-about one season or another in my walks: wild azalea, wild honeysuckle, wild roses, golden rod, larkspur, early crocus, sweet flag (great patches of it), creeper, trumpet-flower, scented marjoram, snakeroot, Solomon's seal, sweet balm, mint (great plenty), wild geranium, wild heliotrope, burdock, dandelions, yarrow, coreopsis, wild pea, woodbine, elderberry, poke-weed, sun-flower chamomile, violets, clematis, bloodroot, swamp magnolia, milk-weed, wild daisy (plenty), wild chrysanthemum."

Then he writes, "As testimonal of gratitude for peace in

half-sickness I dedicate last half of *Specimen Days* to the: bees, black-birds, dragon-flies, pond-turtles, mulleins, tansy, peppermint, moths (great and little, some splendid fellows), glow-worms (swarming millions of them indescribably strange and beautiful at night over the pond and creek), water-snakes, crows, millers, mosquitoes, butterflies, wasps and hor-nets, cat birds (and all other birds), cedars, tulip-trees (and all other trees), and to the spots and memories of those days, and of the creek."

And this about horse-mint: "Not a human being, and hardly the evidence of one, in sight. After my brief semi-daily bath, I sit here for a bit, the brook musically brawling, to the chro-matic tones of a fretful cat-bird somewhere off in the bushes. On my walk hither two hours since, through fields and the old lane, I stopt to view, now the sky, now the mile-off woods on the hill, and now the apple orchards. What a contrast from New York's or Philadelphia's streets! Everywhere great patches of dingy-blossom'd horse-mint wafting a spicy odor through the air (especially evenings). Everywhere the flowering boneset, and the rose-bloom of the wild bean."

Of clover and hay perfume he wrote: "Clear, hot, favorable weather—has been a good summer—the growth of clover and grass now generally mow'd. The familiar delicious perfume fills the barns and lanes. As you go along you see the fields of grayish white slightly tinged with yellow, the loosely stack'd grain, the slow-moving wagons passing, and farmers in the fields with stout boys pitching and loading the sheaves. The corn is about beginning to tassel. All over the middle and southern states the spear-shaped battalia, multitudinous, curv-ing, flaunting—long, glossy, dark green plumes for the great horseman, earth. I hear the cheery notes of my old acquaint-ance Tommy quail; but too late for the whippoorwill (though I heard one solitary lingerer night before last). I watch the broad majestic flight of a turkey-buzzard, sometimes high up, sometimes low enough to see the lines of his form, even his spread quills, in relief against the sky. Once or twice lately I have seen an eagle here at early candle-light flying low."

And this about mulleins: "Large, placid mulleins, as summer advances, velvety in texture, of a light greenish-drab color, growing everywhere in the fields—at first earth's big rosettes in their broad-leav'd low cluster plants, eight, ten, twenty leaves to a plant—plentiful on the fallow twenty-acre lot, at the end of the lane, and especially by the ridge-sides of the fences—then close to the ground, but soon springing up—leaves as broad as my hand, and the lower ones twice as long—so fresh and dewy in the morning—stalks now four or five, even seven or eight feet high. The farmers, I find, think the mullein a mean unworthy weed, but I have grown to a fondness for it. Every object has its lesson, enclosing the suggestion of everything else—and lately I sometimes think all is concentrated for me in these hardy, yellow-flower'd weeds. As I come down the lane early in the morning, I pause before their soft wool-like fleece and stem and broad leaves, glittering with countless diamonds. Annually for three summers now, they and I have silently return'd together; at such long intervals I stand or sit among them, musing—and woven with the rest, of so many hours and moods of partial rehabilitation—of my sane or sick spirit, here as near at peace as it can be."

And the meadow-lark: "Fine, clear, dazzling morning, the sun an hour high, the air just tart enough. What a stamp in advance my whole day receives from the song of that meadow-lark perch'd on a fence-stake twenty rods distant! Two or three liquid simple notes, repeated at intervals, full of careless happiness and hope. With its peculiar shimmering-slow progress and rapid noiseless action of the wings, it flies on a ways, lights on another stake, and so on to another, shimmering and singing many minutes."

As to crows: "As I sit here by the creek, resting after my walk, a warm languor bathes me from the sun. No sound but a cawing of crows, and no motion but their black flying figures from overhead, reflected in the mirror of the pond below. Indeed a principal feature of the scene today is these crows, their incessant cawing, far or near, and their countless flocks and processions moving from place to place, and at times almost darkening the air with their myriads. As I sit a moment writing this by the bank, I see the black, clear-cut reflection of them far below, flying through the watery looking-glass, by ones, twos, or long strings. All last night I heard the noises from their great roost in a neighboring wood."

And the butterflies: "A pretty sight! Where I sit in the shade—a warm day, the sun shining from cloudless skies, the forenoon well advanc'd—I look over a ten-acre field of luxuriant clover-hay (the season crop)—the livid-ripe red blossoms and dabs of August brown thickly spotting the prevailing dark-green. Over all flutter myriads of light-yellow butterflies, mostly skimming along the surface, dipping and oscillating, giving a curious animation to the scene. The beautiful, spiritual insects! straw-color'd Psyches! Occasionally one of them leaves his mates, and mounts, perhaps spirally, perhaps in a straight line in the air, fluttering up, up, till literally out of sight. In the lane as I came along just now I noticed one spot, ten feet square or so, where more than a hundred had collected, holding a revel, a gyration-dance, or butterfly good time, winding and circling, down and across, but always keeping within the limits. The little creatures have come out all of a sudden the last few days, and are now very plentiful."

Of birds and birds and birds: "An unusual melodiousness, these days (last of April and first of May) from the black-birds; indeed all sorts of birds, darting, whistling, hopping or perch'd on trees. Never before have I seen, heard, or been in the midst of, and got so flooded and saturated with them and their performances, as this current month. Such oceans, such successions of them. Let me make a list of those I find here: Black birds (plenty) . . Wrens, Kingfishers, Quails, Turkey-buzzards, Hen-hawks, Yellow birds, Thrushes, Reed-birds, Meadow-larks (plenty) . . . Cat-birds (plenty) . . . Cuckoos, Pond snipes (plenty) . . . Chee-winks, Quawks, Ground robins, Ravens, Gray snipes, Eagles, High-holes, Herons, Tits, Woodpigeons. Early came the blue birds, killdeer, plover, robin, woodcock, meadow-lark, white-bellied swallow, sandpiper, Wilson's thrush, flicker."

And the stars: "I am studying the stars, under advantages, as I cross tonight. (It is late in February, and again extra clear.) High toward the west, the Pleiades, tremulous with delicate sparkle, in the soft heavens. Aldebaran, leading the V-shaped Hyades—and overhead Capella and her kids. Most majestic of all, in full display in the high south, Orion, vast-spread, roomy, chief histrion of the stage, with his shiny yellow rosette on his shoulder, and his three Kings—and a little to the east, Sirius, calmly arrogant, most wondrous single star."

Of distant sounds: "The axe of the wood-cutter, the measured thud of a single threshing-flail, the crowing of chanticleer in the barn-yard (with invariable responses from other barn-yards), and the lowing of cattle—but most of all, or far or near, the wind—through the high treetops, or through low bushes, laving one's face and hands so gently, this balmy-bright noon, the coolest for a long time (Sept. 2)—I will not call it *sighing,* for to me it is always a firm, sane, cheery expression, though a monotone, giving many varieties, or swift or slow, or dense or delicate. The wind in the patch of pine woods off there—how sibilant. Or at sea, I can imagine it this moment, tossing the waves, with spirits of foam flying far, and the free whistle, and the scent of the salt—and that vast paradox somehow with all its action and restlessness conveying a sense of eternal rest."

And the earth: "The soil, too—let others pen-and-ink the sea, the air (as I sometimes try)—but now I feel to choose the common soil for theme—naught else. The brown soil here (just between winter-close and opening spring and vegetation)—the rain-shower at night, and the fresh smell next morning—the red worms wriggling out of the ground—the dead leaves, the incipient grass, and the latent life underneath—the effort to start something—already in shelter'd spots some little flowers—the distant emerald show of winter wheat and the rye-fields—the yet naked trees, with clear interstices, giving prospects hidden in summer—the tough fallow and the plow-team, and the stout boy whistling to his horses for encouragement—and there the dark fat earth in long slanting stripes upturn'd."

Whitman described one of his sun-baths as follows: "Another day quite free from mark'd prostration and pain. It seems indeed as if peace and nutriment from heaven subtly filter into me as I slowly hobble down these country lanes and across fields, in the good air—as I sit here in solitude with Nature—open, voiceless, mystic, far-removed, yet palpable, eloquent Nature. I merge myself in the scene, in the perfect day. Hovering over the clear brook-water, I am sooth'd by its soft gurgle in one place, and the hoarser murmurs of its three-foot fall in another. Come, ye disconsolate, in whom any latent eligibility is left—come get the sure virtues of creek-shore, and wood and field. Two months (July and August, '77) have I absorb'd them, and they begin to make a new man of me. Every day, seclusion—every day at least two or three hours of freedom, bathing, no talk, no bonds, no dress, no books, no manners.

"Shall I tell you, reader, to what I attribute my already much-restored health? That I have been almost two years, off and on, without drugs and medicines, and daily in the open air. Last summer I found a particularly secluded little dell off one side by my creek, originally large dug-out marl-pit, now abandon'd, fill'd with bushes, trees, grass, a group of willows, a straggling bank, and a spring of delicious water running right through the middle of it, with two or three little cascades. Here I retreated every hot day, and follow it up this summer. Here I realize the meaning of that old fellow who said he was seldom less alone than when alone. Never before did I get so close to Nature; never before did she come so close to me. By old habit, I pencill'd down from time to time, almost automatically, moods, sights, hours, tints and outlines, on the spot. Let me specially record the satisfaction of this current forenoon, so serene and primitive, so conventionally exceptional, natural."

So passed the days of Whitman's convalescence. One day in December, 1876, he was moved to go to the New Jersey seaside and renew the happiness he had had in the long ago when he was living in Brooklyn and went to the West Hills country. This is his note about that excursion:

"Even as a boy, I had the fancy, the wish, to write a piece, perhaps a poem, about the sea-shore—that suggesting, dividing line, contact, junction, the solid marrying the liquid —that curious, lurking something, as doubtless every objective form finally becomes to the subjective spirit), which means far more than its mere first sight, grand as that is—blending the real and ideal, and each made portion of the other. Hours, days, in my Long Island youth and early manhood, I haunted the shores of Rockaway or Coney Island, or away east to the Hamptons or Montauk. Once, at the latter place (by the old lighthouse nothing but sea-tossings in sight in every direction as far as the eye could reach), I remember well, I felt that I must one day write a book expressing this liquid, mystic theme. Afterward, I recollect, how it came to me that instead of any special lyrical or epical or literary attempt, the sea-shore should be an invisible *influence,* a pervading gauge and tally for me, in my composition. (Let me give a hint here to young writers. I am not sure but I have unwittingly follow'd out the same rule with other powers besides sea and shores—avoiding them, in the way of any dead set at poetizing them, as too big for formal handling—quite satisfied if I could indirectly show that we have met and fused, even if only once, but enough—that we have really absorb'd each other and understand each other.)

"There is a dream, a picture, that for years at intervals (sometimes quite long ones, but surely again, in time), has come noiselessly up before me, and I really believe, fiction as it is, has enter'd largely into my practical life—certainly into my writings, and shaped and color'd them. It is nothing more or less than a stretch of interminable white-brown sand, hard and smooth and broad, with the ocean perpetually, grandly rolling in upon it, with slow-measured sweep, with rustle and hiss and foam, and many thump as of low bass drums. This scene, this picture, I say, has risen before me at times for years. Sometimes I wake at night and can hear and see it plainly."

In winter, spring, summer and fall Whitman spent long hours by Timber Creek during the years 1873 to 1878, staying with his friends the Staffords. But often during this time he was in Philadelphia, where Mrs. Gilchrist was for that year, 1876–77. He does not mention her name anywhere in these notes.

By June, 1878, he was well enough to take a journey to see John Burroughs at Esopus, New York, paying a visit to some friends in 86th Street, New York City on the way. Judging from Mrs. Gilchrist's letters she was in Massachusetts at this time, though in early January, 1879, she was domiciled at 112 Madison Avenue, New York. On the way from Jersey City to New York Whitman read of the death of William Cullen Bryant. He wrote, "I had known Mr. Bryant over thirty years ago, and he had been markedly kind to me. We were both walkers, and when I work'd in Brooklyn he several times came over, middle of afternoons, and we took rambles miles along till dark out towards Bedford or Flatbush in company. On these occasions he gave me clear accounts of scenes in Europe—the cities, looks, architecture, art, especially Italy—where he had travel'd a good deal." Whitman attended Bryant's funeral, "a solemn, impressive, simple scene," where gray heads and celebrities were gathered together.

184

Then Whitman took the boat *Mary Powell,* up the Hudson, and had happiness and raspberries at John Burroughs, and rides about the country observing and delighting in nature. Always Whitman had such capacity for enjoyment. Mrs. Burroughs' coffee delighted him, and he listened rapturously to the rolling music of the trains across the Hudson and watched the sunrise upon the waters of that beautiful palisaded river.

The visit to Burroughs ended, Whitman came back to New York City, sailing the bay around Staten Island, and observing the city scenes. "The general subjective view of New York and Brooklyn," he noted ("will it not the time hasten when the two shall be municipally united in one and named Manhattan?)" Then: "To-day I should say—defiant of cynics and pessimists, and with a full knowledge of all their exceptions—an appreciative and perceptive study of the current humanity of New York gives the directest proof yet of successful Democracy, and of the solution of that paradox, the eligibility of the free and fully developed individual with the paramount aggregate. In old age, lame and sick, pondering for years on many a doubt for this republic of ours—fully aware of all that can be said on the other side—I find in this visit to New York, and the daily contacts and rapport with its myriad people, on the scale of the oceans and tides, the best, most effective medicine my soul has yet partaken—the grandest physical habitat and surroundings of land and water the globe affords, Manhattan Island and Brooklyn, which the future shall join in one city—city of superb democracy, amid superb surroundings."

By July, 1878, Whitman was living down in the New Jersay country again wandering and resting about Timber Creek, watching butterflies, waking to see the marvellous dawns, gazing by night at the moon and the stars, naming the trees, the flowers, the weeds, the birds, sitting in the sun, and bathing in the creek. In the spring of 1879 he was riding the ferries across the Delaware from Camden to Philadelphia, talking with the ferrymen and the pilots, Hand, Walton and Gibberson by name, and watching the crows fly over the river. In the waiting rooms he noted what he called the "homeward bound ladies," their bright eyes and glowing faces—a charming sight, he said. In the reception room there was flirting, and business talk as "'pleasant sober faced Phil (or Jo or Charley) came in with his burden of afternoon papers." Always his interest in humanity and love of people of whatever station asserted itself. He was again at the home of Burroughs in April of 1879, when they had turf fires, and where Whitman indulged his love of nature and wrote in his journal:

"April 26.—At sunrise, the pure clear sound of the meadowlark. An hour later, some notes, few and simple, yet delicious and perfect, from the bush-sparrow—towards noon the reedy trill of the robin. To-day is the fairest, sweetest yet—penetrating warmth—a lovely veil in the air, partly heat-vapor and partly from the turf-fires everywhere in patches on the farms. A group of soft maples near by silently bursts out in crimson tips, buzzing all day with busy bees. The white sails of sloops and schooners glide up or down the river; and long trains of cars, with ponderous roll, or faint bell notes, almost constantly on the opposite shore. The earliest wild flowers in the woods and fields, spicy arbutus, blue liverwort, frail anemone, and the pretty white blossoms of the bloodroot."

The two men rode about that beautiful country near Burroughs' home along the Hudson River. Then Whitman returned to New York City wandering about Fourteenth Street, Broadway and Fifth Avenue, watching the streams of people, and taking in the glitter and magnetism of the city. Up in Central Park he made the acquaintance of a policeman and talked much with him as he observed the passing show, of riders on horses, carriages, "private barouches, cabs and coupes . . . lap dogs, footmen, fashions, foreigners, cockades on hats, crests on panels . . . and gentility."

Here was the Gilded Age in full swing after the luxury of

pre-war days, the munificence of the Planters and the splendor of the slavocracy in New Orleans. Whitman saw the great steamers, great for that day, depart—and he boarded the school-ship *Minnesota* at Twenty-third Street to look it over, being welcomed and entertained by the captain with plenty to eat and drink. A boat had been sent for Whitman to take him to the *Minnesota*. He was treated with distinction. By August he was in Philadelphia looking at the Exposition Building before crossing the Delaware on his return to Camden. In another month he was starting his long trip west and was well enough for the ordeal.

CHAPTER TWELVE

ILLNESS did not deter Whitman from his literary work. The very fact that he was not well received by the public, that he had a sort of catch-as-catch-can chance with publishers seemed to spur him on with a determination not to be effaced, but to put himself on record. He began in 1855 with placing a picture of himself in his books, and he continued that practice in subsequent editions of *Leaves of Grass*. Whitman's egotism, his vain self-assertion, crop up at every point—and as things were going and have turned out, that was well enough.

In 1875 Whitman brought out *Memoranda of the War*, a cloth-bound book of sixty-eight pages. It was published in Camden. The title page was preceded by a personal note and two portraits of the author. Then in 1876 Whitman saw the sixth edition of his poems through the press. It is known as the *Centennial Edition*, and was in two volumes. The first volume was *Leaves of Grass*; the second *Autumn Rivulets*. The latter contained both prose and poetry. This work was bound in half-leather. *Leaves of Grass* also contained two portraits of the author: one a steel-cut from the edition of 1855 facing the poem "Song of Myself," and the other the wood-cut by Linton from the edition of 1871, and was placed to face the poem "The Wound Dresser." The book contained 384 pages.

Autumn Rivulets had 348 pages in all. It included "Democratic Vistas," "Centennial Songs," and "Passage to India." On the title page were the words: "For the eternal ocean bound these ripples, passing surges, streams of Death and Life." There was a portrait of Whitman, and the book was autographed. There were eighteen new poems among which were: "Eidolons," "Prayer of Columbus," "Out from Behind this Mask," "Song of the Redwood Tree," and the "Ox-Tamer."

In 1881 Whitman published through James R. Osgood & Company of Boston, the seventh edition of *Leaves of Grass,* containing 382 pages and a portrait of himself facing "Song of Myself." There were twenty new poems. One was "The Dalliance of the Eagles," for which Burroughs gave him the material. There were also "Patroling Barnegat," "Italian Music in Dakota," "From Far Dakota's Canyons" (no doubt inspired by his trip west in September of 1879), and "The Sobbing of the Bells" (a poem in memory of Garfield). These new poems did not add to Whitman's reputation, though they are suggestive and thoughtful. Boston did not take kindly to the birth of this edition in its midst and an interference from the law authorities made it stumble. But Whitman was not discouraged.

In 1882 he brought out an author's edition of his works in two volumes, returning to his town of Camden to do it. The first volume contained *Leaves of Grass*—382 pages. It was identical with the edition a year earlier except that the title page contained the note Author's Edition, and named Camden as the place of publication.

Volume two contained "Specimen Days" and "Collect." There were 374 pages and the book bore the imprimatur of Rees, Welsh & Company, Philadelphia. There was a portrait of Whitman seated examining a butterfly. "Specimen Days" included "Memoranda During the War," and notes published in *The Critic* and other magazines. Under the title "Collect" Whitman grouped his prefaces, "Democratic Vistas," "Poets of To-day in America," "Death of Abraham Lincoln," and other papers, "Notes Left Over" and "Pieces in Early Youth." Later copies of this edition bore the imprimatur of David McKay, Philadelphia.

Altogether Whitman had a stumpy row to hoe. He made staunch friends in England. Even Tennyson by this time was writing him occasionally, addressing him, "Dear Old Man." But in America only the stoutest heart and the greatest self-confidence would have braced him to continue the fight. Thus we find Whitman giving report of his own difficulties:

"That I have not gained the acceptance of my own time, but have fallen back on fond dreams of the future—anticipations—('still lives the song, though Regnar dies')—That from a worldly and business point of view *Leaves of Grass* has been worse than a failure—that public criticism on the book and myself as author of it yet shows marked anger and contempt more than anything else—('I find a solid line of enemies to you everywhere'—letter from W. S. K., Boston, May 28, 1884)—And that solely for publishing it I have been the object of two or three pretty serious special official buffetings—is all probably no more than I ought to have expected."

Once in a talk with Traubel, Whitman is reported to have said:

"Don't you remember how Wanamaker used to treat the *Leaves* in his store when McKay first published it? I understood from McKay that they originally had the *Leaves* in the store—considered it—but decided finally that it would not do for them in any way to seem to back up the book. I can see how all this should be all right from the dyed-in-the-wool shop-keeper point of view. The store is full of goody-goody girls and men—full of them: people who have been foully taught about sex, about motherhood, about the body. It is easy to see what *Leaves of Grass* must look like to people with such eyes. The *Leaves* do not need any excuse; they do need to be understood. If I did not understand them I would dislike them myself, God knows! But all this fear of indecency, all this noise about purity and sex and the social order and the Comstockism particular and general is nasty—too nasty to make any compromise with. I never come up against it but I think of what Heine said to a woman who had expressed to him some suspicion about the body. 'Madam,' said Heine, 'are we not all naked under our clothes?'"

In 1890 when Whitman was senile he made a memorandum which might lead one to believe he had uniform bad luck with magazine editors. He noted that a magazine had sent back one of his poems and remarked, "So I am now set out in the cold by every big magazine and publisher, and may as well understand and admit it—which is just as well, for I find I am palpably losing my sight and ratiocination."

This was by no means the story when his whole career is considered. He had some luck with magazines, perhaps as good as any genius of poetry then or today, save sonneteers, and writers of the caste of Longfellow, Lowell, and Whittier. Whitman was in the habit of naming his price when he sent a poem, and he was by no means modest as to the figure. He made some money along the way, as in February, 1869, when *The Atlantic Monthly,* through the intercession of Emerson, published "Proud Music of the Storm" and paid Whitman $100 for it. That would be a good price today.

Oscar Lovell Triggs canvassed this matter of his success with magazines and newspapers, finding that Whitman published variously as follows: "Out of the Cradle Endlessly Rocking," under the title of "A Child's Reminiscence" in *The New York Saturday Press,* December 24, 1859; "Elemental Drifts" under the title "Bardic Symbols," in *The Atlantic Monthly,* April, 1860; "The Return of the Heroes," called a "Carol of Harvest" in *The Galaxy* for September, 1867; "Whispers of Heavenly Death" in *The Broadway* for October, 1868; "Proud Music of the Storm," under the title "Proud Music of the Sea Storm" in *The Atlantic Monthly* for February, 1869; "After all not to Create Only" in *The New York Evening Post, Commercial Advertiser, Washington Evening Star,* and other dailies, September 7, 1871; "O Star of France" in *The Galaxy* for June, 1871; "The Mystic Trumpeter" in *The*

Kansas Magazine for February, 1872; "The Prayer of Columbus" in *Harper's Monthly* for March, 1874; "Patroling Barnegat" and "My Picture Gallery" in *The American* in June and October, 1880; "The Dalliance of the Eagles" in *Copes's Tobacco Plant,* November, 1880; "Patroling Barnegat" republished in *Harper's,* April, 1881; "The Sobbing of the Bells" in *The Boston Daily Globe,* September 27, 1881; "Old Age's Lambent Peaks" in *The Century Magazine,* September, 1883; "With Husky Haughty Lips O Sea" in *Harper's Monthly,* March, 1884; "Of that Blithe Throat of Thine" in *Harper's Monthly,* January, 1885; "To the Sunset Breeze" in *Lippincott's Magazine,* December, 1890; "Sounds of the Winter," "The Unexpress'd," "Sail Out for Good Eidolon Yacht," "After the Argument," in *Lippincott's* for March, 1891; "The Commonplace" in facsimile in *Munyon's Magazine* for March, 1891; "The Pallid Wreath" in *The Critic,* January 10, 1891; and "Death's Valley" in *Harper's Monthly* of April, 1896. Whitman's prose stories, essays and notes, as observed by Triggs, were published quite generally in current periodicals of his time. The foregoing list rather contradicts Whitman's statement that he had been rejected by the magazines. Still he had some rejections and was severely buffeted by critics. To be fair one must admit that very many of Whitman's so-called poems were merely scrawls, improvisations, that and nothing more. Yet let us read what he wrote about his bad luck:

"An editor of (or in) a leading monthly magazine (*Harper's Monthly,* July, 1890) asks: 'A hundred years from now will W. W. be popularly rated a great poet—or will he be forgotten?' . . . A mighty ticklish question—which can only be left for a hundred years hence—perhaps more than that. But whether W. W. has been mainly rejected by his own times is an easier question to answer.

"All along from 1860 to '91, many of the pieces in *L. of G.* and its annexes were first sent to publishers or magazine editors before being printed in the *L.,* and were peremptorily rejected by them, and sent back to their author. 'The Eidolons' was sent back by Dr. H., of *Scribner's Monthly* with a lengthy, very insulting and contemptuous letter. 'To the Sun-Set Breeze' was rejected by the editor of *Harper's Monthly* as being 'an improvisation' only. 'On, On Ye Jocund Twain' was rejected by *The Century* editor as being personal merely. Several of the pieces went the rounds of all the monthlies, to be thus summarily rejected."

He continues: "Who has had more experience of the nether kind than I have? I think everything that could happen to a rejected author has happened one time or another to me. I could tell you some interesting stories. I just think of this one. John Swinton came to see me soon after I had settled in Camden—urged me to offer something to Dr. Holland, for *Scribner's*—was very strenuous about it. I demurred but John persisted. 'Do it, do it!' he said. 'Why should I do it?—why?' I asked John. He still insisted. 'For certain reasons,' he said. I sent a poem, which was rejected—not rejected mildly, noncommittedly, in the customary way, but with a note of the most offensive character. I was sick and blue at the time: the note provoked me: I threw it into the fire. I was always sorry I destroyed it: had I been well I should not have done so: it was a good specimen insult for the historian—for Horace, here, who likes something that piques in his sauce now and then. Of course this ended my relations with Holland." (Does any one remember now that Holland was the author of *Bitter Sweet,* a poem in the manner of *Lucille?*)

And Whitman has this to say in a talk as recorded by Horace Traubel: " 'The Harpers once accepted a poem, which induced me to send them others, but five or six were rejected in succession, some of them accompanied on their return with palliating notes: then I saw I was not wanted: I shut the door and withdrew. That was years ago. Latterly I have had verses in the *Weekly.* I never have any fight with the editors—they know what they are about—they know what they want: if they don't want Walt Whitman who can blame them?' 'They don't like to see you loafing around the throne' [Traubel remarked]. 'That's so: and why should I criticise them for that? I don't blame myself for being Walt Whitman—neither do I blame them for thanking God they are not as I am! Some of my friends have quarrelled with the editors but they have never done it with my consent. The fact is I have been about as well received as I expected to be, considering the proposition I set forth in the *Leaves,* considering the rumpus I made, considering my refusal to play in with the literary gang.'"

In 1870 Bret Harte was the editor of *The Overland Monthly,* and to Harte Whitman sent "Passage to India," which Harte rejected saying that the poem was too long, and too abstract for the hasty and material-minded readers of his magazine. Also *The Nineteenth Century* in May, 1887, rejected "November Boughs"; and H. M. Alden, editor of *Harper's,* returned to Whitman "The Voice of the Rain," as not tempting. However, as has been mentioned, many of these poems were suggestions rather, and materials for poems, but not wrought into poetic substance or form.

Whitman had the good fortune to sell sets of his works in England and to be hailed there. "Curiously," he writes in his *Prose Works,* "the sale abroad proved prompt, and what one might call copious: the names came in lists and the money with them, by foreign mail. The price was $10 a set. Both the cash and the emotional cheer were deep medicines; many paid double or treble price (Tennyson and Ruskin did), and many sent kind and eulogistic letters; ladies, clergymen, social leaders, persons of rank, and high officials. Those blessed gales from the British Islands probably (certainly) saved me. Here are some of the names, for I w'd like to preserve them: Wm. M. and D. G. Rossetti, Lord Houghton, Edwd. Dowden, Mrs. Anne Gilchrist, Keningale Cook, Edwd. Carpenter, Therese Simpson, Rob't Buchanan, Alfred Tennyson, John Ruskin, C. G. Oates, E. T. Wilkinson, T. L. Warren, C. W.

Reynell, W. B. Scott, A. G. Dew Smith, E. W. Gosse, T. W. Rolleston, Geo. Wallis, Rafe Leicester, Thos. Dixon, N. Mac-Coll, Mrs. Matthews, R. Hannah, Geo. Saintsbury, R. S. Watson, Godfrey and Vernon Lushington, G. W. Lewes, G. H. Boughton, Geo. Fraser, W. T. Arnold, A. Ireland, Mrs. M. Taylor, M. D. Conway, Benj. Eyre, E. Dannreather, Rev. T. E. Brown, C. W. Sheppard, E. J. A. Balfour, P. B. Marston, A. C. De Burgh, J. H. McCarthy, J. H. Ingram, Rev. R. P. Graves, Lady Mount-Temple, F. S. Ellis, W. Brockie, Rev. A. B. Grosart, Lady Hardy, Hubert Herkomer, Francis Hueffer, H. G. Dakyns, R. L. Nettleship, W. J. Stillman, Miss Blind, Madox Brown, H. R. Ricardo, Messrs. O'Grady and Tyrrel; and many, many more."

So now we take up Whitman's outer life again. In 1872 he had visited Boston where he talked with Emerson, and we have already recorded the visits he paid Burroughs. Lowell, as I remember it, was once in Chicago; but it was not the way of the eastern poets to pay heed to the country west of the Hudson, not to say west of the Mississippi. Whitman had a continental interest, and in 1879, having by that time measurably recovered his health, he set forth, "fetching up at Denver, Colorado, and penetrating the Rocky Mountain region enough to get a good notion of it all."

In the middle of September he left West Philadelphia, taking a sleeper, and remaining oblivious of the hundreds of miles onward to Pittsburgh. There he saw coal barges amid smoke and fog, and miles of discolored houses. Then he rode through West Virginia until the Ohio River was crossed, then through Ohio and Indiana and through Illinois, "rocked to slumber for a second night, flying like lightning." The run from Philadelphia to St. Louis, he observed, should have been made in thirty-six hours, but there was a wreck which delayed the train. Hence he had but one night in St. Louis. "What a fierce weird pleasure to lie in my berth at night in the luxurious palace car, drawn by the mighty Baldwin—embodying and filling me, too, with swiftest motion and most resistless strength."

He thought his eyes had never looked upon such scenes of pastoral beauty as when he crossed Missouri. And in truth there is no more beautiful country than that along the Missouri River all the way from St. Louis to Kansas City. Arriving at Kansas City he was whirled on to Lawrence, Kansas, and Topeka. In Lawrence he was entertained by a Judge Usher, and he was hospitably treated everywhere there. At Topeka he was billed for a speech in a meeting which celebrated the Kansas Silver Wedding. Whitman was enjoying himself so much at the house of the Ushers that he neglected to go to the meeting to deliver the speech which he had prepared. One suspects that he was not very happy on the platform. The word has come to us that he did not enunciate clearly—his voice was called falsetto by some, baritone by others.

We have a record of the speech as he wrote it in his book *Specimen Days*. He entitled it "The Prairies," and among other things he said: "But if you care to have a word from me, I should speak it about these very prairies; they impress me most of all the objective shows I see or have seen on this my first real visit to the West." He called the prairies that "vast Something, stretching out on its own unbounded scale, unconfined . . . combining the real and the ideal, and beautiful as dreams . . . I wonder indeed if the people of this continental inland West know how much of first class art they have in these prairies—how original and all your own—how much of the influences of a character for your future humanity. . . . Then is it not subtly they who have given us our leading Americans, Lincoln and Grant?—vast-spread, average men—their foregrounds of character altogether practical and real . . . this favor'd central area of (in round numbers) two thousand miles square seems fated to be the home both of what I would call America's distinctive ideas and distinctive realities."

Then he went on to Denver and to the mountains. "I have

found the law of my poems," he noted, "was the unspoken but more and more decided feeling that came to me," when observing the fantastic forms of rocks and the reds, grays, browns, russets and purples all about him in chasms, gorges and crystal streams. Here were new scenes and new joys for the enfeebled Whitman. He journeyed up ten thousand feet above sea level and looked at the mountains about him. He visited the natural parks. "Talk again, I say, of going to Europe, of visiting the ruins of feudal castles, or Coliseum remains, or kings' palaces—when you can come here" and see "beauty, terror, power more than Dante or Angelo ever knew."

He wanted to go farther west and see the National Park; and to travel over the Santa Fe Trail to New Mexico. Instead he turned south from Denver to Pueblo, then east to the Mississippi River, making notes on the prairies and the great plains as subjects of poetry. Bryant wrote a very good poem on the prairies, rather cold and formal, but eloquent. It is regrettable that Whitman did not write one of exclusive treatment on that subject.

When resting in Missouri on his way east he made this note:

"Lying by one rainy day in Missouri to rest after quite a long exploration—first trying a big volume I found there of *Milton, Young, Gray, Beattie and Collins,* but giving it up for a bad job—enjoying however for awhile, as often before, the reading of Walter Scott's poems, *Lay of the Last Minstrel, Marmion,* and so on—I stopp'd and laid down the book, and ponder'd the thought of a poetry that should in due time express and supply the teeming region I was in the midst of, and have briefly touch'd upon. One's mind needs but a moment's deliberation anywhere in the United States to see clearly enough that all the prevalent book and library poets, either as imported from Great Britain, or follow'd and doppel-gang'd here, are foreign to our States, copiously as they are read by us all. But to fully understand not only how absolutely in opposition to our times and lands, and how little and cramp'd, and what anachronisms and absurdities many of their pages are, for American purposes, one must dwell or travel awhile in Missouri, Kansas and Colorado, and get rapport with their people and country."

And in St. Louis he wrote this journal entry:

"Oct. 17, '79.—To-day one of the newspapers of St. Louis prints the following informal remarks of mine on American, especially Western literature: 'We called on Mr. Whitman yesterday and after a somewhat desultory conversation abruptly asked him: "Do you think we are to have a distinctly American literature?" "It seems to me," said he, "that our work at present is to lay the foundations of a great nation in products, in agriculture, in commerce, in networks of intercommunication and in all that relates to the comforts of vast masses of men and families, with freedom of speech, ecclesiasticism, &c. These we have founded and are carrying out on a grander scale than ever hitherto, and Ohio, Illinois, Indiana, Missouri, Kansas and Colorado seem to me to be the seat and field of these very facts and ideas. Materialistic prosperity in all its varied forms, with those other points that I mentioned, intercommunication and freedom, are first to be attended to. When those have their results and get settled, then a literature worthy of us will begin to be defined. Our American superiority and vitality are in the bulk of our people, not in a gentry like the old world. The greatness of our army during the secession war was in the rank and file, and so with the nation. Other lands have their vitality in a few, a class, but we have it in the bulk of the people. Our leading men are not of much account and never have been, but the average of the people is immense, beyond all history. Sometimes I think in all departments, literature and art included, that will be the way our superiority will exhibit itself. We will not have great individuals or great leaders, but a great average bulk, unprecedentedly great." ' "

Four years later Whitman received a letter from Santa Fe asking him to express himself about the Spanish element in

American nationality. His trip west had given him ideas on that subject and he replied as follows:

"We Americans have yet to really learn our own antecedents, and sort them, to unify them. They will be found ampler than has been supposed, and in widely different sources. Thus far, impress'd by New England writers and schoolmasters, we tacitly abandon ourselves to the notion that our United States have been fashion'd from the British Islands only, and essentially form a second England only—which is a very great mistake.

"To that composite American identity of the future, Spanish character will supply some of the most needed parts. No stock shows a grander historic retrospect—grander in religiousness and loyalty, or for patriotism, courage, decorum, gravity and honor. (It is time to dismiss utterly the illusion-compound, half raw-head-and-bloody-bones and half Mysteries-of-Udolpho, inherited from the English writers of the past 200 years. It is time to realize—for it is certainly true—that there will not be found any more cruelty, tyranny, superstition, &c., in the *résumé* of past Spanish history than in the corresponding *résumé* of Anglo-Norman history. Nay, I think there will not be found so much.)"

Whitman was not favorably impressed with the women of the West. In Kansas City and the prairie cities they were well enough dressed but lacked the mentality and physique appropriate to them. They looked dyspeptic, though doll-like and fashionable, he thought. While Whitman was on this trip (and how he enjoyed his nights on the Mississippi!) Grant returned from his trip around the world. Whitman pondered this and thought Grant's reception in foreign capitals by czar, mikado, and other monarchs, transcended Plutarch.

So back he came at last to Camden, to listen to symphony concerts in Philadelphia and to loaf in the woods of Timber Creek. In June he went to visit Doctor Bucke at London, Canada—viewing Niagara and the St. Lawrence on the way.

Doctor Bucke escorted Whitman through the asylum where it was his duty to examine patients. Here he heard a Sunday religious service and listened with great feeling to the singing of *Lead, Kindly Light.* Then up the savage Saguenay, and finally back to Camden.

Carlyle died in February, 1881, and Whitman has written a long note on him in *Specimen Days.* Carlyle had unquestionably exercised a great influence on Whitman, as Emerson had, and as Hegel had, of whom he wrote when recording his thoughts on Carlyle.

In April, down at Timber Creek, Whitman found his kingfisher but not its mate. Later when the mate *did* come along he finished the day's memorandum by quoting Coleridge's melancholy lines:

> All Nature seems at work — slugs leave their lair,
> The bees are stirring — birds are on the wing,
> And winter slumbering in the open air
> Wears on his smiling face a dream of spring;
> And I the while, the sole unbusy thing,
> Nor honey make, nor pair, nor build, nor sing.

The sun had somewhat restored Whitman there in the country, but at intervals he had bad days. Now he was facing very definitely ten years and more of languor, and pain. However, he was not through with his travels. In May of this year he went to Boston, there to deliver his lecture on Lincoln which he sometimes delivered in New York and Philadelphia in these later years. It must be noted again that Whitman knew no more about Lincoln than any one else who could read about him; nor for that matter does he really pretend that he had any intimate contact with Lincoln—nothing but the morning bow as he saw Lincoln driving into Washington from his summer home. Yet if the record be not carefully scrutinized one might gather the impression that Whitman knew Lincoln.

William E. Barton combed this material pretty thoroughly

and arrived at the conclusion that Lincoln did not see Whitman passing the White House and make the remark "there goes a man," or "that looks like a man." Moreover Whitman was not at Ford's Theatre the night that Lincoln was assassinated. He got the details of that from Peter Doyle, who was present.

So Whitman was in Boston again calling it joyous, receptive, full of ardor and sparkle. He went to the house of Quincy Shaw to see the pictures of Millet, and stood long before "The Sower," and "Watering the Cow." Three years before this Longfellow had called upon Whitman in Camden. Now Whitman paid his respects to Longfellow, who was the only "particular eminence" that he sought out. Whitman always spoke favorably of Longfellow, Whittier, and Bryant. He went to see Memorial Hall and then on the 23d of April he left Boston in fair order, saying that another week of kindness, of eating and drinking, would have killed him. By May 14 he was again at Timber Creek observing and making notes about robins.

Was Whitman getting restless or merely feeling the strength of better health? For in late July he went away from Camden again and visited Far Rockaway on Long Island to listen to the noise of the surf and watch the curling crest of the waves amid "the sand and the salt." He went to Long Branch by steamer and there driving along Ocean Avenue observed the fine houses of the rich, but remarked that none equalled that of his friend George W. Childs whom we shall mention again in connection with his generosity toward the "good gray" and invalided poet.

When, after all these diversions, he was at "home" it was at the house of friends at Mott Haven. Here he more or less escaped the intense heat that sometimes comes to New York City in mid-summer, and the beauty of upper Manhattan, above 100th Street, took his heart. It was a habit with him to go down to the Hudson to observe the fine yachts at anchor and to be thrilled by the laughter, the shouts, the calls and responses of young bathers. Here in this temporary home, and all homes were now temporary to him, he was putting the last touches on *Leaves of Grass* and reading proofs.

At the time a painting of Custer's Last Rally by the artist John Mulvaney was being exhibited in New York. Whitman went to see it, finding it "typical, deadly heroic to the uttermost—nothing in the books like it, nothing in Homer, nothing in Shakespeare; more grim and sublime than either. All native, all our own, all a fact." Always with him the American scene and epos!

Ah, yes! how good for the old man to get down to Pfaff's again and to breakfast there. Pfaff himself "quickly appear'd on the scene to welcome me," wrote Whitman, "and bring up the news . . . first opening a big fat bottle of the best wine in the cellar." And then "talk about ante-bellum times, '59 and '60, and the jovial suppers at his then Broadway place, near Bleecker Street. Ah, the friends and names and frequenters, those times, that place. Most are dead—Ada Clare, Wilkins, Daisy Sheppard, O'Brien, Henry Clapp," and so on, "all gone. And there Pfaff and I, sitting opposite each other at the little table, gave a rememberance to them in a style they would themselves have fully confirm'd, namely, big brimming, fill'd up champagne glasses, drained in abstracted silence, very leisurely to the last drop."

By autumn of this year, 1881, Whitman was in Boston again and went out to Concord to see Emerson. It was well, for the next year Emerson died, and now, on this visit, the philosopher was losing or had altogether lost his memory. He was like an early winter day that broods and seems to think much, but is mystically still. Whitman now saw Emerson several times at the Sanborns' there in Concord and at Emerson's own house, in company with the Alcotts and others.

At these gatherings there was a good deal of talk of Thoreau and Hawthorne, both dead by this time twenty years. Whitman

recorded "my seat and the relative arrangement was such that
without being rude, or anything of the kind, I could just look
squarely at E., which I did a good part of two hours. On entering he had spoken very briefly and politely to several of the
company, then settled himself in his chair, a trifle push'd back,
and though a listener, and apparently an alert one, remain'd
silent through the whole talk and discussion. . . . A good
color in his face, eyes clear, with the well known expression of
sweetness, and the old clear peering aspect quite the same."
The same, no doubt he means, as when years before he had
walked about with Whitman importuning him to modify the
vulgarity of *Leaves of Grass* so that the book would have the
full chance with the public which he thought it deserved.

Whitman dined with Emerson again at his own home and
studied him further. Then he did the usual things, made a
pilgrimage to Concord, a call at the statue of the Minute Man
and read Emerson's verses already inscribed there—visited the
Concord battlegrounds, and Hawthorne and Thoreau's graves
there in the loveliest cemetery in America, Hawthorne the
Democrat too and son of Jefferson whom the war had hurt
and broken as it had sent Whitman into a long illness and
perhaps into a deflection of his creative life. Thoreau, the
philosophical anarchist, was Jeffersonian in the purest quintes-
sential.

Whitman strolled into Boston Common and there recalled
that twenty-one years before he had walked there with Emerson and listened to his expostulations. "More precious than
gold," he called that dissertation, saying, "it afforded me, ever
after, this strange, and paradoxical lesson; each point of E.'s
statement was unanswerable, no judge's charge ever more complete or convincing, I could never hear the points better put
—and then I felt down in my soul the clear and unmistakable
conviction to disobey all, and pursue my own way. 'What have
you to say then to such things?' said E., pausing in conclusion.
'Only that while I can't answer them at all, I feel more settled

than ever to adhere to my own theory, and exemplify it.'
Whereupon we went and had a good dinner at the American
House."

Thus the two wisest, most inspired and consecrated men of
their times met and compared points of view, touched and
took a soft rebound and parted in friendship.

By November Whitman was back in Camden; and soon now
he was to be installed in his own house to which he brought his
books, papers, clippings, the vast refuse and fag-ends of things
with which he surrounded himself, and his chair for that window from which he looked into Mickle Street for the ten years
of life that yet remained to him.

CHAPTER THIRTEEN

CAMDEN, made populous since Whitman's day by manufacturing and canning works, had by the census of 1930 about 120,000 people. In 1884 it was a comparatively small place. From the sales of books Whitman had accumulated about $1400, and with the help of George W. Childs, the rich philanthropist of Philadelphia, Whitman added to that sum enough to buy for about $1700, the house numbered 328 Mickle Street—now numbered 330.

Mickle Street in '84 was a residence street of Americans of middle class fortune and some standing. When I saw it in June, 1936, it was a street of old houses interspersed with shops, and mainly inhabited by Italian laborers employed in the nearby factories.

In 1909 I journeyed all the way from Chicago to Whitman's Mickle Street house and his tomb at Harleigh Cemetery. I wandered about in great confusion in Camden inquiring for the house. No one seemed to know where it was or what it was. At last driven into a corner grocery store by a snow storm I asked the proprietor and his wife where the house was. They didn't know—but a laborer standing by the stove, warming himself, gave me the direction. I wish this were a symbol of the fact that the common man, whom Whitman loved and sang, knew about him—but such is not the case. When I did find the house it was closed and I didn't get in. I saw only its commonplace exterior and the hitching stone on the walk marked "W. W."

205

But in June, 1936, I found the house sustained by public funds and in the care of Mrs. Martha Lippincott Davis, who welcomed me cordially and showed me through the rooms now filled with Whitman treasures. When I first saw this house I wondered why Whitman would settle himself in such an unpoetic place. Why didn't he go to the beautiful country around Camden, down to Timber Creek, and buy a house? That is what I asked myself then. Why did Whitman plant himself in the midst of dusty and noisy surroundings, near the railroad and the ferry, where crashing cars and whistles and bells and mad din filled the air? In 1936 I understood better why he did this.

He was thus convenient to the ferry and could get to Philadelphia easily; he was thus amid the streams of humanity which he loved; and it may be that the silence of the country would have been too much for him. Perhaps he would have been lonesome without this accessibility of people in these years when the silence of his own soul, his pain and languor troubled him to his full endurance. Besides there were doctors in Camden as there were in nearby Philadelphia, and people who ministered to him.

The house of two stories, of plain boards, with flat roof, standing jammed to the brick walk in front, yet having an attractive door, is like a hundred that might be seen in many eastern villages. There are seven rooms, four downstairs and three upstairs. The front room is charming, and well lighted by windows with small panes. The back rooms, dining-room and kitchen suggest comfort. The front upstairs room, where Whitman slept, read and rested in his rocking-chair with its white wolf robe, is also well lighted by good windows. In the east wall of this room as in the front room below it, there is a mantel which lends beauty to the room. The pleasant narrow hallway has a staircase with banister of pickets and dark railing, walnut or mahogany. Altogether the house is quaint and comfortable. There is a back yard large enough to raise a few flowers in and delightful enough to sit in at the close of day or any time when the sun is not too hot or the air too cool.

Whitman had a good home. I no longer wonder why he bought this house for he probably passed it many times on his way to the ferry in those days when he was living with his brother George in the large brick house in Stevens Street.

On the occasion of my happy visit to Mickle Street these rooms once occupied by Whitman were bright and clean and freshly papered in paper of the same pattern, I was told, as when he lived there. Cases with manuscripts, photographs, souvenirs and books of one kind and another stood in the back division of the front room downstairs. Among the interesting framed pictures on the walls was a painting of Walter Whitman, the poet's father, showing a face not unlike Emerson's in its upper portion, very blue eyes and straw-colored hair, with no beard and no mustache. There was also a painting of Whitman's mother revealing her Dutch ancestry in all its lineaments.

On the wall in another place was a framed writing by Whitman, evidently the title of some book he was meditating. "Airs and Echoes of Lilac Time" were the words, and Whitman's comment followed to the effect that the work was to reconcile and make harmonious in many moral ideas that part of himself which was physical nature, to express the effort to fuse man and nature, to realize the conscience, the moral laws, the sense of right.

In another place hung Whitman's first will, dated October 23, 1872, made at the age of fifty-three when he was a clerk in the Department of Justice The will bequeathed to Whitman's mother, Louisa, in trust for Edward, his brother, "all my property, being personal, between ten and eleven hundred dollars" in the Brooklyn Savings Bank; also what was due from the sale of books from J. L. Redfield, 140 Fulton Street, and the plates of the books. He provided that in case his mother died, his brother, George, should act as trustee in place of his mother. The brother, Edward, of defective mind, was thus affectionately remembered by the poet.

To better visualize the house as it looked when Whitman occupied it we can take his own words jotted down as he was accustomed to make casual records:

"Today in the upper story of a little wooden house of two stories near the Delaware River, east shore, sixty miles up from the sea, is a rather large 20-by-20 low ceiling'd room something like a big old ship's cabin. The floor, three quarters of it with an ingrain carpet, is half cover'd by a deep litter of books, papers, magazines, thrown-down letters and circulars, rejected manuscripts, memoranda, bits of light or strong twine, a bundle to be 'express'd,' and two or three venerable scrap books. In the room stand two large tables (one of ancient St. Domingo mahogany with immense leaves) cover'd by a jumble of more papers, a varied and copious array of writing materials, several glass and china vessels or jars, some with cologne-water, others with real honey, granulated sugar, a large bunch of beautiful fresh yellow chrysanthemums, some letters and envelope paper ready for the post office, many photographs, and a hundred indescribable things besides. There are all around many books, some quite handsome editions, some half cover'd by dust, some within reach, evidently used (good-sized print, no type less than long primer), some maps, the Bible (the strong cheap edition of the English crown), Homer, Shakspere, Walter Scott, Emerson, Ticknor's *Spanish Literature,* John Carlyle's *Dante,* Felton's *Greece,* George Sand's *Consuelo,* a very choice little Epictetus, some novels, the latest foreign and American monthlies, quarterlies, and so on. There being quite a strew of printer's proofs and slips, and the daily papers, the place with its quaint old-fashion'd calmness has also a smack of something alert and of current work. There are several trunks and depositaries back'd up at the walls (one well-bound and big box came by express lately from Washington City, after storage there for nearly twenty years). Indeed the whole room is a sort of result and storage collection of my own past life. I have here various editions of my own writings, and sell them upon request; one is a big volume of complete poems and prose, 1,000 pages, autograph, essays, speeches, portraits from life, &c. Another is a little *Leaves of Grass,* latest date, six portraits, morocco bound, in pocket-book form."

Those who entered the Mickle Street house when Whitman was living in it found the rooms in the same condition that Whitman described them himself as being in. They uniformly say that the room where Whitman sat was a riot of confusion, and that Whitman's feet were surrounded with books, old shoes, newspapers, pamphlets, stools and what-not in wild disorder. To the last he kept to his habit of eating at any and all hours, of sleeping according to whim; and when he began to have young men of eighteen or so acting as nurse and attendant to him, he got them into the same irregular ways. When he went to see Burroughs up the Hudson River he took the particular young man he had in his service at the time, with whom he slept and walked. Mrs. Burroughs was greatly annoyed at the careless, unpunctual ways of Whitman and his boy friend, and their antics and playfulness in the kitchen disturbed her not a little.

In going through the Whitman bibliography I found a book by Elizabeth Leavitt Keller, entitled *Walt Whitman in Mickle Street,* published in 1926. The author was born in Niagara Falls, was married to a man named Keller, lost her husband and in 1876 became a nurse. She took care of Whitman for a short time during his illness in 1892, and long afterward wrote this book. It was a sort of vindication of Mary O. Davis, one infers, who was Whitman's housekeeper in February, 1885, and remained such to his death.

This book on its face seems not entirely trustworthy. People in Camden say that it is full of mis-statements. Nevertheless as in all such cases, what the author said and what others said and now say, about the matters touched upon, would have to be subjected to almost impossible cross-examination to find the real truth. The result would be that little more would be actually known than the extent to which these witnesses differ. With this explanation the book may be drawn upon for whatever it reveals.

First, then, according to this book, after George Whitman removed from Camden, sometime before 1884, Whitman was living in a rented room and in a bad state—even without money. This last item is hardly true, for Whitman's bank book showed that in 1873, the year he came to Camden from Washington, he opened an account with the National State Bank of Camden with a deposit of $704. At the end of 1874 he had $2,671.80 on deposit and on January 1, 1884, $2,798.39. That Whitman at this time was alone and ill and in need of some human help may well be believed, and that he had little aptitude for taking care of himself is equally credible. But that he was without money is not true.

To go on with the book, Whitman is alleged to have been wandering about Camden and going to the door of Mary O. Davis for breakfast and for meals. Once being served on a morning Mrs. Davis' kitchen became his haven. Then Whitman bought the Mickle Street house, which at the time was occupied by tenants, and Whitman made arrangements to live with them. He attempted to keep house for himself, sleeping in a scantily furnished bed, and using a homemade table to eat from and a rickety chair to sit in. He cooked on an oil stove at the risk of his life, due to his unmanageable hands and legs.

All this drove him to the kitchen door of Mrs. Davis, who sometimes, to save Whitman, went to Mickle Street to cook for him and to serve him. This lasted until Whitman induced Mrs. Davis to come to live with him and save the rent she was paying for her own house. The statement of this book that the house was dreadfully noisy is, of course, the fact, for it was near the depot and the ferry where there was continuous racket from passing freight and excursion trains. And that it had a bad odor from a guano factory in Philadelphia may not be devoid of truth. That Mrs. Davis found the house littered with papers which Whitman jealously guarded is also true, and that it remained in such disorder to the end may be believed. That Mrs. Davis carpeted the rooms at her own expense and set up stoves and put in shelves from outlays of her own money may be judged as to their truthfulness by considering the story as a whole. That she brought with her her robin and canary may be believed, since Whitman wrote a poem to *his* canary, which doubtless belonged to Mrs. Davis.

Were the neighbors curious about the relationship between Whitman and Mrs. Davis? This book says so. And also that Mrs. Davis sewed his threadbare garments and made shirts for him, which he cut out himself and superintended while they were being sewed. At this time Whitman could not walk without a cane and could not carry his cane in his left hand, so that he went forth leaning heavily on Mrs. Davis' arm. The late Francis Wilson, who was an actor of note, told me that he often saw Whitman in these days about the streets of Philadelphia with a market basket on his arm, in which he was carrying copies of his books to sell wherever he could sell them. The book under discussion says that Whitman did this; but also that months passed after Mrs. Davis became his housekeeper, during which time Whitman did not mention the subject of the housekeeping expenses. He left Mrs. Davis to pay them, though she knew that Whitman had money enough to pay one-half the cost of keeping the defective Edward in an institution. Nor did Whitman pay for the repairs on the house, nor for fuel wood, until compelled to do so.

By way of testing the truth of these things it may be set down as a fact here that Whitman in 1857 borrowed $200 from James Parton, and not repaying it was sued for it by Parton, who secured a judgment against him and siezed Whitman's copies of Jefferson's *Works* and Carlyle's *Cromwell*. It is the fact that

Whitman accepted subscription money with which to buy a horse and buggy, that he sold this and bought a better horse—and that all the time he had money in the bank. He lectured on Lincoln in Philadelphia in March, 1886, and again in April, 1887, and made several hundred dollars. In April, 1887, he lectured on Lincoln in New York City at which time he netted $600. *The New York Tribune* stated that, "The lecturer was dressed in a dark sack-coat, with dark waistcoat and trousers, low shoes and gray woolen socks. The spotless linen of his ample cuffs was turned up over the end of his sleeves."

In October, 1890, Robert G. Ingersoll delivered a benefit lecture for Whitman at Philadelphia which brought in about $900. On this occasion Whitman is charged with having borrowed $9 from Thomas Bailey Aldrich, which he never repaid. How can this story be possibly run down? Meanwhile, according to this book, Whitman's bust was being made by Sidney Moore, and his picture being painted by Anne Gilchrist's son, and the house was in the great confusion of plaster and scattered papers and waste. The summer of 1887 was fearfully hot and Mrs. Davis was overworked by serving guests and callers whom Whitman always pressed with invitations to stay and eat—and for all of this Mrs. Davis paid. Is this true? If false, the author, Mrs. Keller, must have had some deep animus. If she had an animus what was it? Mrs. Davis is alleged to have felt that the guests attributed the disorder of the house to her negligence, and that greatly embarrassed her, though she could do nothing about it in the face of Whitman's incorrigible habits. This hot summer and the work of the house permanently impaired Mrs. Davis' health; for in addition to everything else she had to take proofs to the printer for Whitman and do it in a hurry and get them back to him with speed.

Bucke came to see Whitman, also Burroughs and others. Dinners were given to Whitman in the house. Whitman was ill from overexertion and excitement; people streamed to the door for autographs and to gaze on the author of *Leaves of*

Grass. A man nurse was brought in and Mrs. Davis had to carry meals to him. Finally Warry Fritzinger, a son of Mrs. Davis, was installed as the man nurse for Whitman. Warry took a course in massage at Philadelphia and after that was used to rub and pummel Whitman every night before he went to bed. Whitman neglected, to Warry's amazement, to pay for this instruction. Is this true?

At last Whitman was overseeing the building of his tomb in Harleigh Cemetery. He sat by writing poems and reading them to the stone cutters. Mrs. Davis was not satisfied with the bequest of $1000 which Whitman made to her in his will. After his death she brought a suit which was tried in April, 1894, at which Mrs. Keller testified. Mrs. Davis won this suit for services to Whitman which had not been paid for—but the bill had been repudiated by Whitman's executors.

Notwithstanding Whitman's physical condition and the confusion of his life as above detailed, he was not idle about writing and publishing. In 1888 he brought out *November Boughs,* through David McKay of Philadelphia, a book of 140 pages of poetry and prose with a picture of himself for a frontispiece, taken in his seventieth year. All the poems, sixty-one in number, were new, except "Small the Theme of My Chant," which is from the 1867 edition of his poems, and "Stronger Lessons." Among the new poems were "My Canary Bird," "Old Salt Kassabone," "A Prairie Sunset." The prose was "A Backward Glance O'er Travel'd Roads" and many of the notes from the 1872 edition of his prose works. The group of poems was under the general titles of "Sands at Seventy," and "Fancies at Navesink."

In 1888–'89 Whitman published the eighth edition of his poems, which was the third edition of his complete works. It was a one-volume quarto of 900 pages, the complete poems and prose, and contained *Leaves of Grass, Specimen Days* and *Collect, November Boughs,* and *Sands at Seventy.* There was a portrait from life and the book was autographed. The new pieces in this edition were taken from *November Boughs.*

In 1889 there was a special edition of *Leaves of Grass,* a book of 422 pages bound in morocco, which also included "Sands at Seventy" and "A Backward Glance O'er Travel'd Roads." It had this personal note, "Doubtless anyhow the volume is more a person than a book." The book was autographed. It was a special edition in honor of the poet's seventieth birthday.

In 1891 there was *Good Bye My Fancy,* a book of sixty-six pages published by David McKay. It had for a frontispiece a reproduction of Whitman's bust. There were thirty-one new poems, such as "Sail Out for Good Eidolon Yacht," "Good Bye My Fancy," "Apparitions," "Osceola," and "Grand Is the Scene." In 1892 there was the ninth edition of *Leaves of Grass,* and the fourth edition of *Whitman's Complete Works.* And thus his work was done.

This is a good time to call upon those who saw Whitman in these Camden days for some intimate idea of his appearance and manner. In 1877 Doctor Bucke made a journey to Camden to see Whitman and found him in the house of George Whitman in Stevens Street. "I rang the bell," wrote Bucke in *Calamus,* already referred to, "the door was opened by Mrs. George Whitman. She called upstairs, 'Walt, Walt, here is some one to see you' and showed me into a very comfortable sitting room. I had only sat a few minutes . . . when Walt Whitman entered. He walked slowly leaning on a cane—his left leg manifestly weaker than the right, making him quite lame. He was suffering from the paralysis mentioned in the letters. He was a man of about 6 feet in height and weighing about 200 pounds, erect, broad-chested, dressed in a light gray suit—a white shirt with broad turned down collar open at the throat and no necktie. His face was broad and red, the picture of robust health, his hair and beard long and almost white. After he had welcomed me, which he did with cordiality, and we had sat down to talk I saw that his eyes, which were a good part of the time half covered by heavy lids, were pale blue, that his nose was strong and straight, his lips full and more expressive of tenderness than firmness, his cheeks rosy and smooth almost as a boy's— his ears large, fleshy and extraordinarily handsome, his head massive and well rounded both from front and back, and from side to side, his brows prominent and very high arched. His open shirt showed the gray hair on his chest. Head and body somewhat proudly carried. His ruddy face, his flowing almost white hair and beard, his spotless linen, his plain, fresh looking gray garments exhaled an impalpable odor of purity. Almost the dominant, initial feeling was: here is a man who is absolutely clean and sweet—and with this came upon me an impression of the man's simple majesty, such as might be produced by an immense handsome tree, or some large, magnificent, beautiful animal. The poet's voice, which was soft, clear and sympathetic added much to the charm of his presenec. In his speech there was no attempt at smartness or cleverness—the reverse indeed of all that. His language was simple, sincere and direct."

After a brief visit Bucke and Whitman took the street car to the ferry, and the ferry to Philadelphia; then they rode in a car several miles up Market Street. All the working people recognized Whitman as they went along. They then came back to the river where Whitman took the ferry back to Camden and Bucke returned to his hotel in Philadelphia.

Bucke then recorded as a finale: "It would be nothing more than the simple truth to state that I was by it [this interview] lifted to and set upon a higher plane of existence, upon which I have more or less continuously lived ever since—that is for a period of eighteen years. And my feeling toward the man Walt Whitman from that day to the present has been and is that of the deepest affection and reverence."

When Bucke wrote *Cosmic Consciousness* he gave this description of Whitman in person and these reminiscences of his habits:

"At first sight he looks much older, so that he is often supposed to be seventy or even eighty. He is six feet in height, and quite straight. He weighs nearly two hundred pounds. His body and limbs are full-sized and well proportioned. His head is large and rounded in every direction, the top a little higher than a semi-circle from the front to the back would make it. Though his face and head give the appearance of being plentifully supplied with hair, the crown is moderately bald; on the side and back the hair is long, very fine, and nearly snow white. The eyebrows are highly arched, so that it is a long distance from the eye to the center of the eyebrow (this is the facial feature that strikes one most at first sight). The eyes themselves are light blue, not large—indeed, in proportion to the head and face they seem rather small; they are dull and heavy, not expressive—what expression they have is kindness, composure, suavity. The eyelids are full, the upper commonly droops nearly half over the globe of the eye. The nose is broad, strong, and quite straight; it is full-sized, but not large in proportion to the rest of the face; it does not descend straight from the forehead, but dips down somewhat between the eyes with a long sweep. The mouth is full-sized, the lips full. The sides and lower part of the face are covered with a fine white beard, which is long enough to come down a little on the breast. The upper lip bears a heavy moustache. The ear is very large, especially long from above downwards, heavy and remarkably handsome. I believe all the poet's senses are exceptionally acute, his hearing especially so; no sound or modulation of sound perceptible to others escapes him, and he seems to hear many things that to ordinary folk are inaudible. I have heard him speak of hearing the grass grow and the trees coming out in leaf. His cheeks are round and smooth. His face has no lines expressive of care, or weariness, or age—it is the white hair and beard, and his feebleness in walking (due to paralysis) that make him appear old. The habitual expression of his face is repose, but there is a well-marked firmness and decision. I have never seen his look, even momentarily, express contempt, or any vicious feeling. I have never known him to sneer at any person or thing, or to manifest in any way or degree either alarm or apprehension, though he has in my presence been placed in circumstances that would have caused both in most men. His complexion is peculiar—a bright maroon tint, which, contrasting with his white hair and beard, makes an impression very striking. His body is not white like that of all others whom I have seen of the English or Teutonic stock—it has a delicate but well-marked rose color. All his features are large and massive, but so proportioned as not to look heavy. His face is the noblest I have ever seen. . . .

"Walt Whitman's dress was always extremely plain. He usually wore in pleasant weather a light gray suit of good woolen cloth. The only thing peculiar about his dress was that he had no necktie at any time, and always wore shirts with very large turndown collars, the button at the neck some five or six inches lower than usual, so that the throat and upper part of the breast were exposed. In all other respects he dressed in a substantial, neat, plain, common way. Everything he wore and everything about him was always scrupulously clean. His clothes might (and often did) show signs of wear, or they might be torn or have holes worn in them, but they never looked soiled. Indeed, an exquisite aroma of cleanliness has always been one of the special features of the man; it has always belonged to his clothes, his breath, his whole body, his eating and drinking, his conversation, and no one could know him for an hour without seeing that it penetrated his mind and life, and was in fact the expression of a purity which was physical as much as moral and moral as much as physical. . . .

"Though he would sometimes not touch a book for a week, he generally spent a part (though not a large part) of each day in reading. Perhaps he would read on an average a couple of hours a day. He seldom read any book deliberately through, and there was no more (apparent) system about his reading than in anything else that he did; that is to say, there was no system about it at all. If he sat in the library an hour, he would have half a dozen to a dozen volumes about him, on the table, on chairs and on the floor. He seemed to read a few pages here and a few pages there, and pass from place to place, from volume to volume, doubtless pursuing some clue or thread of his own. Sometimes (though very seldom) he would get sufficiently interested in a volume to read it all. I think he read almost, if not quite the whole, of Renouf's *Egypt,* and Bruschbey's *Egypt,* but these cases were exceptional. In his way of reading he dipped into histories, essays, metaphysical, religious and scientific treatises, novels and poetry—though I think he read less poetry than anything else. He read no language but English, yet I believe he knew a great deal more French, German and Spanish than he would own to. But if you took his own word for it, he knew very little of any subject.

"He had a way of singing, generally in an undertone, wherever he was or whatever he was doing, when alone. You would hear him the first thing in the morning while he was taking his bath and dressing (he would then perhaps sing out in full, ballads or martial songs), and a large part of the time that he sauntered outdoors during the day he sang, usually tunes without words, or a formless recitative. Sometimes he would recite poetry, generally, I think, from Shakespeare or Homer, once in a while from Bryant or others. He spent very little time in writing. It is probably that he never did give much time to that occupation. He wrote few private letters. While he was with us he would write a letter to a Canadian paper, about his travels, his condition, and his latest doings and thought, and get fifty or a hundred copies and send them to his friends and relations, especially the girls and young folks, and make that do for correspondence. Almost all his writing was done with a pencil in a sort of loose book that he carried in his breast pocket. The book consisted of a few sheets of good white paper, folded and fastened with a pin or two. He said he had tried all sorts of note-books and he liked that kind best. The literary work that he did was done at all sorts of times, and generally on his knee, impromptu, and often outdoors. Even in a room with the usual conveniences for writing he did not use a table; he put a book on his knee, or held it in his left hand, laid his paper upon it and wrote so. His handwriting was clear and plain, every letter being perfectly formed.

"He was very fond of flowers, either wild or cultivated; would often gather and arrange an immense bouquet of them for the dinner-table, for the room where he sat, or for his bed-room; wore a bud or just-started rose, or perhaps a geranium, pinned to the lapel of his coat, a great part of the time; did not seem to have much preference for one kind over any other; liked all sorts. I think he admired lilacs and sunflowers just as much as roses. Perhaps, indeed, no man who ever lived liked so many things and disliked so few as Walt Whitman. All natural objects seemed to have a charm for him; all sights and sounds, outdoors and indoors, seemed to please him. He appeared to like (and I believe he did like) all the men, women and children he saw (though I never knew him to say that he liked any one), but each who knew him felt that he liked him or her, and that he liked others also. He was in this and in everything entirely natural and unconventional. When he did express a preference for any person (which was very seldom) he would indicate it in some indirect way; for instance, I have known him to say: 'Goodbye, my love,' to a young married lady he had seen only a few times.

"Walt Whitman is the best, most perfect, example the world has so far had of the Cosmic Sense, first because he is the man in whom the new faculty has been, probably, most perfectly developed, and especially because he is, par excellence, the man who in modern times has written distinctly and at large from the point of view of Cosmic Consciousness, and who also has referred to its facts and phenomena more plainly and fully than any other writer either ancient or modern."

Justin McCarthy visited America in 1871. In his reminiscences you will find these words concerning Whitman: "Through the kindness of a friend in Washington I made the acquaintance of Walt Whitman. . . . Walt Whitman was then living in the most unpretentious sort of way. He was lodged in rooms like a garret, up several flights of stairs in a thickly populated building. . . . Even as I stood in Walt Whitman's room for the first time and looked at the stately figure of the iron gray poet himself, I could not keep out of my mind a whimsical sort of idea that if I were asked then to decide at once as to the comparative accuracy of the two descriptions I should be a little puzzled as to the answer I ought to give [namely, a man of utterly simple and even poor tastes, and a man who went in for being a penniless poet]. . . . There was the humble bed, there was the poor washstand, there were the two or three rickety chairs, there was the shelf with the cut loaf of bread, there was the staggery writing desk, and there were leaves of paper strewn over the desk and the table. . . . If ever sincerity and candour shone from the face of a man, these qualities shone from the face of Walt Whitman. There was an unmistakable dignity about the man despite his poor garb, and his utterly careless way of life. He had a fine presence with his broad rugged forehead, and his iron gray hair, giving the idea of premature old age. . . . He claimed no mission, he said, and he had only written poems because they came into his mind, and he wrote them in the form which they had won when they presented themselves to his imagination. But he rejected with perfect good humor the idea of his ever having set himself up to be the prophet or the herald of a new order of things in American literature. . . . Nothing could be less like the manner of a man who desires to attitudinize than was the whole bearing of Walt Whitman."

As to whether he did attitudinize or not the reader will remember the prefaces which Whitman by this time had given to the world, and there is more to come concerning his intentions in writing *Leaves of Grass.*

Notice how people differ when trying to describe a man from memory. Some called Whitman's voice deep or barytone, some high, thin and feminine. Burroughs said that Whitman's voice was a tender barytone, and further "he was in no sense a muscular man, an athlete. His body though superb was curiously the body of a child; one saw this in its form, in its pink color, and in the delicate texture of the skin. He took little interest in feats of strength, or in athletic sports. He walked with a slow, rolling gait, indeed moved slowly in all ways; he always had an air of infinite leisure. . . . He was his mother's child, unmistakably. With all his rank masculinity there was a curious feminine undertone in him, which revealed itself in the quality of his voice, the delicate texture of his skin, the gentleness of his touch and ways, the attraction he had for children, and the common people."

So Whitman appeared to Burroughs in the Camden days, when he was wont to visit Burroughs at Esopus on the Hudson. In 1877 Burroughs made this record in his journal:

"A great event! Walt came home with me from New York Friday night, the 16th, and stayed till 4 this afternoon. Harry Stafford came with him. They cut up like two boys and annoyed me sometimes. Great tribulation in the kitchen in the morning. Can't get them up to breakfast in time.

"Walt takes Harry with him as a kind of foil or refuge from the intellectual bores. Walt is mending, and said he walked better the morning he left than he had for five years."

The late James Huneker (1859–1921), noted for his musical and literary criticism, left us the following picture of Whitman, in his book *Ivory Apes and Peacocks:*

"I was a boy, and seeing Walt on Market Street, as he came from the Camden ferry, I resolved to visit him. It was some time after the Fourth of July 1877, and I soon found his little house on Mickle Street. A policeman at the ferry-house directed me. I confess I was scared after I had given the bell one of those pulls that we tremblingly essay at a dentist's door. To my amazement the old man soon stood before me and cordially bade me enter.

" 'Walt,' I said, for I had heard that he disliked a more ceremonious prefix, 'I've come to tell you how much the *Leaves* have meant to me.' 'Ah!' he simply replied, and asked me to take a chair. To this hour I can see the humble room, but when I try to recall our conversation I fail. That it was on general literary subjects I know, but the main theme was myself. In five minutes Walt had pumped me dry. He did it in his quiet, sympathetic way, and, with the egoism of my age, I was not averse from relating to him the adventures of my soul. That Walt was a fluent talker one need but read his memoirs by Horace Traubel. Witness his tart allusion to Swinburne's criticism of himself: 'Isn't he the damndest simulacrum?' But he was a sphinx the first time I met him. I do recall that he said Poe wrote too much in a dark cellar, and that music was his chief recreation—of which art he knew nothing; it served him as a sounding background for his pencilled improvisations. I begged for an autograph. He told me of his interest in a certain asylum or hospital whose name has gone clean out of my mind, and I paid my few dollars for the treasured signature. It is now one of my literary treasures.

"If I forget the tenor of our discourse I have not forgotten the immense impression made upon me by the man. As vain as a peacock, Walt looked like a Greek rhapsodist. Tall, imposing in bulk, his regular features, mild, light-blue or grey eyes, clear ruddy skin, plentiful white hair and beard, evoked an image of the magnificently fierce old men he chants in his book. But he wasn't fierce, his voice was a tenor of agreeable timbre, and he was gentle, even to womanliness. Indeed, he was like a receptive, lovable old woman, the kind he celebrates so often. He never smoked, his only drink was water. I doubt if he ever drank spirits. His old friends say 'No,' although he is a terrible rake in print. Without suggesting effeminacy he gave

me the impression of a feminine soul in a masculine envelope. . . .

"I left the old man after a hearty hand-shake, a So Long!
just as in his book, and returned to Philadelphia. Full of the
day, I told my policeman at the ferry that I had seen Walt.
'That old gas-bag comes here every afternoon. He gets free
rides across the Delaware,' and I rejoiced to think that a soul-
less corporation had some appreciation of a great poet, though
the irreverence of this 'powerful uneducated person' shocked
me. When I reached home I also told my mother of my visit.
She was plainly disturbed. She said that the writings of the
man were immoral, but she was pleased at my report of Walt's
sanity, sweetness, mellow optimism, and his magnetism, like
some natural force. I forgot, in my enthusiasm, that it was
Walt who listened, I who gabbled. My father, who had never
read *Leaves,* had sterner criticism to offer: 'If I ever hear of you
going to see that fellow you'll be sorry!' This coming from the
most amiable of parents, surprised me. Later I discovered the
root of his objection, for, to be quite frank, Walt did not bear
a good reputation in Philadelphia, and I have heard him
spoken of so contemptuously that it would bring a blush to the
shining brow of a Whitmaniac. Yet dogs followed him and
children loved him. I saw Walt accidentally at intervals, though
never again in Camden. I met him on the streets, and several
times took him from the Carl Gaertner String Quartet Concerts
in the foyer of the Broad Street Academy of Music to the
Market Street cars. He lumbered majestically, his hairy breast
exposed, but was a feeble old man, older than his years;
paralysis had maimed him. . . .

"Truth is, Walt was not the healthy hero he celebrates in
his book. That he never dissipated we know; but his husky
masculinity, his posing as the Great God Priapus in the garb
of a Bowery boy is discounted by the facts. Parsiphallic, he was,
but not of Pan's breed. In the 'Children of Adam,' the part most
unfavourably criticised of *Leaves,* he is the Great Bridegroom,

and in no literature, ancient or modern, have been the mysteries of the temple of love so brutally exposed."

From no one have we of this day received a fuller and more interesting description of Whitman than from Edward Carpenter. This man was twenty-five years younger than Whitman, and in his early thirties fell under Whitman's influence. Coming from England in 1877 he made a pilgrimage in May to Camden, finding Whitman living with his brother, Colonel George Whitman, at 431 Stevens Street. Whitman was called, and soon came downstairs, leaning heavily on the banister, dragging his paralyzed leg. He seemed to Carpenter quite an old man with his almost white beard, and shaggy head and neck. He was in gray dress. He was tall and erect, of florid fresh complexion, pure gray-blue eyes, not old eyes. His hands were strong and well formed. On closer view he seemed not so old. At the foot of the stairs he took Carpenter by the hand, and in a leisurely manner directed him to a seat. Carpenter was at once impressed with Whitman's vista and background of personality. He wrote:

"I remember how I was most struck, in his face, by the high arch of the eyebrows, giving a touch of child-like wonder and contemplation to his expression; yet his eyes, though full of a kind of wistful tenderness, were essentially not contemplative but perceptive—active rather than receptive—lying far back, steady, clear, with small definite pupils and heavy lids of passion and experience. A face of majestic simple proportion, like a Greek temple as some one has said; the nose Greek in outline, straight (but not at all thin or narrow, rather the contrary), broad between the brows, and meeting the line of the forehead without any great change of direction; the forehead high, with horizontal furrows, but not excessively high; the head domed, and rising to a great height in the middle, above the ears—not projecting behind; ears large and finely formed; mouth full, but almost quite concealed by hair. A head altogether impressing one by its height, and by a certain untamed 'wild hawk' look, not uncommon among the Americans."

Whitman proposed a jaunt to Philadelphia. He put on his grey slouch hat and sallied forth with pleasure, took Carpenter's arm as a support, walked slowly the best part of a mile to the ferry. The men on the ferry were evidently old friends. "On the Philadelphia side," Carpenter relates, "we were quite besieged by a man or woman selling fish at the corner of the street, the tramway conductor, the loafers on the pavement. Presently a cheery shout. . . . He was an old Broadway 'stager' who had not seen Walt for three or four years; tears were in his eyes as he held his hand." Whitman had messages for children, and in his pocket the poet discovered one or two packets of sweetmeats for absent little ones. But for the most part his words were few. It was the others who spoke, and apparently without reserve.

Whitman could not walk far, but all the while he was restfulness and calmness. In a few days after this Carpenter went to see Whitman at Timber Creek, where he was with his friends the Staffords. He found Stafford to be a Methodist, who sometimes preached, and Mrs. Stafford to be a woman of cultured expression. There was a son Harry Stafford, a great favourite of Whitman's, a grown-up daughter and two children. Whitman was very fond of them all. Mrs. Stafford told Carpenter that Whitman was "a good man; I think he is the best man I ever knew." And so Carpenter found that this was the house, the creek and the woods to which Whitman was then repairing to overcome his paralysis. Whitman said to Carpenter, "I had hardly realized that there was so much interest in me in England. I confess I am surprised that America, to whom I have especially addressed myself, is so utterly silent. Lowell and indeed most of the critics, say that I am crude, inartistic—do you think that?"

Carpenter reports Whitman as follows regarding the composition of *Leaves of Grass:* "'I did, in fact, re-write and destroy much before I published; I cannot think that I have alto-

225

gether attained, but I have planted the seed; it is for others to continue the work. My original idea was that if I could bring men together by putting before them the heart of man, with all its joys and sorrows and experiences and surroundings, it would be a great thing; up to this time I have had America chiefly in view, but this appreciation of me in England makes me think I might perhaps do the same for the old world also. I have endeavoured from the first to get free as much as possible from all literary attitudinising—to strip off integuments, coverings, bridges—and to speak straight from and to the ear.' "

Then Whitman invited Carpenter to meet Anne Gilchrist and her children, living then at 1929 North 22nd Street, Philadelphia, where Mrs. Gilchrist had provided a sort of prophet's chamber for Whitman. Carpenter wrote: "When I arrived . . . the whole family was sitting out on the doorsteps—Whitman in the midst, in an arm chair, his white beard and hair glistening in the young moonlight, looking like some old god—the others grouped around him or at his feet. After this for a week of evenings I made one of the party. How pleasant it was! Whitman had a knack of making ordinary life enjoyable, redeeming it from commonplaceness. Instead of making you feel that the Present is a kind of squalid necessity to be got over as best may be, in view of something always in the future, he gave you that good sense of nowness, that faith that the present is enjoyable, which imparts color and life to the thousand and one dry details of existence. No great talker, and would generally let the conversation ebb and flow at its own will, without effort ready apparently for grave or gay alike.

"Unlike many highly important people who seem to enjoy holding forth to a general audience, Whitman, as I thought, preferred to let conversation turn on the pivot of personal relationship. Often as not he would have his listener by the hand; and his words too had an attractive force, from their very simplicity and purity from affectation or display. I think he did not really care to have conversational dealings with people except on such a basis of personal affection. To such as he did not like—to all mere gabblers, bores, spying and prying persons —he became as a precipice, instantly and utterly inaccessible. Certainly it was one of the pleasures of his society that you always felt he was there in person, *bona fide,* not by deputy; and no current notion of politeness could make him do a thing he did not enjoy doing. One evening we were looking over some fine engravings, mostly portraits, Gainsboroughs, Reynolds, Lelys, and others, from Mrs. Gilchrist's collection. He enjoyed them greatly and very deliberately, dwelling long and long over some of them, criticising style, workmanship, composition, character,—but when he had had enough of it all— Well, he said so! I have never known any one so cordial and near to detach and withdraw himself at times more decisively than he did, or on the whole spent more time in solitude."

Carpenter observed that no judgment of Whitman was complete which failed to take into account Whitman's Quaker element of obstinacy which existed to such a marked degree in him. The conversation at the Gilchrist house turned upon the Chinese, and he records Whitman's remarks:

" 'I fancy they are like the Germans, only more refined. My notion is that the Germans are simple, true, affectionate folk, but there is a kind of roughness, one may almost say brutishness, about them; the Chinese have the same good qualities, with a certain alertness and grace which the Germans lack.' "

When Mrs. Gilchrist spoke of the degradation of women among Orientals and its effect on their races, Whitman replied, " 'I suppose that among the *masses* of the people the women (and men too) live, after all, much as they do in the West, and as they must do in all times and climes; and that the special treatment of women in the East only applies to the upper classes. The masses in every part of the globe are dominated by the necessities of Nature. Thus also among the Greeks and Romans the peasant-life must have had its races of fine women.' And here he cited Juvenal, and his comparison of the effeminate lady of his time with the 'stern magnificent mother' of the early days of Rome."

Carpenter continues, "Whitman spoke of 'Sakuntala,' the Indian drama, its 'modernness'—the comic scenes especially being as of the times of Shakespeare; and of the great Hindu epic, the 'Ramayana'; and told the story of Yudisthura, which occurs as an episode in the latter. There was conversation in reference to the cramped life of the 'high-born' women in the East—to the shoddiness and vulgarity of modern well-to-do life. Whitman said, 'It seems a strange thing to me, this love of gilt and upholstery among the Americans—that people leading a free natural open-air life should, directly they make a little money, want to go in for sofas, expensively furnished rooms, dress, and the like; yet it seems to be a law, a kind of necessity, that they should do so. . . . I suppose it is partly that each man wishes to feel himself as good as others, to feel that he can have of the 'best' too; democracy showing itself for a time in that way, reducing the borrowed old-world standard of superiority to an absurdity; and I guess it will not last for ever.'

"We did not generally sit up later than eleven. Breakfast was at 7:30 or 8. Walt's arrival in the morning was as exhilarating as a fine sunrise. After breakfast and a chat we would separate to our respective occupations. In the afternoon, almost every day I was there, the poet went off to Camden to visit his sister-in-law, who was at that time confined to the house, and to whom, I believe, he was much attached. As I have said, Walt was very simple and domestic in his ways; and would quite enjoy, on a rainy afternoon, having a game of twenty questions such as he had 'often played in camp with the soldiers during the war,' or would take pleasure in preparing some little dish of his own devising for the evening meal. One evening we pressed him to read. He would not recite anything of his own; but he read out Tennyson's 'Ulysses'—in a clear, strong, and rugged tone. He said: 'I guess it is about the best Tennysonian poem.' Another evening, I remember, he told us how, when living at New York, he had had a 'fancy' to visit Sing-sing Prison. He obtained permission to do so, got to know one or two of the wardens, and for some time went there pretty frequently. He wrote letters for the prisoners, &c. 'It was a whim.'

"We had a long talk on manual labour. Most of us agreed it would be a good thing for all classes to take part in—not to be left to one class only. Walt maintained with regard to reforms and the like, that it was not good trying to benefit people (labouring people for instance) who did not feel the need of any change. He said 'Many people came to me at one time about slavery, and "wondered" that I was so quiet about it; but, in truth, I felt that abolitionists were making quite noise enough, and that there were other things just as important which had to be attended to.' We got talking of Abraham Lincoln—I suppose in reference to slavery—and I mentioned the story that Lincoln went out of his mind and nearly committed suicide over a love affair. Walt, who always was a great admirer of Lincoln, and who knew a good deal about him and his history gave this a most emphatic denial, saying that Lincoln was 'never even near being crazy.'

"I told Walt about a visit paid to Oliver Wendell Holmes, and the criticisms of *Leaves of Grass* which I heard on that occasion. I saw the 'Autocrat of the Breakfast Table' at his house in Boston. He was then about 70 years of age—a dapper active little man, full of life and go, rather enjoying the visits of strangers—saying 'Oh yes, I have a large "parish"—people write to me and come and call from all parts of the world— we authors are rather vain, you know, and quite enjoy a little homage; but my parish is not as big as Longfellow's—not as big as Longfellow's. But this is not a good time for you to see Boston. Boston is very empty now—(getting up and glancing through the window) very empty; you might almost see a fox run down the street'; I said something about American literature and *Leaves of Grass*. 'Oh! Whitman,' he said, 'well-well-well—Whitman is all very well—he has capacity, but it won't do—it won't do. I tell you what, it's something like this: you know, skilful cooks say that the faintest odour, the merest whiff, of *assafœtida,* will give a piquant flavour to a dish—and I can believe that; but to drench it in *assafœtida,* no that won't do. The poets *coquette* with Nature and weave garlands of roses for her; but Whitman *goes at her* like a great hirsute man —no, it won't do. Now,' he continued, 'the other day Lowell and Longfellow and I were chatting together, and the subject of Whitman turned up. Said Lowell, "I can't think why there is all this stir about Whitman; I have read a good deal of his poetry, but I can't see anything in it—*I can't see anything in it."* "Well," said Longfellow, "I believe the man might have done something if he had only had a decent training and education." As to my own opinion, why,' said Holmes, 'I have already given you that. So you see what we think of him in America.' Whitman was a good deal amused, and took it all in good part, saying he knew pretty well already what they thought.

"As the days went by I began to see more clearly the depths which lay behind the poet's simple and unconcerned exterior. Literary persons, as a rule, write over their own heads; they talk a little bigger than themselves. But Whitman seemed to fill out *Leaves of Grass,* and for an interpretation of it. I began to see that all he had written there was matter of absolute personal experience—that you might be sure that what was said was meant. There was the same deliberate suggestiveness about his actions and manners that you find in his writings—only, of course, with the added force of bodily presence; and far down, too, there were clearly enough visible the same strong and contrary moods, the same strange omnivorous egotism, controlled and restrained by that wonderful genius of his for human affection and love. 'Who has the most enamoured body?' were words which somehow his presence often suggested. It was with real reluctance that, a week after my arrival, I bade adieu to all that friendly household."

So ended Carpenter's contacts with Whitman in 1877. In June of 1884 he was back in America again and down to Mickle Street to see his friend. Carpenter wrote that Whitman had "at that time for housekeepers, an elderly workman and his wife, Mr. and Mrs. Lay, with whom he was on easy terms, and with whom he had his meals. In appearance I thought him much the same as in 1877—a trifle thinner perhaps, and certainly more infirm. Some expression of weariness, too, I thought I saw, which would likely arise from the increased confinement of his life. 'I keep going,' he said, 'much the same. Visits from English friends are perhaps my chief diversion.' Then, after tender inquiries, especially for Mrs. Gilchrist (who was now in London), 'have just had a visit from Oscar Wilde—who told me about England; I made him do the talking—rather liked him. I have occasional letters from Dowden—a steady friend— and others. Bucke's book is going off slowly—not much cared for by my friends—but I like it. I opposed the book all along, till Bucke, getting fairly out of patience, came one day and said 'Now I am just as obstinate as you, and I intend to bring it out whether you like it or no—so you had better make the best of the matter and help to make it authentic as far as you can'; whereupon I caved in, laughing heartily, and wrote the account of my birthplace and antecedents which occupies the first twenty-four pages of the book.' Whitman continued 'I thought that there was a germinal idea in Bucke's book—the idea that *Leaves of Grass* was above all an expression of the Moral Nature. As to O'Connor's letters—I must say I like them. They are comforting. Just as any woman likes a man to fall in love with her—whether she returns it or not—so to have once aroused so eloquent and passionate a declaration is reassuring and a help to me.' We then spoke of the money-making and gentility business at New York—I remarking that I thought it had all increased considerably since I was there in '77, and he corroborating, though holding that I probably had to be gone through 'for reasons.' "

Carpenter, commenting on Whitman's character, wrote: "I am impressed more than ever with W's contradictory, self-willed, tenacious, obstinate character, strong and even extreme moods, united with infinite tenderness, wistful love, and studied tolerance; also great caution (he says: 'the Phrenologists always say that caution is my chief characteristic—did you know that?') and a certain artfulness, combined with keen, penetrating and determined candour; the wild-hawk look still there, 'untamable, untranslatable,' yet with that wonderful tenderness at bottom."

One day they went to Fairmount Park, Philadelphia. The conversation drifted to social questions. Whitman said he believed, like Carlyle, in *Men,* and continued, "I think that notwithstanding all set-offs the great capitalists and masters of private enterprise have, in America at least, been useful. I have myself had all along a tender feeling for Co-operation, but for that doubt whether a committee or an elected person could or would do the work." As to England he seemed to think that emigration would relieve it, and he looked upon the law and custom of *entail* as the "hard-pan underlying your social institutions." Whitman went on, "I like and welcome all agitation, even the fiercest, but like Carlyle have little belief in reform talk. Society like a person in middle life, is set, and you have to make the best of it. I am, I hope, a bit of a reformer myself. Yes, we must *grow* generous, ungrasping masters of industry; absurd as the idea would seem to most now-a-days, I believe that is the upshot of what is going on. The creation of a large, independent, democratic class of small owners is the main thing—though it is never once mentioned by our economists and politicians. I am satisfied that for America Free Trade and open admission of all foreigners is an integral part of its theory; the future of the world is one of open communication and solidarity of all races; and if that problem cannot be solved in America it cannot be solved anywhere."

Carpenter observed that Whitman was absorbed and quiet on the visit to Fairmount Park. He was recognized by a few among the well-dressed crowd, but seemed to hold himself aloof with almost an air of hauteur. He looked distinguished in his gray suit, and with his gray uncovered head, though he gave evidence of weariness. Whitman broke silence to ask Carpenter about his life and ways at home in England.

"The following evening," Carpenter records, "I stayed to supper with Whitman in the little kitchen of his home, in company with Mr. and Mrs. Lay. They seemed homely decent people, rather dull and quiet. Walt, who was dressed just in shirt and trousers—for the weather was hot—kept things going. Afterwards we sat in the front room with Golger McKinsey, a young Philadelphian of literary leanings, who had come in. Walt talked about Shakespeare, the Bacon theory, the greatness of the historical plays, the 'dragon-rancours' of the barons, King Lear, &c. 'I will not be positive about Bacon's connection with the plays,' Whitman said, 'but I am satisfied that behind the historical Shakespeare there is another mind, guiding, and far, far reaching, giving weight and permanent value to what would otherwise have been only two plays a year written for a wittily, alert, jocose audience—chiefly of young gallants.'

"The conversation turned somehow on death. W. said: 'It is in reality a very different affair from the romantic stage view of it; deathbed speeches and "scenes" are of the rarest occurrence. I have witnessed hundreds of deaths, and as a rule it seems just a matter of course—like having your breakfast, or any other event of the day, and met with indifference at the last, and with apathy, or unconsciousness.'"

On another occasion the two men walked around the streets of Camden—Walt as usual with plentiful greetings to passers-by. "Walt," writes Carpenter, "insisted on our having some refreshment, left us a few minutes later, left us with that queer brusque manner of his which so often offended his friends—

just coldly saying 'Ta-ta,' and going off as if he didn't care if he never saw us again!"

On June thirtieth Carpenter had his last visit with Whitman and writes in conclusion: "He was very friendly and affectionate, and sat by the open window downstairs enjoying the wafts of fragrant air, while he talked about *Leaves of Grass.* 'What lies behind *Leaves of Grass,*' Whitman said, 'is something that few, very few, only one here and there, perhaps oftenest women, are at all in a position to seize. It lies behind almost every line; but concealed, studiedly concealed; some passages left purposely obscure. There is something in my nature furtive like an old hen! You see a hen wandering up and down a hedgerow, looking apparently quite unconcerned, but presently she finds a concealed spot, and furtively lays an egg, and comes away as though nothing had happened! That is how I felt in writing *Leaves of Grass.* Sloane Kennedy calls me 'artful'—which about hits the mark. I think there are truths which it is necessary to envelop or wrap up.' I replied that all through history the old mysteries, or whatever they may have been called, had been held back; and added that probably we had something yet to learn from India in these matters. W.: 'I do not myself think there is anything more to come from that source; we must rather look to modern science to open the way. Time alone can absolutely test my poems or any one's. Personally, I think that the "something" is more present in some of my small later poems than in the "Song of Myself."'"

And there is this last glimpse of Whitman: "I left him sitting there by the window in his downstairs room, close to the street and the passers-by—his clear eye undimmed by age, his rugged, loving nature unaltered; though there was a certain grave weariness in his otherwise majestice presence, which gives one a touch of sadness when one thinks that he had still nearly eight years to pass of increasing physical disablement and of

continually diminishing vitality, culminating at last in serious
bodily misery and wretchedness."

First and last Whitman was honored by the calls of many
distinguished men such as John Morley in 1867, Justin Mc-
Carthy, already mentioned, Edmund Yates in 1872, Lord
Houghton, Sir Edwin Arnold, Henry Irving, Oscar Wilde,
Bram Stoker, Ernest Rhys, and Edmund Gosse. In America he
drew about him more and more friends and admirers. Though
Whittier was averse to Whitman at first the two men became
more cordial, and especially did Whitman give Whittier his
due. One regrets the failure of the Emerson relationship to
have grown deeper and stronger. On Whitman's part he
showed he was not incapable of returning criticism for criticism.

In 1872 Whitman wrote to Dowden that Emerson was drawing on the same theme that he had done twenty-five years before. "It all seems quite attenuated (the first drawing of a good
pot of tea you know—and Emerson's was the heavenly herb
itself—but what must we say to a second, and even third or
fourth infusion?)" Emerson had said in 1871 that he was not
satisfied with Whitman. He had expected him to make the
songs of the nation, but he was doing nothing but making inventories. Also William Douglas O'Connor was estranged
from Whitman, but returned friendly and devoted enough
later.

Whitman was greatly fortuned by the friendship from 1888
on of Horace Traubel, who was connected with a bank in
Philadelphia. Traubel at this time was thirty years old, and a
poet by nature. He married Anne Montgomerie in Whitman's
house in Camden at the request of Whitman who desired to
attend the wedding, but was too ill to leave home. Day by day
Traubel sat and talked with Whitman, and took down what
he said. We thus have a report of Whitman's ideas and opin-

235

ions on a great variety of subjects, by which we are able to judge his nature, and the richness of his mind. When Whitman died Traubel wrote, "O My Dead Comrade" from which these lines are taken:

O my dead comrade — my great dead!
I sat by your bedside — it was the close of day —
I heard the drip of the rain on the roof of the house

. . . .

I sat by your bedside. I held your hand:
Once you opened your eyes: O look of recognition!
O look of bestowal!
From you then passed to me the commission of the future . . .

And now we turn to Traubel with whom we combine Whitman's own writings, notes and memoranda to see what the man thought and planned, and to examine the inner workings of his mind.

CHAPTER FOURTEEN

AMERICA has no treasury of profound opinion or judgment of literature and men surpassing that in Whitman's prefaces, his memoranda and notes, and his conversations with Traubel. His judgment of men and lives is wonderfully refreshing, and in order to look into his thinking mind some of his comments on great works and men need citation. Whitman in his unfettered originality shook off stock verdicts of his day. He knew that Shakespeare, the Bible and any book whatever, can be so constantly studied that it takes on elements of beauty and greatness which it does not really possess. For myself, I am sure that Shakespeare and the Bible have reached their pre-eminence as the result of long years of study, propagandum and commentation. In the meantime the surpassing greatness of Homer, and Aeschylus diminish and fall away, for lack of careful appraisal. Whitman thought Aeschylus a greater poet than Shakespeare, and in that judgment I fully concur. Carlyle was moved to the highest praise of Job; I think *Prometheus Bound* strikes a profounder and more philosophical and uplifting note. From *Whitman's Prose Works* I take this note of his on Shakespeare:

"Superb and inimitable as all is, it is mostly an objective and physiological kind of power and beauty the soul finds in Shakspere*—a style supremely grand of the sort, but in my opinion stopping short of the grandest sort, at any rate for fulfilling and satisfying modern and scientific and democratic American purposes. Think, not of growths as forests primeval, or Yellow-

*Whitman spelled Shakespeare's name three different ways in his writings.

237

stone geysers, or Colorado ravines, but of costly marble palaces, and palace rooms, and the noblest fixings and furniture, and noble owners and occupants to correspond—think of carefully built gardens from the beautiful but sophisticated gardening art at its best, with walks and bowers and artificial lakes, and appropriate statue-groups and the finest cultivated roses and lilies and japonicas in plenty—and you have the tally of Shakspere. The low characters, mechanics, even the loyal henchmen—all in themselves nothing—serve as capital foils to the aristocracy. The comedies (exquisite as they certainly are) bringing in admirably portray'd common characters, have the unmistakable hue of plays, portraits, made for the divertisement only of the élite of the castle, and from its point of view. The comedies are altogether non-acceptable to America and Democracy."

And to Horace Traubel he said: "Do you suppose I accept the almost luny worship of Shakespeare—the cult worship, the college-chair worship? Not a bit of it—not a bit of it. I do not think Shakespeare was the all in all of literature. I think there were twenty thousand things coming before him and at his time and since—things, men, illuminati—and everything has to be counted. Shakespeare was the greatest of his kind—but how about his kind?"

And this from Traubel's Boswellian book: "Reference having been made to Shakespeare, W. said: 'Shakespeare shows undoubted defects: he often uses a hundred words where a dozen would do: it is true that there are many pithy terse sentences everywhere: but there are countless prolixities: though as for the overabundances of words more might be said: as, for instance, that he was not ignorantly prolific: that he was like nature itself: nature, with her trees, the oceans: nature, saying "there's lots of this, infinitudes of it—therefore, why spare it? If you ask for ten I give you a hundred, for a hundred I give you a thousand, for a thousand I give you ten thousand."

It may be that we should look at it in that way: not complain of it: rather understand its amazing intimation.'

"Frothingham had somewhere said that Shakespeare 'lacked the religious as distinguished from the poetic faculty.' W. said: 'That seems to me to be profoundly true. The highest poetic expression demands a certain element of the religious—indeed, should be transfused with it. Frothingham has hit upon the truth: scholars will not, dare not, admit it, but it is the truth. The time will come when Shakespeare will be given his right place—will be put on a low shelf, as the esthetic-heroic among poets, lacking both in the democratic and spiritual: a master, sure enough: yes, a master: but subject to severe deductions. People don't dare face the fact Shakespeare. They are all tied to a fiction that is called Shakespeare—a Shakespearean illusion. This is the idea in substance that I tried to exploit in the *Critic:* tried, I say (I reckon I didn't say the thing in the best style). I never have regarded Shakespeare as the heroic-heroic, which is the greatest development of the spirit: I call the heroic-heroic men the greatest men: Shakespeare is rather the poet of lords and ladies and their side of life. Even the Greeks were a little tinged with the same quality. It's very difficult to talk about Shakespeare in a frank vein: there's always somebody about with a terrific prejudice to howl you down.'

"In speaking of the Shakespeare sonnets W. said: 'Their origin was a thought-origin—that I feel, acknowledge: but they are often over-done—over-ornate—their elaboration is extreme, at times utterly obscuring the idea, which might be assumed to be of the first importance.' "

Under the heading of "Preparatory Reading and Thought" in Volume IX (page 269) of Whitman's *Complete Works,* there is this note:

"Many little things are too much over-colored in Shakespeare —far too much. The features of beloved women, compliments, the descriptions of moderately brave actions, professions of service, and hundreds more, are painted too intensely. It is no answer to this to say that a lover would so state the case about a woman he loved, or that a strong, rich nature would be apt to describe incidents in that manner; and that Shakespeare is therefore correct in so presenting them. Immensely too much is unnaturally colored—the sentiment is piled on, similes, comparisons, defiances, exaltations, immortalities, bestowed upon themes certainly not worthy the same, thus losing proportion. (Also most of the discursive speeches of the great and little characters are glaringly inappropriate, both words and sentiments such as could not have come from their mouths in real life and therefore should not in the plays.) Yet on great occasions the character and action are perfect. This is what saves Shakespeare. Is he imitative of Homer? If so where and how?"

From Whitman's notes of preparation and reading one learns that Whitman was reading Virgil's *Bucolics, Eclogues* and the *Æneid,* in 1857, and he expressed himself thus:

"Of the *Æneid,* it seems to me well enough except for the fatal defect of being an imitation, a second-hand article—Homer's *Iliad* being the model. It is too plain an attempt to get up a case, by an expert hand, for Roman origin and for the divine participation in old Italian affairs just as much as in those of besieged Troy and in mythical Greece. The death of Turnus, at the conclusion, seems to me a total failure as a piece of invention, description, etc. . . . The *Bucolics* and *Georgics* are finely expressed—they are first rate.

"Sustenance for the great geniuses of the world is always plenty and the main ingredients of it are perhaps always the same. Yet nothing ever happened to former heroes, sages and poets so inspiring to them, so fit to shine resplendent, light upon them and make them original creators of works, newer, nobler, grander, as the events of the last eighty years. I mean the advent of America."

But Homer was Whitman's delight, his profound admira-

240

tion—and he had ideas, and excellent ones, about translating Homer, though he did not know Greek. He knew intuitively how that greatest poem of the world needed to be rendered in another language.

Traubel records this conversation: "'I have had different opinions about Palmer's prose Homer—have liked it and not liked it and liked it again and so on—it comes and goes like indigestion. I think Buckley's translation the best extant— I read it many years ago: the impression it made upon me has proved to be indelible. Bryant's and Derby's are damnable— I don't know which is worse than the other—they are both so stiff, so bad, it hardly seems anything could be worse than either. John Swinton sent me Derby's, for what reason I can't imagine. Pope was of course a machine—he wrote like a see-saw.'"

Here is another Whitman-Traubel conversation: "'Bucke is fond of ranking *Faust* and *Leaves of Grass* together,' said Whitman. I expressed doubts. W. himself spoke of Goethe. 'I suppose humility should restrain me: it might be said I have no right to an opinion: I know nothing of Goethe at first hand: hit upon translations, pick up a poem, a glint, here and there. I have read *Faust*—looked into it—not with care, not studiously, yet intelligently, in my own way.' Now he 'had an opinion of Goethe,' and, having it 'might as well own up.' 'Goethe impresses me as above all to stand for essential literature, art, life—to argue the importance of centering life in self—in perfect persons—perfect you, me: to force the real into the abstract ideal: to make himself, Goethe, the supremest example of personal identity: everything making for it: in us, in Goethe: every man repeating the same experience.' Goethe would ask: 'What are your forty, fifty, hundred, social, national, phantasms? This only is real—this person.' While W. felt that 'all the great teachers—the Greek, the Roman—Plato, Seneca, Epictetus (I remember Epictetus says a very like thing) in some respects placed a related emphasis on personality, identity,' yet he observed a break in the fact that 'all those eminent teachers were superbly moral (I confess they quite satisfy me as being so) while Goethe was not. Goethe seemed to look upon personal development as an end in itself; the old teachers looked for collective results. I do not mean that Goethe was immoral, bad—only that he laid stress upon another point. Goethe was for beauty, erudition, knowledge—first of all for culture. I doubt if another imaginist of the first order in all literature, all history so deeply put his stamp there. Goethe asked: ' "What do you make of your patriotism, army, state, people?" It was all nothing to him.' Here W. stopped and laughed. 'So you see I have an opinion while I confess I know nothing about Goethe.' Further: 'I do not think Burns was bad any more than I think Goethe was bad, but Burns was without morale, morality.' Goethe always 'looked askant' at patriotism. 'Burns was as little a patriot in any large sense as any man that ever lived. You know it is very easy to get up a hurrah—call it freedom, patriotism: but none of that is patriotism in any sense I accept.'

"W. said: 'Goethe suggests books—carries the aroma of books about with him—seems to be a great man with books, by books, from books. Now, whatever Shakespeare was or was not, he was not that sort of man: he came, with all his scholarship, direct from nature. To me that means oh! so much: to come straight from life—to be rooted in an immediate fact. Bucke sees a great deal more in Goethe than I do—sees Goethe as if come fresh from the soil—regards him in a more liberal light: insists that he articulates the soundest philosophy of the modern world. Bucke says my trouble is in the fact that I cannot read German—that Goethe cannot be translated.' "

This is what Whitman wrote after looking over Goethe's complete works:

"Here is now (January, 1856) my opinion of Goethe. (Had I not better read more of Goethe before giving an opinion?) He is the most profound reviewer of life known. To him life, things, the mind, death, people, are all studies, dissections, exhibitions. These he enters upon with unequalled coolness and depth of penetration. As a critic he stands apart from all men and criticises them. He is the first great critic and the fountain of modern criticism. Yet Goethe will never be well beloved of his fellows. Perhaps he knows too much. I can fancy him not being well beloved of Nature for the same reason. A calm and mighty person whose anatomic considerations of the body are not enclosed by superior considerations makes the perfect surgeon and operator upon the body upon all occasions. So Goethe operates upon the world . . . his office is great . . . what indeed is greater? He shall have the respect and admiration of the whole. There is however what he cannot have from any."

Whitman thought well of Kant, and took pains to write down Kant's definition of metaphysics, namely that which considers the whole concrete show of things, the world, man himself, either individually or aggregated in history, as resting on a spiritual, invisible basis, continually shifting, yet the real substance, and the only immutable one. This, observed Whitman, was the doctrine of Hegel a "philosopher in the domain of metaphysics, who has rendered greater service than any man we know."

"Only Hegel," wrote Whitman, "is fit for America—is large enough and free enough. Absorbing his speculations and imbued by his letter and spirit, we bring to the study of life here and the thought of hereafter, in all its mystery and vastness, an expansion and clearness of sense before unknown. As a face in a mirror we see the world of materials, nature with all its objects, processes, shows, reflecting the human spirit and by such reflection formulating, identifying, developing and proving it. Body and mind are one; an inexplicable paradox, yet no truth truer. The human soul stands in the centre, and all the universes minister to it, and serve it and revolve round it. They are one side of the whole and it is the other side. It

243

escapes utterly from all limits, dogmatic standards and meas-
urements and adjusts itself to the ideas of God, of space, and
to eternity, and sails them at will as oceans, and fills them as
beds of oceans.

"The varieties, contradictions and paradoxes of the world
and of life, and even good and evil, so baffling to the superficial observer, and so often leading to despair, sullenness or
infidelity, become a series of infinite radiations and waves
of the one sea-like universe of divine action and progress,
never stopping, never hasting. 'The heavens and the earth'
to use the summing up of Joseph Gostick whose brief I en-
dorse: 'The heavens and the earth and all things within their
compass—all the events of history—the facts of the present and
the development of the future (such is the doctrine of Hegel)
all form a complication, a succession of steps in the one eternal
process of creative thought.' "

Here are his thoughts about Tennyson:

"Let me assume to pass verdict, or perhaps momentary judgment, for the United States on this poet—a remov'd and distant
position giving some advantages over a nigh one. What is
Tennyson's service to his race, times, and especially to America? First, I should say—or at least not forget—his personal
character. He is not to be mention'd as a rugged, evolution-
ary, aboriginal force—but (and a great lesson is in it) he
has been consistent throughout with the native, healthy, patriotic spinal element and promptings of himself. His moral line
is local and conventional, but it is vital and genuine. He reflects
the upper crust of his time, its pale cast of thought—even its
ennui. Then the simile of my friend John Burroughs is entirely true, 'his glove is a glove of silk, but the hand is a hand
of iron.' He shows how one can be a royal laureate, quite
elegant and 'aristocratic,' and a little queer and affected, and
at the same time perfectly manly and natural. As to his non-
democracy, it fits him well, and I like him the better for it.
I guess we all like to have (I am sure I do) some one who

presents those sides of a thought, or possibility, different from our own—different and yet with a sort of home-likeness—a tartness and contradiction offsetting the theory as we view it, and construed from tastes and proclivities not at all his own. . . . Tennyson is the imitation of Shakespeare, through a refined, educated, traveled, modern English dandy."

Traubel records Whitman's opinion of Browning:

"I asked W. whether he had read Browning's *Paracelsus.* He talked then of Browning: 'You should read *The Ring and The Book.* That, at least, it would repay anybody who had the leisure to read. Browning is in some respects utterly free— free not to explain: free to put down his statement where it may be seen and then let the world find its own way to a meaning—free of the desire to be at once or ever understood. Browning was also free of humor as an architect of verse, though I feel that his freedom here drifts him rather towards an angular than a facile result. Browning has what O'Connor calls "elements"—powers of the first class—virility, fibre. I think it would mean a hard tussle for anyone to take Browning up in the bulk—attempt to take him in in the large—the whole of him for better or for worse. I don't believe I could do it. I don't find Browning's technique easy—it beats me sore, bruises me—though I don't make much of that: the fault is mainly my own . . .

" 'I have read Browning but I do not feel that I know him. I realize him—that is, I see him for a great figure—I see him for a proud achievement—O yes—I do—but do not feel that I know his books. I have read *The Ring and the Book, Paracelsus,* some scattering poems (many of them, in fact)—that is all. My impression has been not that he was not for anybody but that he was not for me, though Professor Corson, who has been here to pay me a visit, says that I am mistaken, that Browning is my man, only that I have not so far got at him the right way. I do not assent to that—Corson does not know my appetite and my capacity as well as I know it my-

self. One thing I always feel like saying about Browning—
that I am always conscious of his roominess: he is noway a
small man: all his connections are big, strong.' "

And as to Keats—Traubel writes:

"W. went on talking on the question of 'lights' in literature.
'I had a letter from a fellow last week: did I show it to you?
I [Whitman] intended that you should see it. The letter was
from England: some one, not a célèbre—not even literary,
markedly, I suppose—yet a man of considerable cuteness, writing it. His fad is Keats: he thinks Keats is the man. He
offered me some very free criticisms of *Leaves of Grass*. Oh!
I wish I had the letter here: I must have sent it to Bucke: I did
not intend to—I wanted you to see it, know about it, before it
went.' 'How do you regard Keats, on the whole, anyway?
You don't refer to him often or familiarly.' He replied: 'I
have of course read Keats—his works: may be said to have read
all: he is sweet—oh! very sweet—all sweetness: almost lush:
lush, polish, ornateness, elegancy.' 'Does he suggest the Greek?
He is often called Greek.' 'Oh, no! Shakespeare's Sonnets, not
the Greek: you know, the Sonnets are Keats and more—all
Keats was then a vast sum added. For superb finish, style,
beauty, I know of nothing in all literature to come up to these
Sonnets: they have been a great worry to the fellows: and to
me, too: a puzzle: the Sonnets being of one character, the
Plays of another. Has the mystery of this difference suggested
itself to you? Try to think of the Shakespeare plays: think of
their movement: their intensity of life, action: everything hell-
bent to get along: on: on: energy—the splendid play of force:
across fields, mire, creeks: never mind who is splashed—spare
nothing: this thing must be done, said: let it be done, said:
no faltering.' He shot this out with the greatest energy of
manner and tone, accompanying animated gestures, saying in
conclusion: 'The Sonnets are all that is opposite—perfect of
their kind—exquisite, sweet: lush: eleganted: refined and refined then again refined—again: refinement multiplied by

refinement.' Then he saw no vigor in them? 'No: vigor was not called for: they are personal: more or less of small affairs: they do their own work in their own way: that's all we could ask and more than most of us do, I suppose.' He regarded the Plays as being 'tremendous with the virility that seemed so totally absent from the Sonnets . . .'

" 'Keats' poetry is ornamental, elaborated, rich in wrought imagery, it is imbued with the sentiment, at second-hand, of the gods and goddesses of twenty-five hundred years ago. Its feeling is the feeling of a gentlemanly person lately at college, accepting what was commanded him there, who moves and would only move in elegant society, reading classical books in libraries. Of life in the nineteenth century it has none any more than the statues have. It does not come home at all to the direct wants of the bodies and souls of the century.' "

Traubel writes Whitman's expressions on Ibsen dated September, 1888:

"W. reading Ibsen's *Pillars of Society*. 'Some one in the Walter Scott Company sent it over to me.' Laid it down. Shook hands with me. 'Perhaps it was Rhys. I am not greatly impressed. It seems to me to have been too prettily done though it is no doubt much more powerful in the Norwegian—hardly seems apposite when rendered in English. I doubt whether I would ever care for the play.' "

In October, 1888—Traubel continues of Whitman on Ibsen:

"Advised me to take Ibsen's *The Pillars of Society* and read it: 'Take it—take it for a long while, take it for a long while'— then, laughingly: 'Take it for good if you can make good out of it.' 'You don't seem to take any great shine to Ibsen?' 'No—it seems that way: and yet I realize him to be an immense power: he is dynamic, vital: I do not seem to find the exact place for him.' 'But you think he has a place?' 'Do you?' 'Sure —don't you?' He said quickly: 'Sure—sure—but where is it?' I remarked: 'You don't often give puzzles up: you generally find some way to solve them.' He shook his head: 'Did I say I gave Ibsen up? I'm a little slower than common making him out—that's all.' "

Whitman had this to say of Carlyle in May, 1882:

"Yet Carlyle could never have understood me—could never have comprehended the *Leaves,* which are outside his spiritual latitude and longitude altogether. Carlyle was not an apt student of the modern, of literary rebellion—he was raised, imbedded, in older routines. He did not understand humanity—had no faith in humanity, in fact—more than that, he lacked unction: don't you think that's the word to describe it?—he had no religious faith—I am sure he lacked conviction in the triumph of good. I do not intend to say Carlyle did not contribute—did not do this and that for which humanity will be eternally richer and grateful. What I am trying to say is that he had no avenue of approach to the people; he lost his way in the jungle: the people were not a beautiful abstraction—they were an ugly fact; he shrank from the people. Carlyle was incapable of seeing men generously, even his friends. One thing Carlyle did understand—the incessant caterwauling of radicals—their unceasing complaints against everything—their inability to appreciate the importance of conservatism, of restraint, even of persecution.' "

Whitman had much to say of Emerson at different times, and in somewhat varied tone. Here is an opinion that is dated 1847, and was a note to a magazine article:

"The superiority of Emerson's writings is in their character—they mean something. He may be obscure, but he is certain. Any other of the best American writers has in general a clearer style, has more of the received grace and ease, is less questioned and forbidden than he, makes a handsomer appearance in the society of the books, sells better, passes his time more apparently in the popular understanding; yet there is something in the solitary specimen of New England that outvies them all. He has what none else has; he does what none else does. He pierces the crusts that envelope the secrets of life. He joins on equal terms the few great sages and original seers. He represents the freeman, America, the individual. He represents the gentleman. No teacher or poet of old times or modern times has made a better report of manly and womanly qualities, heroism, chastity, temperance, friendship, fortitude. None has given more beautiful accounts of truth and justice. His words shed light to the best souls; they do not admit of argument. As a spring from the pine tree or a glimpse anywhere into the daylight belittles all artificial flower work and all the painted scenery of theatres, so are live words in a book compared to cunningly composed words. A few among men (soon perhaps to become many) will enter easily into Emerson's meanings; by those he will be well beloved. The flippant writer, the orthodox critic, the numbers of good or indifferent imitators, will not comprehend him; to them he will indeed be a transcendentalist, a writer of sunbeams and moonbeams, a strange and unapproachable person."

Traubel writes in 1888:

"W. spoke of Emerson: 'I shall never forget the first visit he paid me—the call, the first call: it was in Brooklyn: no, I can never forget it. I can hear his gentle knock still—the soft knock —so (indicating it on the chair-arm)—and the slow sweet voice, as my mother stood there by the door: and the words, 'I came to see Mr. Whitman': and the response, 'He is here'—the simple unaffected greeting on both sides—'How are you, Mr. Whitman,' 'How are you Waldo'—the hour's talk or so—the taste of lovableness he left behind when he was gone. I can easily see how Carlyle should have likened Emerson's appearance in their household to the apparition of an angel.'

"W. got talking of Emerson again: 'The world does not know what our relations really were—they think of our friendship always as a literary friendship: it was a bit that but it was mostly something else—it was certainly more than that—for I loved Emerson for his personality and I always felt that he loved me for something I brought him from the rush of the big cities and the mass of men. We used to walk together, dine together, argue, even, in a sort of a way, though neither one of us was much of an arguer. We were not much for repartee or sallies or what people ordinarily call humor, but we got along together beautifully—the atmosphere was always sweet, I don't mind saying it, both on Emerson's side and mine: we had no friction—there was no kind of fight in us for each other—we were like two Quakers together. Dear Emerson! I doubt if the literary classes which have taken to coddling him have any right to their god. He belonged to us—yes, to us—rather than to them.' Then after a pause: 'I suppose to all as well as to us—perhaps to no clique whatever.'

"Of Emerson again, and also of Shakespeare, Shelley and Milton: 'That the most of those who wrote agreed upon Emerson should occasion neither surprise nor disappointment: that seems as it should be: Emerson is great—oh! very great: I have not attempted to decide how great, how vast, how subtle: but very, very: he was a far-reaching force: a star of the first, the very first, magnitude maybe: without a doubt that.' I spoke of the wariness of the writers. W. said: 'That I noticed too: they are too wary: dropping out Shakespeare, Byron, Shelley, perhaps—some of them of the very topmost rank—I am not afraid to say our fellows, the best of them deserve an equal rank with the rest: I dare even say Milton.' Then further: 'I could never go Milton: he is turgid, heavy, over-stately.' I said: 'Take *Paradise Lost:* don't its vogue come mainly from a sort of Christian theological self-interest rather than from pure delight in its beauty?' He responded at once: 'Oh! an immense lot! Besides, it seems to me that Milton is a copy of a copy—not only Homer but the Æneid: a sort of modern repetition of the same old story: legions of angels, devils: war is declared, waged: moreover, even as a story it enlists little of my attention: he seems to me like a bird—soaring yet overweighted: dragged down, as if burdened—too greatly burdened: a lamb in its beak: its flight not graceful, powerful, beautiful, satisfy-

ing, like the gulls we see over the Delaware in midwinter—
their simple motion a delight—attracting you when they first
break upon your sight: soaring, soaring, irrespective of cold or
storm. It is true, Milton soars, but with dull, unwieldy motion.'
Then after a slight repetition of points accented above: 'There's
no use talking, he won't go down with me: I have sometimes
questioned myself: have I not been too hasty? have I not
rejected unfairly?—was it humor, whim, that stood in the
way? Then I would re-examine my premises. Yet each attempt
was fruitless. In this way I have gone back to the book repeatedly. Only the other day the same question returned.' He
pointed to the floor: a pile of books was at his feet—he pulled
out a Milton. 'I have a volume here containing "Paradise Lost":
I have had it about me for twenty years: but it never attracts
or exalts me.'"

Later Whitman indulged this critical attitude toward Emerson as a philosopher:

"For a philosopher, Emerson possesses a singularly dandi-
fied theory of manners, etc.. . . . No, no, dear friend; though
the States want scholars, undoubtedly, and perhaps want ladies
and gentlemen who use the bath frequently, and never laugh
loud, or talk wrong, they don't want scholars, or ladies and
gentlemen, at the expense of all the rest. They want good
farmers, sailors, mechanics, clerks, citizens—perfect business
and social relations—perfect fathers and mothers. If we could
only have these, or their approximations, plenty of them, fine
and large and sane and generous and patriotic, they might
make their verbs disagree from their nominatives, and laugh
like volleys of musketeers, if they should please. Of course
these are not all America wants, but they are first of all to
be provided on a large scale. And, with tremendous errors and
escapades, this, substantially, is what the States seem to have
an intuition of, and to be mainly aiming at. The plan of a select
class, superfined (demarcated from the rest) the plan of Old
World lands and literature, is not so objectionable in itself,

but because it chokes the true plan for us, and indeed is death to it.

"At times it has been doubtful to me if Emerson really knows or feels what Poetry is at its highest, as in the Bible, for instance, or Homer or Shakspere. I see he covertly or plainly likes best superb verbal polish, or something old or odd—Waller's *Go, lovely rose,* or Lovelac's lines 'to Lucusta'—the quaint conceits of the old French bards, and the like. Of *power* he seems to have a gentleman's admiration—but in his inmost heart the grandest attribute of God and Poets is always subordinate to the octaves, conceits, polite kinks, and verbs. The reminiscence that years ago I began like most youngsters to have a touch (though it came late, and was only on the surface) of Emerson-on-the-brain—that I read his writings reverently, and address'd him in print as 'Master,' and for a month or so thought of him as such—I retain not only with composure, but positive satisfaction. I have noticed that most young people of eager minds pass through this stage of exercise."

Of Longfellow, Whittier and others Whitman writes in Volume III of his *Complete Works:*

"Longfellow, reminiscent, polish'd, elegant, with the air of finest conventional library, picture-gallery or parlor, with ladies and gentlemen in them, and plush and rosewood, and ground-glass lamps, and mahogany and ebony furniture, and a silver inkstand and scented satin paper to write on.

"Whittier stands for morality (not in any all accepting philosophic or Hegelian sense, but) filter'd through a Puritanical or Quaker filter—is incalculably valuable as a genuine utterance (and the finest)—with many local and Yankee and *genre* bits—all hued with anti-slavery coloring—(the genre and anti-slavery contributions all precious—all help). Whittier's is rather a grand figure, but pretty lean and ascetic—no Greek —not universal and composite enough (don't try—don't wish to be) for ideal Americanism. Ideal Americanism would take the Greek spirit and law, and democratize and scientize and (thence) truly Christianize them for the whole, the globe, all history, all ranks and lands, all facts, all good and bad. Ah this *bad*—this nineteen-twentieths of us all! What a stumbling-block it remains for poets and metaphysicians—what a chance (the strange, clear-as-ever inscription on the old dug-up tablet) it offers yet for being translated—what can be its purpose in the God-scheme of this universe, and all?

"Then William Cullen Bryant—meditative, serious, from first to last tending to threnodies—his genius mainly lyrical—when reading his pieces who could expect or ask for more magnificent ones than such as "The Battle-Field," and "A Forest Hymn"; Bryant, unrolling, prairie-like, notwithstanding his mountains and lakes—moral enough (yet worldly and conventional)—a naturalist, pedestrian, gardener and fruiter—well aware of books, but mixing to the last in cities and society. I am not sure but his name ought to lead the list of American bards. Years ago I thought Emerson pre-eminent (and as to the last polish and intellectual cuteness maybe I think so still)—but, for reasons, I have been gradually tending to give the file-leading place for American native poesy to W. C. B.

"Of Emerson I have to confirm my already avow'd opinion regarding his highest bardic and personal attitude. Of the galaxy of the past—of Poe, Halleck, Mrs. Sigourney, Allston, Willis, Dana, John Pierpont, W. G. Simms, Robert Sands, Drake, Hillhouse, Theodore Fay, Margaret Fuller, Epes Sargent, Boker, Paul Hayne, Lanier, and others, I fitly, in essaying such a theme as this, and reverence for their memories, may at least give a heart-benison on the list of their names . . .

"Started out by that item on 'Old Poets and Poetry' for chyle to inner America sustenance—I have thus gossip'd about it all, and treated it from my own point of view, taking the privilege of rambling wherever the talk carried me. Browning is lately dead; Bryant, Emerson, and Longfellow have not long pass'd away; and yes, Whittier and Tennyson remain, over eighty years old—the latter having sent out not long since a fresh volume, which the English-speaking Old and New Worlds are yet reading. I have already put on record my notions of T. and his effusions: they are very attractive and flowery to me—but flowers, too, are at least as profound as anything; and by common consent T. is settled as the poetic cream-skimmer of our age's melody, *ennui* and polish—a verdict in which I agree, and should say that nobody (not even Shakspere) goes deeper in those exquisitely touch'd and half-hidden hints and indirections left like faint perfumes in the crevices of his lines. Of Browning I don't know enough to say much; he must be studied deeply out, too, and quite certainly repays the trouble—but I am old and indolent, and cannot study (and never did)."

Once in talking to Traubel Whitman spoke concerning Bryant as follows:

" 'I remember that he always expressed wonder that with what he called my powers and gifts and essential underlying respect for beauty I refused to accept and use the only medium which would give me complete expression. I have often tried to think of myself as writing *Leaves of Grass* in Thanatopsian verse. Of course I do not intend this as a criticism of Bryant— only as a demurrer to his objection to me: "Thanatopsis" is all right in Thanatopsis verse. Bryant said to me: "I will admit that you have power, sometimes great power." But he would never admit that I had chosen the right vehicle of expression. We never quarreled over such things. I liked Bryant as a man as well as a poet; he I think liked me as a man: at least I inferred so from his way.' 'As you have challenged the whole world,' said Bryant to Whitman on a time, 'I don't suppose you are surprised or resentful when you find the whole world out against you.' "

Then as to Poe, Traubel records this as of September, 1888:
"W. stopped a bit—then cried: 'Poe—poor wonderful Poe.' and quoted: 'And the fever called living is conquered at last' —saying pathetically and looking at me: 'How full that seems!

how true, far-reaching!' He added then: 'Shelley is interesting to me as Burns is, chiefly as a person: I read with most avidity not their poems but their lives: the Burns letters, for instance.'"

In *Specimen Days* Whitman has expressed himself about Poe:

"Almost without the first sign of moral principle, or of the concrete or its heroisms, or the simpler affections of the heart, Poe's verses illustrate an intense faculty for technical and abstract beauty, with the rhyming art to excess, an incorrigible propensity toward nocturnal themes, a demoniac undertone behind every page—and, by final judgment, probably belong among the electric lights of imaginative literature, brilliant and dazzling, but with no heat. There is an indescribable magnetism about the poet's life and reminiscences, as well as the poems. To one who could work out their subtle retracing and retrospect, the latter would make a close tally no doubt between the author's birth and antecedents, his childhood and youth, his physique, his so-call'd education, his studies and associates, the literary and social Baltimore, Richmond, Philadelphia and New York, of those times—not only the places and circumstances in themselves, but often, very often, in a strange spurning of, and reaction from them all."

And here is a tribute from *Specimen Days* to Emerson, Longfellow, Bryant and Whittier:

"If anybody cares to know what I think—and have long thought and avow'd—about them, I am entirely willing to propound. I can't imagine any better luck befalling these States for a poetical beginning and initiation than has come from Emerson, Longfellow, Bryant, and Whittier. Emerson, to me, stands unmistakably at the head, but for the others I am at a loss where to give any precedence. Each illustrious, each rounded, each distinctive. Emerson for his sweet, vital-tasting melody, rhym'd philosophy, and poems as amber-clear as the honey of the wild bee he loves to sing. Longfellow for rich color, graceful forms and incidents—all that makes life beautiful and love refined—competing with the singers of Europe on their own ground, and, with one exception, better and finer work than that of any of them. Bryant pulsing the first interior verse-throbs of a mighty world—bard of the river and the wood, ever conveying a taste of open air, with scents as from hayfields, grapes, birch-borders—always lurkingly fond of threnodies—beginning and ending his long career with chants of death, with here and there through all, poems, or passages of poems, touching the highest universal truths, enthusiasms, duties—morals as grim and eternal, if not as stormy and fateful, as anything in Eschylus. While in Whittier, with his special themes—(his outcropping love of heroism and war, for all his Quakerdom, his verses at times like the measur'd step of Cromwell's old veterans)—in Whittier lives the zeal, the moral energy, that founded New England—the splendid rectitude and ardor of Luther Milton, George Fox—I must not, dare not, say the wilfulness and narrowness—though doubtless the world needs now, and always will need, almost above all, just such narrowness and wilfulness. . . .

"*The Song of Hiawatha* by H. W. Longfellow. A pleasing ripply poem—the measure, the absence of ideas, the Indian process of thought, the droning metre, the sleepy, misty, woody character, the traditions, pleased me well enough."

Whitman speaks concerning Bryant and others, to Horace Traubel:

"'Well—Cooper has guts. I never met Cooper—I never met him to talk with: at least I think I did not; but I heard him. He was a good, sturdy, man in appearance: had the appearance of a farmer—a brainy farmer: not very tall, not very stout: good belly—carried himself well. Unlike Irving, Cooper had a remarkable personality, and, as I have said, he had Carlyle's cynicism to some extent, though he was never gloomy—was always as strong and sweet as sunlight. Irving, on the other hand, suggested weakness, if he was not weak: was pleasant, as you say, but without background. I never enthused over him: Irving was suckled on the Addisonian-Oxford-Cambridge milk.'

"I quoted something Bryant said about Cooper—that he was 'our first man,' &c. W. said: 'Ah! Bryant! did he say that? Bryant is himself the man! Of all Americans so far, I am inclined to rank Bryant highest. Bryant has all that was knotty, gnarled, in Dante, Carlyle: besides that, has great other qualities. It has always seemed to me Bryant, more than any other American, had the power to suck in the air of spring, to put it into his song, to breathe it forth again—the palpable influence of spring: the new entrance to life. A feature in Bryant which is never to be under-weighed is the marvelous purity of his work in verse. It was severe—oh! so severe! never a waste word—the last superfluity struck off: a clear nameless beauty pervading and overarching all the work of his pen. Bryant the man I met often—often. He was not much of a talker, would not impress or attract as such. His voice was a good one—not deep—not fascinating—not moving, eloquent. Bryant tried lecturing. He was a great homeopathist—a great Unitarian: at the time of the homeopathic excitement he delivered two or three lectures on the subject. But I don't think he liked lecturing himself, and he did not prove a success with others. He was an American: that is one of the palpable facts: thoroughly American, patriotic: moreover, he had a tint of the Scotch left—a trifle hypochondriac—a bit irascible. I have often observed marked traces running through the Scotch character of general hypochondriacism: Burns? yes: and Carlyle. Bryant bore the marks of it. I know it is not invariable: there are exceptions: but in the main its existence cannot be questioned.'"

And this about Voltaire:

"W. quoted a Voltairean hit at the Index of the Catholic Church and remarked: 'I have been prohibited in Russia—under ban: John Swinton, who has a good deal to do with the Nihilists there, told me of it.' 'How did it occur—what was the ground for it?' 'I cannot tell positively in detail.' 'Because of your democracy?' 'Not exactly that, I should suppose, though also that after all, it may be: probably because I am understood to excuse the assassination of emperors.'

"Talked of Voltaire. 'Now there was a great man, too,' said W.: 'an emancipator—a shining spiritual light: a miraculous man whose ridicule did more for justice than the battles of armies. . . . Voltaire never was of a mind to condone Shakespeare: Shakespeare's crudities were offensive to him: there was something crude, powerful, drastic, in the Shakespeare plays: Voltaire could not reconcile his nerves to their brutal might. But you cannot shift such luminaries from their orbit by a sneer—by an adjective. Do you think *Leaves of Grass* was ever really hurt by the people who went at it with a club?' "

Whitman counsels Traubel about Grote:

"Oh! read Grote: don't believe those who tell you he was only a scholar, a pedant—anything of either in a bad sense: you must not take him en passant; take him up at a moment when you are prepared to tackle a big job: there are volumes of him: not one only, or even two or three but eight or nine: I have read them all—carefully, fully, more than once—more deliberately than usual for me: there is no work near the equal of it treating of the Greeks. Some people class Grote with Southey: that's a mistake: there's not the slightest resemblance: Grote is all that we mean by vigor, originality, force; Southey in every way contrasts with him. Picture to yourself a sailor, a first mate—strong, lithe—standing at the wheel: his raincoat, rainproof—the skies clouded: a great storm: this man at his post: no ornament—every stitch he wears necessary, useful, protective; then think of a man all perfumes—silk coated: all his appointments elegant, scarce: hangings, courtesies, parlors: kid gloves: think of him, of all that he implies: Well, Grote is no more like Southey than this sailor is like this dandy. Grote's integrity was absolute: I know of no historic writer who is more guarded, more subtly straightforward: as a young man you should particularly read Grote: he is an equipment in himself."

Whitman wrote of Burns: "Thus, while Burns is not at all great for New World study, in the sense that Isaiah and Eschylus and the book of Job are unquestionably great— is not to be mention'd with Shakspere—hardly even with current Tennyson or our Emerson—he has a nestling niche of his own, all fragrant, fond, and quaint and homely—a lodge built near but outside the mighty temple of the gods of song and art—those universal strivers, through their works of harmony and melody and power, to ever show or intimate man's crowning, last, victorious fusion in himself of Real and Ideal."

Conversing with Traubel, Whitman mentioned Arnold and others:

"W. talked of Arnold. 'Arnold had no genius—only a peculiarly clever order of refined talent. Arnold is much that sort of man who would be in his place as Keeper of Her Majesty's Despatches, careful that never a word be misapplied or misspelled—or he might serve as a tutor for gentlemen's sons, or sons of lords: but as for genius—no—no—not at all—that is not there. These men have their functioning to do—they are not waste, they are not useless: but they do not inspire—they do not lift you off your feet—they are without inspiration. They make more fuss over foliage than root—neglect the root. Well—I mustn't go on too much about Arnold. I do not feel myself to be against him in any way: but so much is made of the Arnold type of man that we are liable to miss our normal gauge of value. . . .

"'Arnold has been writing new things about the United States. Arnold could know nothing about the States—essentially nothing: the real things here—the real dangers as well as the real promises—a man of his sort would always miss. Arnold knows nothing of elements—nothing of things as they start. I know he is a significant figure—I do not propose to wipe him out. He came in at the rear of a procession two thousand years old—the great army of critics, parlor apostles, worshippers of hangings, laces, and so forth and so forth—they never have anything properly at first hand. Naturally I have little inclination their way.'

"I found a poem by Swinburne—'A Double Ballad of August.' W. said: 'Oh yes, I did see that. And if Swinburne had a few grains of thought with all his music wouldn't he be the greatest charmer of all? I never liked him from the first—Swinburne—from the very first: could not take him in, adapt myself to him. I know of nothing I think of so little account as pretty words, pretty thoughts, pretty china, pretty arrangements. I have a friend, a woman—a cute one, too: one of the very cutest—who takes most to *Bothwell:* thinks *Bothwell* the one thing most to Swinburne's credit and likely to last, if any: and it is true of *Atalanta,* as you say, that it is rich in particulars and esteemed by scholars. My taste is alien—on other currents: I do not seem to belong in the Swinburne drift. I find it difficult to account for my dear woman's taste. Did you not hear it said somewhere that Schiller was very fond of rotten apples—had them always about him—the rottener the better? Maybe that is a story which explains her taste. . . .

"'He is always the extremist—always all pro or all con: always hates altogether or loves altogether: as the boys say, he goes the whole hog or nothing: he knows no medium line.' 'When he loved you he loved you too much. Now he hates you he loves you too little.' 'I suppose that's so: I don't know what I deserve or what I don't deserve. Tom said the other day: "Swinburne either insults you or hugs you—he knows nothing between": that's just the point—yet that *between* something or other is more worth while than all the rest.' "

And speaking of Lowell, Lanier, Miller, and Tolstoy:

"'Lowell was not a grower—he was a builder. He *built* poems: he didn't put in the seed, and water the seed, and send down his sun—letting the rest take care of itself: he measured his poems—kept them within the formula.' And yet?' 'I know what you mean to say. He was a man of great

260

talent—I do not deny it: and skill, yes, skill—I do not deny that. But inspiration? I doubt it.' . . . Corning referred to something Lowell had written about Thoreau. W. said: 'I have never read it: I do not seem to care much about Lowell's work.

" 'Lanier was tragic in life and death. He had the soul of the musician—was a flute player: indeed, in the accounts, was phenomenally fine. This extreme sense of the melodic, a virtue in itself, when carried into the art of the writer becomes a fault. Why? Why, because it tends to place the first emphasis on tone, sound—on the lilt, as Rhys so often puts it. Study Lanier's choice of words—they are too often fit rather for sound than for sense. His ear was over-sensitive. He had genius—a delicate, clairvoyant genius: but this over-tuning of the ear, this extreme deference paid to oral nicety, reduced the majesty, the solid worth, of his rhythms.'

"We exchanged some few words about Joaquin Miller. W. was very willing to say good things about him. 'Miller is wholesome: he is a bit of his own West done up in print. I ought to be very grateful to him. He has always gone out of his way to show that he stood with me—that the literary class would not find him aligned with them in their assaults on me. Miller never quite does the work I expected him to do. He may yet do it. . . .

" 'I feel about literature what Grant did about war. He hated war. I hate literature. I am not a literary West Pointer: I do not love a literary man as a literary man, as a minister of a pulpit loves other ministers because they are ministers: it is a means to an end, that is all there is to it: I never attribute any other significance to it. Even Goethe and Schiller, exalted men, both, very, very, were a little touched by the professional consciousness.' 'Then you do not accept the notion of art for art's sake?' 'Not a bit of it—that would be absurd on the face: the phrase seems to me to mean nothing. Take Tolstoy: there are things about him that do not attract me—some that are even offensive—his asceticism, for instance—and yet Tolstoy comes to about the right amount: he counts up to a high figure.'

"W. discussed Stedman's *American Poets* again. 'The book is too deliberate—holds back too much: is like a conservative charge to a jury. There are touches in Stedman that seem like genius—but just as you are about to accept him as a luminary he snuffs the light out himself. Have you got as far as the Poe yet? Do I like Poe? At the start, for many years, not: but three or four years ago I got to reading him again, reading and liking, until at last—yes, now—I feel almost convinced that he is a star of considerable magnitude, if not a sun, in the literary firmament. Poe was morbid, shadowy, lugubrious—he seemed to suggest dark nights, horrors, spectralities—I could not originally stomach him at all. But today I see more of him than that—much more. If that was all there was to him he would have died long ago. I was a young man of about thirty, living in New York, when "The Raven" appeared—created its stir: everybody was excited about it—everybody reading it: somehow it did not enthuse me. Oh—I was talking of Stedman. I wanted to say I do not think Stedman did full justice to Bryant or Longfellow or Whittier—not even to Poe. I think that if Stedman had let himself go a little he would have made a book calculated for a long life. I have such personal respect, love, for Stedman, I wish his book made a stronger appeal to me. Now, if we could get Stedman himself into a book we would all bow down to it. . . .

" 'Stedman would I think be freer and easier with me if it was not for the rabid crowd of literary wolves by which he is surrounded in New York—that crowd of yellers and screamers who declare that Walt Whitman is no good—is to be in no way endorsed, tolerated, commended. Even Stedman could not resist all that pressure. Yet he is noble, generous, lavish of his love. I shall never forget his kindness to me—his many kindnesses: why, he once paid thirty dollars I am told for a single special copy of *Leaves of Grass*. That was surely an act of great faith. The worst I hear about Stedman is not that he has failed in business but that he is sick.' " This comment was in August, 1888.

"He got talking about New York—its literary men. 'They are mainly a sad crowd: take the whole raft of them—Stoddard, Fawcett, the rest—what are they saying or doing that is in the least degree significant? I am told that Stoddard is pretty sour on me—hates even to have my name mentioned in his presence, never refers to me with respect. I do not blame him. But—I am sorry for Walt Whitman. There is Taylor. He was first rather friendly. Then he went to New York and experienced a change of heart. Yet I have been told by a man who was very near to Taylor that he was melting towards me again when he died. I had a couple of letters from Taylor back, back, years and years ago. I don't know where they are: they were good letters. When they turn up, if they turn up, you shall have them. They will add a bit to the material you have collected about me. Did I tell you that I dined with Stoddard at the house of a Mrs. Bleecker? He was courteous but not friendly on that occasion. New York gives the literary man a touch of snow: he is never quite the same human being after New York has really set in: the best fellows have few chances of escape. Take John himself. Burroughs, I mean. He lives just far enough off. Even John barely got off with his skin. Stedman? Stedman is all right—I love him. But after all I do not think that Stedman ever drew very deep water. His estimate of the American poets misses the chief points—is wide of the truth: he is too judicial, too much concerned about being exactly just. The man who tries a too delicate operation with his scales breaks the scales. Don't Stedman break down in the process of his own criticism? He is generous, inclusive, hospitable, a bit over-ripe here and there, too much cultivated, too little able to be foolish, to be free, (we must all be foolish at times—it is the one condition of liberty)—is always precisely so, always according to

263

program.' W. still talked on, hitting at different themes: 'I sometimes waver in opinion as between Emerson and Bryant. Bryant is more significant for his patriotism, Americanism, love of external nature, the woods, the sea, the skies, the rivers, and this at times, the objective features of it especially, seems to outweigh Emerson's urgent intelligence and psychic depth. But after every heresy I go back to Emerson. Stedman is cute but he has not attached to Whittier, Emerson and Bryant anything like the peculiar weight that I should, rebel as I am. Stedman is cute but hardly more than cute—not a first hander—a fine scholar, with great charms of style, fond of congregating historic names, processional, highly organized, but not in the windup proving that he is aware of what all his erudition, even all his good will (he has plenty of that, God bless him!), leads up to. I should not say such things, should I? I am a hell of a critic.'

"Had I read Ossian? Was very circumstantial in talking about the book. 'Macpherson was a sort of a rascal—had scamp qualities. There was a great Ossianic debate. I have always had an Ossian about me, though I can't say I ever read it with any great fervor. It was a curious controversy—there were great men on both sides of it—many things were said both pro and con—ideas it did no harm to ventilate. Ossian is of the Biblical order —is best to one who would come freshly upon it—to one who knew nothing of the Hebrew Bible. I don't think Ossian would satisfy the modern young man—the radical—the new man with the new spirit. Ossian's fame lasts—he is still sold—I am told he has been highly thought of by continental critics—very highly. You say you can no longer read Milton—the bigger poems. Well you mustn't feel bad and guilty about that—you're not alone in that fix: there are plenty like you: you may count your uncle here in for the same complaint.' He laughed.

"Talked an hour or more about Symonds. W. very frank, very affectionate. 'Symonds is a royal good fellow—he comes along without qualifications: just happens into the temple and

takes his place. But he has a few doubts yet to be quieted
—not doubts of me, doubts rather of himself. One of these
doubts is about *Calamus*. What does *Calamus* mean? What do
the poems come to in the round-up? That is worrying him a
good deal—their involvement, as he suspects, is the passional
relations of men with men—the thing he reads so much of in
the literatures of southern Europe and sees something of in his
own experience. He is always driving at me about that: is that
what *Calamus* means? because of me or in spite of me, is that
what it means? I have said no, but no does not satisfy him.
But read this letter—read the whole of it: it is very shrewd,
very cute, in deadliest earnest: it drives me hard—almost compels me—it is urgent, persistent: he sort of stands in the road
and says: "I won't move till you answer my question." You see,
this is an old letter—sixteen years old—and he is still asking
the question: he refers to it in one of his latest notes. He is
surely a wonderful man.

" 'The story writers do not as a rule attract me. Howells is
more serious—seems to have something to say—James is only
feathers to me. What do you make of them?—what is their
future significance? Have they any? Don't they just come and
go—don't they just skim about, butterfly about, daintily, in
fragile literary vessels, for awhile—then bow their way out?
They do not deal in elements: they deal only in pieces of
things, in fragments broken off, in detached episodes.'

"Asked me: 'Do you know much about Aaron Burr? There's
a man, now, who is only damned and damned again in history
and yet who had his parts. I have always designed writing
something about him to show I did not stand in the jam of his
vilifiers. I had a piece on him which should have gone into
this book. You don't know (I guess I never told you) that
when I was a lad, working in a lawyer's office, it fell to me to
go over the river now and then with messages for Burr. Burr
was very gently—persuasive. He had a way of giving me a
bit of fruit on these visits—an apple or a pear. I can see him

clearly, still—his stateliness, gray hair, courtesy, consideration. Two or three years ago I wrote up some reminiscences but the manuscript got buried with other manuscripts down stairs. Sometime I must hunt it up.' "

Traubel quotes Whitman on Thomas Paine:

" 'Of the foul and foolish fictions yet told about the circumstances of his decease, the absolute fact is that as he lived a good life, after its kind, he died calmly and philosophically, as became him. He served the embryo Union with most precious service—a service that every man, woman and child in our thirty-eight States is to some extent receiving the benefit of today—and I for one here cheerfully, reverently throw my pebble on the cairn of his memory. As we all know, the season demands—or rather, will it ever be out of season?—that America learn to better dwell on her choicest possession, the legacy of her good and faithful men—that she fail not to dissipate what clouds have intruded on that fame, and burnished it newer, truer and brighter, continually.'

"I quoted Henry George as calling Jefferson 'among the greatest of the great.' W. added: 'Yes, greatest of the great: that names him: it belongs to him: he is entitled to it.'

"Some one had sent W. Ingersoll's *The Gods* in a pamphlet. W. was happy over it. 'I wonder if anybody ever hit back at the orthodox God better than our dear Bob? Ever spit upon it with such necessary and effective derision? I read this superb thing today: it seems just perfect. Of course Bob does not go far enough: he gets rid of the old thing—does it without a quaver —ends it forever. But God? God? Well, there are other divinities: they are not of the hell and damnation sort: they are not of the legs and arms sort—the personal sort: they yet remain, more firmly on their thrones, in the race, than ever: they continue their supremacy. Bob does not intellectually account for them: he has them in his heart: they are one part of his noble protest —whether he knows it or not. I sometimes ask: Why does Bob not see more? Then I say: If he saw more maybe he could not do his work? I ask myself that question over and over again. He lives more: the chief matter is living. The main thing is that he has done his divinely appointed job: O, the dear wonderful man! He was sent by high heaven to save the race and he has done it. We talk about salvation: we need most of all to be saved from ourselves: our own hells, hates, jealousies, thieveries: we need most to be saved from our own priests —the priests of the churches, the priests of the arts: we need that salvation the worst way. The Colonel has been the master craftsman in this reconstruction: he has taken us by the ears and shaken the nonsense out of us: the criminal institutions we have built up on our already overburdened backs. As I read this old piece over again my first impression of the sanity, the health, the virile humanity, of it all was renewed in me. Some things—some systems—requiring to be removed, can't be got rid of with a too kind law: they have to be rejected scornfully —with a species of almost ghoulish delight. Hell is such a system: the revengeful gods—they are such a system: they should be summarily ejected: they should be stamped out without equivocation.' I said: 'You spoke of the priests of religion and the priests of the arts. We still have the priests of commerce to contend with.' 'So we have: doubly so: the priests of commerce augmented by the priests of churches, who are everywhere the parasites, the apologists, of systems as they exist.' "

In 1833 when Andrew Jackson passed through Brooklyn, Whitman saw him and paid him this tribute in *The Brooklyn Eagle:* "Massive, yet most sweet and plain character! In the wrangle of party and the ambitious strife after political distinction, which mark so many even of our most eminent men how grateful it is to turn to your unalloyed patriotism. Your great soul never knew a thought of self in questions which involved your country. Ah, there has lived among us but one purer."

Finally Horace Traubel records this conversation of Whitman regarding himself:

"I asked W.: 'Are you the last of your race?' 'Neither the last nor the first.' 'Will there be more poets or less?' 'More—more: and greater poets than have ever been.' 'What kind? Your kind?' 'I don't know about that: some *free* kind, sure: they are bound to come—to come soon.' After a silent minute or two: 'I think I'll get there. The stylists object to me—but they lack just what Matthew Arnold lacks. They talk about form, rule, canons, and all the time forget the real point, which is the substance of poetry. I do not look for a vast audience—for great numbers of endorsers, absorbers—just now—perhaps not even after awhile. But here and there, every now and then, one, several, will raise the standard. *Leaves of Grass* will finally make its way. The book is like the flukes of a whale—if not graceful at least effective: never super-refined or ashamed of the animal energy that imparts power to expression . . . I do say with regard to myself that I must be judged elementally —that the Arnolds, the disciples of books as books, the second and third hand men, the scholars pure and simple, the lovers of art for art's sake, cannot understand me—cannot take me in —I elude their circumscriptions. Even Goethe, in loving beauty, art, literature, for their own inherent significance, is not as close to nature as I conceive he should be. I say this with all due respect for Dr. Bucke, who reads Goethe in the German and declares to me that I have but very little conception of Goethe's real place in the spiritual history of the race. Well, maybe I have. I care less and less for books as books—more and more for people as people.'"

All these glimpses of Whitman's mind and thinking lead to helpful observations of Whitman, the man.

CHAPTER FIFTEEN

As MENTIONED before Whitman began life as a Jeffersonian Democrat and never, in the main, departed from that faith. He detested slavery as Jefferson did, and the Free Soil movement swept him along without, however, making him an enthusiast. One feels that the oncoming of the Civil War affronted his deeper convictions. He probably doubted the necessity of that war. He saw and later recorded that secession could be as much laid to the doors of Northern States as to the Southern. He denounced all war with vehement hatred and in his *Collect* will be found a long note in which his position on secession is fully set forth. He was for the sovereignty of the states, and he was a free trader.

In 1888 he said, "that tariff taffy gives me the belly-ache." In talking to Traubel he declared himself as follows: "Why am I a free trader? A free trader in the large sense? It is for solidarity: free trade makes for solidarity: the familiar, full, significant word: and I hope, oh I hope there has been no failure to manifest the fact in my books. I know in my own heart that every line I ever wrote—every line—not an exception—was animated by that feeling."

Again he expressed himself: "The protectionists are fond of flashing to the public eye the glittering delusion of great money-results from manufactures, mines, artificial exports—so many millions from this source, and so many from that—such a seductive, unanswerable show—an immense revenue of annual cash from iron, cotton, woolen, leather goods, and a hundred other things, all bolstered up by 'protection.' But the really important point of all is, *into whose pockets does this plunder really go?* It would be some excuse and satisfaction if even a fair proportion of it went to the masses of laboring-men—resulting in homesteads to such, men, women, children—myriads of actual homes in fee simple, in every State, (not the false glamour of the stunning wealth reported in the census, in the statistics, or tables in the newspapers), but a fair division and generous average to those workmen and workwomen—*that* would be something. But the fact itself is nothing of the kind. The profits of 'protection' go altogether to a few score select persons—who, by favors of Congress, State legislatures, the banks, and other special advantages, are forming a vulgar aristocracy, fully as bad as anything in the British or European castes, of blood, or the dynasties there of the past. As Sismondi pointed out, the true prosperity of a nation is not in the great wealth of a special class, but is only to be really attain'd in having the bulk of the people provided with homes or land in fee simple. This may not be the best show, but it is the best reality."

Ingersoll, who started in life as a Democrat, and then became a Colonel in the Union army, changed his political creed almost completely, and by that fact became a protectionist. In July of 1888 Ingersoll gave out an interview in favor of protection. The campaign was on between Cleveland and Harrison, with Cleveland standing for a tariff for revenue only. Whitman was not wholly satisfied with Cleveland. He saw in him the stiff, rather unvisioned man that he was. At the same time he did not like Ingersoll's preachment of protection. Whitman said:

"I like Ingersoll, sure enough, but his logic in this matter is queer, to say the least. What will America do? Is she for the great mass of men?—the race, the whole globe? No man is a democrat, a true democrat, who forgets that he is interested in the welfare of the race. Who asks only, what is best for America? Instead of, what is best for man—the whole of man?"

In those days there were dreadful and bloody strikes at the steel mills and the mines. Whitman saw that these conditions were produced by special privilege and monopoly, fruitions that did not belong to the America that he loved and had celebrated. He planned to deliver a lecture on the tramp and strike question. He didn't deliver the lecture, but he left notes of what he meant to say, as follows:

"Beneath the whole political world, what most presses and perplexes today, sending vastest results affecting the future, is not the abstract question of democracy, but of social and economic organization, the treatment of working-people by employers, and all that goes along with it—not only the wages-payment part, but a certain spirit and principle, to vivify anew these relations; all the questions of progress, strength, tariffs, finance, &c., really evolving themselves more or less directly out of the Poverty Question, (the Science of Wealth, and a dozen other names are given it, but I prefer the severe one just used). I will begin by calling the reader's attention to a thought upon the matter which may not have struck you before—the wealth of the civilized world, as contrasted with its poverty—what does it derivatively stand for and represent? A rich person ought to have a strong stomach. As in Europe the wealth of today mainly results from, and represents, the rapine, murder, outrages, treachery, hoggishness, of hundreds of years ago, and onward, later, so in America, after the same token—(not yet so bad, perhaps, or at any rate not so palpable—we have not existed long enough—but we seem to be doing our best to make it up)."

The putrid conditions of America after the War of the States were never subjected to such a malediction as Whitman gave it in *Democratic Vistas*. Though Whitman knew that the South was not solely at fault for secession, yet he called secession the foulest crime of time. He should have known that Lincoln could have prevented the war, yet he worshipped Lincoln. He said that the South was legally in the right, yet he made no admission that he might have foreseen with the statesmen of the South that the war would bring centralization and all the corruption which he denounced in *Democratic Vistas*. He showed in the note on secession that he knew what men and influences were back of the war and of reconstruction, yet he said nothing against the war as a preventible tragedy. These are not very grave inconsistencies, but I feel he would have been a greater liberal if he had said with Greeley, "Let the erring sisters go." There was nothing in his political or economic thinking to stay such words in his mouth. It was rather that the Union was a mystical entity with him, as it was with Lincoln, and that he could not bear to have the object of his greatest love, the vision of his prophetical poetry divided and so ruined.

And yet the Union that he loved was lost though the Southern states were forced to come back under the rule of the North. He had to live for the rest of his life in a land that stank with corruption and hypocrisy, with crookedness and despotism, with sophistical courts and twisted laws. He saw no more days like those of the fifties when the country was bursting with vitality and novelty, with progress and hope, with dreams of an America to carry on the prophecies of the New Atlantis. America had become after the war a pot seething with a poisonous compost. Yet Whitman went on. He became more lofty and spiritual. He did not lose his faith. Once his friend Harned asked him, "Have you ever had any experiences to shake your faith in humanity?" Whitman replied, "Never! Never! I trust humanity: its instincts are in the main right: it goes false, it goes true, to its interests, but in the long run it makes advances. Humanity always has to provide for the present moment as well as for the future: that is a tangle, however you look at it. Why wonder, then, that humanity falls down every now and then? There's one thing we have to remember —that the race is not free (free of its own ignorance)—is hardly in a position to do the best for itself: when we get a real democracy, as we will by and by, this humanity will have its chance—give a fuller report of itself." This was in May, 1888.

Whitman made a self-analysis as to the war and the questions involved in it. "All my friends," he said, "are more ardent in some respects than I am: for instance, I was never as much of an abolitionist as Marvin, O'Connor, and some of the others. Phillips—all of them—all of them—thought slavery the one crying sin of the universe. I didn't though I, too, thought it a crying sin. Phillips was true blue—I looked at him with a sort of awe: I never could quite lose the sense of other evils in this evil—I saw other evils that cried to me in perhaps even a louder voice: the labor evil, now, to speak of only one, which to this day has been steadily growing worse, worse, worse. I did not quarrel with their main contention but with the emphasis with which they asserted their particular idea. Some of the fellows were almost as hot with me as with slavery just because I wouldn't go into tantrums on the subject: they said I might just as well be on the other side—which was, of course, not true: I never lost any opportunity to make it plain where I stood, but I did not concentrate all my moral fire on the same spot."

Looking deeper into life than any political or war question directed his eyes, he could see the baneful effect of orthodoxy, and speak these words: "Did you ever think for a moment how so many young men, full of the stuff to make the noblest heroes of the earth, really live—really pass their lives, year after year, and so till death? Constant toil—ever alert to keep the wolf back from the door—no development—no rational pleasure,—sleeping in some cramped dirty place—never knowing once in their whole lives real affection, sweetly returned, the joy, the life of life—always kept down, unaware of religion—no habitual rendezvous except the bar-room—unaware of any amusements except these preposterous theatres, and of a Sunday these and those equally preposterous and painful screamings from the pulpits."

In 1888 Whitman said, "there was a time when New England culture made me sick, mad, rebellious, though now it does not seem to matter—I have become hardened to it." This was undoubtedly his attitude, and in a way continued to be. Yet he constantly lauded the Bible, more or less unconscious of the fact that it had produced that culture, and that it strengthened and perpetuated the opposition to himself as a poet of freedom. He saw that the objection to the nude, and shame of the body were of Asiatic origin, without laying his hands directly upon the Bible as the source in American life of those preposterous prejudices. He could place Jesus over an enlightened mind like Socrates and forget that Jesus cast his rejectors into hell, that Jesus preached asceticism, and no divorce, a doctrine that has been repudiated very largely by the American states, though only so after great struggles. When giving Jesus the great pre-eminence that he did he lagged behind Elizabeth Cady Stanton, an American product of the same times as those which produced Whitman. She was brave enough in her day to declare that Jesus was a celibate who condemned marriage. The dogma of the virgin birth is in the teeth of everything about life for which Whitman stood. Whitman was very far from being a complete Greek. The Hebraic cultus touched him deeply, and gave nourishment to his rôle as a prophet, beard and all. Since Whitman's day psychology and science have shown that mankind came by its consciousness of guilt, through the shame of sex, which makes the story of the Garden of Eden, and the expulsion of Eve and Adam therefrom, when they found themselves naked, so profoundly significant. If this truth occurred to Whitman I have not found the place where he uttered it. Paine began with attacking the authenticity of the Bible; the philosophy of Hebraism and Christianity was not so much under criticism by him, nor by Ingersoll much later. It was well enough to see the fall of man as a fiction, and the atonement an absurdity, and with Jefferson to laugh at the jargon of trinitarian arithmetic. It is something else to see the extent to which the ethics of Christianity are false and enervating, as Nietzsche saw them. Whitman forever lauded the poetry of the

Hebrew prophets, without perceiving, apparently, that they have fostered in Occidental thought, and very much in America, that bitter radicalism and sanguinary reformation which has torn the country and had much to do with the war between the states. Jefferson before him characterized those writings as the ravings of fanatical minds.

On the other hand, while Whitman was constantly talking religion, and declaring that there could be no great poetry without a deep religious basis, it is difficult to see what he meant by religion, unless religion was that principle which produced a solidarity of human beings bound together by love, by the love of comrades. "There can be henceforth no system of religion," he said. And again, "there is something greater (is there not?) than all the science and poems of the world—above all else, like the stars shining eternal—above Shakespeare's plays, or Concord philosophy, or art of Angelo or Raphael—something that shines elusive like beams of Hesperus at evening—high above all the vaunted wealth and pride—prov'd by its practical outcropping of life, each case after its own concomitants—the intuitive blending of divine love and faith in a human emotional character—blending for all, for the unlearn'd, the common and the poor."

This is a lazar philosophy, but it is Whitman's religion. Perhaps there can be nothing better, call it religion, or humanitarianism, than belief in human nature. For how can the world go on if men do not believe, that bad as men are, and absurd as their actions are, they must still be believed in to save human life from catastrophe? There is nothing else to believe in, but gods; and what are they? "Though he slay me still will I believe," must be the viable doctrine in which humanity is substituted for Jehovah. Can this faith be made co-operative with Aristotle's ideal of the magnanimous man? Whitman perhaps thought something about this, without knowing much about Aristotle's *Nichomachean Ethics* and the magnanimous man. Whitman's moral or religious beliefs may be found as well as anywhere in his words in the poem, "Starting from Paumanok" and in the "Song of the Open Road."

In *Whitman's Complete Works,* Volume X, Page iii, may be found this statement: "It was originally my intention, after chanting in *Leaves of Grass* the songs of the body and of existence, to then compose a further, equally-needed volume, based on those convictions of perpetuity and conservation which, enveloping all precedents, make the unseen soul govern absolutely at last. I meant, while in a sort of continuing the theme of my first chants, to shift the slides and exhibit the problem and paradox of the same ardent and fully appointed personality entering the sphere of the resistless gravitation of spiritual law, and with cheerful face estimating death, not at all as the cessation, but as somehow what I feel it must be, the entrance upon by far the greater part of existence, and something that life is at least as much for, as it is for itself."

When talking to Traubel in the summer of 1888 Whitman had this to say about church attendance: "I never made any vows to go or not to go: I went, at intervals, but anywhere—to no one place: was a wanderer: went oftenest in my earlier life—gradually dropped off altogether; today a church is a sort of offense to me. I never had any 'views'—was always free—made no pledges, adopted no creeds, never joined parties or 'bodies.' Many years ago a reporter came to me about some comments *anent* me that appeared in *Appleton's Journal:* how did I dress when I was young, how now, what were my habits —and more like that. I said to him: I always dressed as I do now and spoke and acted as I do now—that's all I know about it—that's all I can tell you. And that's what I could say now about churches and views: I am as I was: I have not changed."

That Whitman fully grasped the beauty and the inspiring philosophy of evolution is shown by a talk he had with Traubel about Huxley. Traubel records the conversation as follows:

"I quoted something Huxley said about evolution—that he did not hold it as a dogma but as a working hypothesis. W.

exclaimed: 'It is beautiful—beautiful—such a confession as that: the most glorious and satisfying spiritual statement of the nineteenth century. Can the churches, the priests, the dogmatists, produce anything to match it? How can we ever forget Darwin? Was ever a great man a more simple man than Darwin? He was one of the *acme* men—he was at the top. I could hope for no better fate for my book than that it should grow strong in so beneficent an atmosphere—breathe the breath of its life.'"

It was a concomitant of cosmic consciousness for Whitman to believe in immortality. In that faith he never wavered from the first. These remarks made to Traubel in 1888 show how Whitman felt:

"W. said: 'I believe in immortality, and by that I mean *identity*. I know I have arrived at this result more by what may be called feeling than formal reason—but I believe it; yes, I know it. I am easily put to flight, I assure you, when attacked, but I return to the faith, inevitably—believe it, and stick to it, to the end. Emerson somewhere speaks of encountering irresistible logic and yet standing fast to his conviction. There is judgment back of judgment—defeat only seems like defeat: there is a fierce fight: the smoke is gone—your enemies are nowhere to be seen—you are placidly victorious after all—the finish of the day is yours. Logic does very little for me: my enemies say it, meaning one thing—I say it, meaning another thing.'"

One of Whitman's remarkable poems is called "The Sleepers." It will not be found in all editions of *Leaves of Grass*. It is contained in the edition of 1882 published by Rees Welsh & Company. This poem shows how Whitman from a youth up lived in a sort of dream world in which he identified himself with everything, himself being both the seer and the seen. His belief in immortality came from his consciousness that all is subject, all is presence, all is one, all is the absolute. His often expressed belief in the oneness of things and the endless relationship of things, is a manifestation of his cosmic consciousness. From this divination resulted his catalogues. He catalogued in order to bring everything into unity, and also because his sympathies and his attempts to identify himself with everything led him into the breasts of all human beings and into the heart of nature. These lines from "The Sleepers" illustrate the point:

> I wander all night in my vision,
> Stepping with light feet, swiftly and noiselessly stopping,
> Bending with open eyes over the shut eyes of sleepers.

While thus sleep-walking he visits the fatigued, he sees the white faces of corpses, the livid faces of drunkards, the wounded upon the battlefield, the insane, the newborn, the newly married couple, and so on. He stands where people are suffering, where men are working and where the young are dancing or swimming. So he wanders through the mysterious night. He is not afraid to trust himself to the night. "I love the rich running day, but I do not desert her in whom I lay so long." That is the night, the mystery of creation, the place of divinations, sympathies and understandings. To dismiss Whitman's catalogues as mere inventories, as Emerson did, is partly to miss the nature of his genius and what it strove to express. His belief in immortality came from his dreams as a dreamer in the night, it was incident to his Uranian love, and to his vital body charged with sex, which made him the glowing influence that he was, the presence that Edward Carpenter and others felt as the emanation of a kind of high purity, flowing from the soul of a saint, a prophet.

Burroughs wrote of Whitman: "He was always the picture of sweetness, sanity, and health, even after his partial paralysis up to within a few months of his death. No man who had led a debauched life in any way could have made the impression of purity and nobility, upon old and young, male and female that he made."

278

Whitman was, in the above particulars, a mystic. But his insistence upon the flesh, his repeated statements that the body is as much as the soul, and his catalogues of material things as he roamed in imagination over America and the world, hide his mystical proclivities. Browning sang:

Let us cry all good things
Are ours, nor soul helps flesh more, now than flesh helps soul.

Whitman carried that doctrine much farther. Hence he laid himself open to the charge of fleshliness, to sensuality, to a kind of materialism. All the while, almost with the reiterated persistence of Heraclitus he was singing that all is divine fire, all is immanent life, mind and creativeness.

Still it is not hard to understand how Whitman affected some minds disagreeably, particularly the Puritan mind, and how his peccadilloes were seized upon to degrade him. When he romanced about the sale of his books, and told "whoppers" about his offspring he laid himself open to attack. Emory Holloway justly enough says that fancy in Whitman was so vivid that he was unable often to distinguish between reality and unreality, and that this faculty in Whitman was strengthened by reading Cooper and *The Arabian Nights*. This he carried over into maturity. Shelley often could not tell the outward world of fact from the inner world of his mind's representations. This is common enough among poets. But while Shelley had a keen intellect for metaphysics, Whitman was incapable of a systematic philosophy; and all his references to Kant and Hegel have the appearance of ostentation concerning things that he knew about in the most fugitive way, and as literary men often known them, who see the difficulty of carrying the *Philosophy of History,* or the *Critique of Pure Reason* in mind. This is a burden which interferes with creativeness, except with men like Goethe. For the writing of poetry, it is not necessary to be weighted down with such intricate erudition.

Then there was Whitman's vast egotism, his invulnerable admiration of and belief in, himself. I quote here from an article written by Emory Holloway for the February, 1922, number of *The Dial*. He said that Whitman in youth was lonely and longing for affection and that his mystical tendencies increased his loneliness and turned him more and more upon himself. And then, "the youth found . . . another way out. I do not mean," writes Holloway, "his somewhat abnormal emotional attraction to his mother . . . and imitation of her. Nor do I mean his romantic attraction to other men, what some psychoanalysts might consider a subconscious defense mechanism against the mild Œdipus complex. . . . But I refer to his discovery of the path Narcissus took. A powerful but repressed sexual nature was, I think, largely responsible for Whitman's egotism; which no explanations concerning its vicarious character have ever succeeded in rendering quite attractive. . . . Why should the subject [of nudeness] have appealed . . . with such strength and persistence? And the simplest answer that psychology can give is that it is a survival of what in childhood may be not abnormal exhibitionism, a narcissistic admiration of his own well formed body first, and a later extension of this unabashed admiration to well made and well functioning bodies everywhere."

To express this otherwise, and perhaps with more general clearness for being put in terms of common experience, it may be said that a sensitive boy of imagination may turn to his mother in order not to be wounded, but to be understood and appreciated. The mother may then return with maternal instinct this tenderness, seeking to protect and comfort her child, and this may lead to egotism and to preoccupation with the affection of that mother. From this might come Narcissism, self-love, and then perhaps a Uranian tendency where the father was disliked or less loved by the child, than the mother.

All this considered, was it wonderful that Whitman did not go to war but instead nursed the suffering and the dying? In

January, 1903, Higginson made an attack on Whitman for not having played a soldier's part in the War of the States. Burroughs commented on this in the following journal entry:

"I see that Higginson, in his Lowell Institute lectures, continues his efforts to belittle Whitman. . . . Think of belittling him because he did not enlist as a soldier and carry a musket in the ranks! Could there be anything more shocking and incongruous than Whitman killing people? One would as soon expect Jesus Christ to go to war. Whitman was the lover, the healer, the reconciler, and the only thing in character for him to do in the War was what he did do—nurse the wounded and sick soldiers—Union men and Rebels alike, showing no preference. He was not an athlete, or a rough, but a great tender mother-man, to whom the martial spirit was utterly foreign."

Whitman's self-puffing does not harmonize with the dignity that he practised in most particulars. It is understandable when considered in connection with his egotism, his stubbornness of character, his will not to be put down, especially as he was so sure that he had a great mission and a great expression. In the *Nation* for February 17, 1874, Whitman had an article about himself from which this sample is pertinent here:

"The immortal Hebraic poems—Homer's, Virgil's, and Juvenal's compositions—Dante's, Shakespear's, and even Tennyson's—from the highest point of view—are all and each such characteristic yet generic growths. Walt Whitman is the same in my opinion. The physiognomy of a race—of each race in the past—has the same old generic type, and yet is markedly different, and is characteristic only of itself."

In August of 1879, Whitman wrote to Burroughs and sent him these paragraphs for an essay on "Nature and the Poets," to be signed by Burroughs:

"Whitman is not remarkable in details or minute finish. But in spirit, in reverence, in breadth, *ensemble,* and in his vistas he stands unmatched. Through all that fluid, weird Nature, 'so far and yet so near,' he finds human relations, human responsions. In entire consistence with botany, geology, science, or what-not, he endues his very seas and woods with passion, more than the old hamadryads or tritons. His fields, his rocks, his trees, are not dead material, but living companions.

"To him all Nature's objectiveness holds a cognizant lurking something, without voice, yet realizing you as much as you realize it. No wonder Addington Symonds, the young Hellenic scholar of England, says, 'Singular as it may appear, Walt Whitman is more thoroughly Greek than any man of modern times!'"

Yet Whitman was not without praise from others and from the highest sources. He was surrounded in his last years by a devoted band of followers, and he was in receipt of encouraging letters from England where *Leaves of Grass* was admired by the best minds. In 1883 Meredith addressed to Whitman the following sonnet:

AN ORSON OF THE MUSE

WALT WHITMAN

Her son, albeit the Muse's livery
And measured courtly paces rouse his taunts,
Naked and hairy in his savage haunts,
To Nature only will he bend the knee;
Spouting the founts of her distillery
Like rough rock-sources; and his woes and wants
Being Nature's, civil limitation daunts
His utterance never; the nymphs blush; not he.
Him, when he blows of Earth, and Man, and Fate,
The Muse will hearken to with graver ear
Than many of her train can waken; him
Would fain have taught what fruitful things and dear
Must sink beneath the tidewaves, of their weight,
If in no vessel built for sea they swim.

In 1882 Swinburne had written Lord Houghton in great praise of "A Voice out of the Sea," and he called "When Lilacs Last in the Dooryard Bloom'd" "the most sonorous nocturne

282

ever chanted in the church of the world." In 1868 in a critique of William Blake, Swinburne commented upon the spiritual kinship between Blake and Whitman, their splendor of stars and storms, their flights across vast spaces of air upon shoreless seas, their passionate love of liberty, and their oceanic quality in common—showing in their short-comings the faults of elemental and eternal things. The poem addressed by Swinburne to Whitman in *Songs before Sunrise* has already been mentioned. It is true that in a short time Swinburne turned upon Whitman, in his book *Under the Microscope* and declared that Whitman took himself too seriously as a "representative poet," and an "official democrat"—and that "the strength forsakes his hand, the music ceases at his lips."

There is something more to say, later, of Swinburne's critical enmity. But all in all Whitman had great praise to sound in his inner ear and to comfort him in the last dark painful days when his mind misted. It was in Whitman's seventy-second year that he wrote to Symonds professing to have fathered six children. His last pictures show a face emptied of all power, wearing the stare of an uncomprehending old man of more than ninety. This premature senility, and all along the way his tendency to seem older than his years, has puzzled many Whitman students.

CHAPTER SIXTEEN

Not only did Whitman have torture of body after 1873, he had torture of mind all along. It is to his credit that his songs were hopeful and uplifting to others despite these drains upon his constitution. In 1860 Whitman published some lines entitled, "Hours Continuing Long Sore and Heavy Hearted," among the *Calamus* group. They were rejected in 1867, but rescued later by Oscar Lovell Triggs: We may insert them here:

Hours of my torment — I wonder if other men ever have the like, out of the like feelings?

Is there even one other like me—distracted—his friend, his lover, lost to him?

Is he too as I am now? Does he still rise in the morning, dejected, thinking who is lost to him? and at night, awaking, think who is lost?

Does he too harbor his friendship silent and endless? harbor his anguish and passion?

Does some stray reminder, or the casual mention of a name, bring the fit back upon him, taciturn and deprest?

Does he see himself reflected in me? In these hours, does he see the face of his hours reflected?

What a cry of loneliness! What an expressed agony for that defeat of the soul, always that defeat of the soul which loses its friend, its lover! Here is a note of his own, much later:

"Christmas Day, 25th Dec., 1888—Am somewhat easier and freer today and the last three days—sit up most of the time—read and write, and receive my visitors. Have now been in-

284

doors sick for seven months—half of the time bad, bad, vertigo, indigestion, bladder, gastric, head trouble, inertia—Dr. Bucke, Dr. Osler, Drs. Wharton and Walsh—now Edward Wilking my help and nurse. A fine, splendid, sunny day. My *November Boughs* is printed and out; and my *Complete Works, Poems and Prose,* a big volume, 900 pages, also. It is ab't noon, and I sit here pretty comfortable."

Whitman's premature old age and his paralysis excited speculation among those in particular who saw in his poems a confession of abnormal sexuality, and of gross indulgence. Thomas Wentworth Higginson was one of the chief enemies who pursued Whitman on these subjects. Higginson accused Whitman of a drench of passions which at the age of fifty-five resulted in paralysis and approaching senility. Burroughs, staunch friend of Whitman that he was, always came to the poet's defense. This is what Burroughs wrote on one of those occasions of championship:

"That Whitman's life was entirely blameless in this respect (sexual irregularities) I am not prepared to say, because I do not know, I think it highly probable that it was not, but that his partial paralysis was in any way traceable to any such cause, I am very sure is not the case. His paralysis resulted from the bursting of a very small blood vessel at the base of the brain— an accident to which all robust full-blooded men are peculiarly liable, especially if they have been subject to great emotional strain, as Whitman was during the war. . . .

"I have known Whitman for nearly thirty years, and a cleaner, saner, more wholesome man, in word and deed, I have never known. If my life depended upon it, I could not convict him of one unclean word, or one immoral act."

However, Whitman was pretty much invalided from February, 1873, to the day of his death. The summer of 1891 was exceedingly hot, and bore upon Whitman heavily. On December 17, 1892, Whitman had a chill and contracted pneumonia. Bucke came and got a nurse for him—she was the Mrs. Keller who wrote the book about Whitman in Mickle Street previously quoted.

On December 24 Whitman made a will. By this testament he bequeathed $1000 to Mrs. Mary Elizabeth Van Nostrand of Greenport, Suffolk County, New York; $1000 to Mrs. Hannah Louise Heyde; $250 to Mrs. Susan Stafford, wife of George Stafford of Glendale, Camden, New Jersey; $1000 to Mrs. Mary O. Davis, of 328 Mickle Street, Camden, New Jersey; $20 to Mrs. Mapes; $50 to Mrs. Nancy Whitman, widow of his brother Andrew. He made Louisa Whitman, the wife of George Whitman, his executrix. To Warren Fritzinger he left $200, and inserted precatory words to allow Mrs. Mary O. Davis to occupy the Mickle Street house without rent.

In a codicil dated January 1, 1892, he left Mrs. Stafford $200 instead of $250, and to Mrs. Van Nostrand $200 instead of $1000. He gave his gold watch to Horace Traubel, and his silver watch to Harry Stafford. No mother of any child, no child, was mentioned in this will.

In late December, Traubel sent word to Burroughs that Whitman was in a critical condition, and Burroughs hastened to Camden. From Burroughs's journal these words are taken:

"Walt on the bed with eyes closed, but he knows me and speaks my name as of old, and kisses me. He asks me to sit beside him a while. I do so, holding his hand. He coughs feebly. . . . Asks about my family and sends his best love to Wife and Julian. Gives me two copies of his complete poems just out. He tells me where to find them. After a while I go out for fear of fatiguing him. He says, 'It is all right, John,' evidently referring to his approaching end. He said his brother George had just been in and it had unnerved him for the first time.

"Xmas . . . Walt . . . rallied considerable during the day. . . . He speaks of Mrs. O'Connor, of Eldridge and his wife, his voice natural and strong. . . . I dined at Harned's and spent the evening there.

"Dec. 26. Walt had a bad night. Doctors think he may live a

day or two yet, or may go any hour. I go up and look at him long and long, but do not speak. His face has steadily refined; no decrepitude or breaking down; never saw the nose so beautiful. He looks pathetic, but how beautiful! At eleven I take a silent farewell."

On February 22 Whitman was seated for the last time in his chair with the white wolf robe. His suffering was very great from this time on. On March 25 at 1:15 A.M. Warren Fritzinger wrote to Mrs. Keller as follows:

"We put him on the water bed at twelve o'clock. I have turned him twice since, and I can assure you from present indications, if it does the old man no good, it will us. He turns just as easy again; can turn him with one hand, and then does it away with the ring. He was turned 63 times in the last 24 hours; how is that for business? Kind of beats when you were here. Mama has one of her headaches, has had it since yesterday . . . we had a run of visitors today, and the old gent had four letters in the morning mail, of which three were applications for autographs."

Doctor Macalister was in attendance upon him, and also Doctor Daniel Longaker of Philadelphia. His close friends like Traubel were with him to the last. His sufferings for the weeks of life that remained to him were very great; but he made no complaint. He lay apparently in sleep or a doze; but it was soon discovered that he was alert to his surroundings. His hearing it may be mentioned remained remarkably acute, while his strength ebbed. For air entered his lungs imperfectly, and his cough was troublesome. His heart was rapid and showed weakness. He had no anxiety about himself, and made no complaint. This attitude he maintained to the last. Meanwhile his breathing was difficult accompanied by rales. This interfered with his talking, and indeed he talked little and showed that he did not wish to be pressed to speak. Once he said, "My friends seem not to realize how weak I am, and what an effort it is for me to talk." At the same time he partook of food satis-

287

factorily. Sometimes in the morning he ate a mutton chop, and during the day he drank several milk punches. All this was in December. On Christmas Day he grew alarmingly weak. His pulse was rapid and irregular, the surface of his body was covered with a cold clammy sweat. A collapse had overtaken him. He rallied from this in a day. Then in a day he relapsed, and lay for hours in what appeared to be a semiconscious state. Yet he promptly replied to any question asked him. Once he murmured, "No pain, but so very miserable." His pulse was now irregular and fast, the beat being one hundred to the minute. By January 7 he had regained a normal pulse respiration ratio, the former seventy-two and the latter eighteen. The alarming symptoms had abated. Doctor Longaker said that Whitman's rally from death in December was the most remarkable experience of his entire medical observation. All this was true, but Whitman never established any real convalescence. He had a troublesome cough, and expectorated much muco-purulent matter, showing that the pneumonia had not undergone complete resolution. Meanwhile he suffered marked loss of flesh. His nights were restless. Hourly, or oftener, he called his nurse Warry to shift his position in bed. He could lie only on his left side, and this position finally tortured him. Whitman said: "I have to choose between two evils: lying on the left side tortures me, on the right side the phlegm chokes me." So the painful days went on. After his morning meal he would have the curtain opposite his bed raised; then he would read the daily papers and his mail. Sometimes he wrote a little. On January 10 he signed two of the Johnston etchings for the attending physicians. Little as he said, even in the way of necessary communication, he surprised all about him by references to the news of the day. His friends talked of getting a new bed for him. "You slip away from us so in this one," they said. He replied, "Some of these fine mornings I shall be slipping away from you forever." One time he talked of the two-hour conversation that he had had with Emerson on Boston Common.

"Emerson talked the finest talk that was ever talked," observed Whitman as he caught his breath. The doctors were in the dark as to the nature and extent of his malady. The question of cancerous disease was considered, and then dismissed. He continued to lose flesh markedly. However, by March 11, he was again reading the daily papers. Still he could not get into a comfortable position in bed. From the 21st to the 22d of March he was shifted forty-one times by Warry. On the 23d his hearing was dull, his respiration twenty-three to the minute, his pulse eighty-four. The death rattle, for some days absent, was again heard by the physicians. By March 26, he was extremely weak. His respiration went up to thirty a minute; his pulse was small and irregular, and the rales grew more distinct. Whitman's last words were, "Shift, Warry." Then the creator of *Leaves of Grass* was gone. Traubel, the good friend, the better for being a poet himself and akin to Whitman through the Muses, gave this account of the end in addressing Doctor Longaker.

"The end came so suddenly this day's evening between six and seven, even after all our anticipation, that we had no time to summon you. Harned, Macalister, Fritzinger, and Mrs. Davis were present when I arrived. There was no sign of struggle on the part of the patient. The light flickered, lowered, was quenched. He seemed to suffer no pain. His heart was strong to the last, and even may be said to have outbeat his life, since for some minutes after the breath was gone the faint throb at his breast, though lessening, continued. He needed no help—indeed help was past avail. A few minor attentions which we fairly reasoned might give him comfort were shown. Elsewise we sat or stood and watched. He said nothing. He lay on his back—the one hand which he had reached to me when I came, and which I held, on the coverlet. He passed away as peacefully as the sun, and it was hard to catch the moment of transition. That solemn watch, the gathering shadows, the painless surrender, are not to be forgotten. His soul went out with the day. The face was calm, the body lay without rigidity, the majesty of his tranquil spirit remained. What more could be said? It was a moment not for the doctor, but for the poet, the seer."

Some months before his death Whitman had consented to an autopsy; and as the doctors were somewhat puzzled by his case as a medical matter, a post mortem was made on March 27 by Henry W. Cattell, demonstrator of morbid anatomy of the Pennsylvania University, in the presence of Doctor Longaker, Professor F. X. Dercum, Doctor Macalister, and Traubel. The brain was found to be remarkably well formed and symmetrical. It weighed forty-five ounces, two hundred and ninety-two and one-half grains avoirdupois. That is a medium weight for a brain, but a brain decreases in weight one ounce for every ten years after fifty years of age. Moreover Whitman had undergone great emaciation. The doctors estimated that Whitman's brain had shrunk six to eight ounces in the last months of his life. They were of the opinion that at Whitman's mental maturity his brain weighed at least fifty-six ounces. The calvarium of the brain was white, and the muscular tissue pale. The dura mater was very adherent to the skull cap and showed recent pachymeningitis on both sides, but especially on the right. The blood in the longitudinal sinus was fluid. The pia and arachnoid were very œdematous. Numerous milky patches, especially over the vertex, were seen, but no miliary tubercles were discernible. The brain substance was excessively soft. The heart, which weighed about nine ounces, was very flabby and well covered with epicardial fat. The pulmonary valves were slightly thickened. The aortic valves were in good condition. The mitral valves good. Only about one-eighth of the right lung was suitable for breathing purposes. The upper and middle lobes were consolidated and firmly bound down to the pleura. Large tubercular nodules and areas of catarrhal pneumonia were found everywhere. The spleen was soft and weighed about eight ounces, the capsule thickened and fibrous, on section pulpy. The kidneys were surrounded by a mass of fat. The left supra-renal capsule was tubercular and contained a cyst the size of a pigeon's egg. The kidney was soft, red and swollen and somewhat granular. The right kidney was a little smaller and the better of the two. Over the whole of the mesentery, especially in its lower portion, were hundreds of minute tubercles varying in size from that of a fine needle point to the head of a good-sized pin. These whitish points were surrounded by a hemorrhagic base.

The cause of death was given as pleurisy of the left side, consumption of the right lung, general miliary tuberculosis and parenchymatous nephritis. There was also found a fatty liver, gall stone, a cyst in the adrenal, tubercular abscesses, involving the bones, and pachymeningitis. The doctors considered it marvelous that respiration could have been carried on for so long a time with the limited amount of useful lung tissue found at the autopsy. They believed that this was largely due to the indomitable will of Walt Whitman. Any one else, they declared, would have died much earlier with one-half of the pathological changes which existed in his body.

These facts are taken from *In Re Walt Whitman,* edited by Traubel, Bucke and Harned, and published in Philadelphia in 1893. There has been such vast talk and speculation about Whitman's invalidism and last sickness that it is well that something definite in a life of Whitman should go forth to the world. This portion of the autopsy report may be included here as an end of the whole matter: "To medical ears, at least, it may seem strange that physicians of even average diagnostic skill should overlook a large pleural effusion like this. There were two reasons for it—the first was the lack of complaint of pain; the second our respect for his disinclination to be disturbed. It seemed a rudeness, almost, to subject him to searching examination. Practically this failure of discovery made little difference, since it is doubtful if the removal of the fluid would have added much to his comfort or succeeded in prolonging life. This pleurisy was due to deposit in the membrane of tubercles, the same as were found in the spleen and the peritoneum of the left side of the abdomen in general. Here they originated peritonitis, and thus accounted for pain. The abscess eroding the sternum must have existed a long time. It also was tubercular, and in all probability was the original point of development of the disease and the focus of subsequent infection. It is a fact now pretty generally known that individuals in apparently perfect health may have tuberculous mediastinal glands, and such this, in all likelihood, was originally. How long it and the other abscess eroding one of the ribs had existed is a matter of surmise, not of certainty. It might have been several years. It certainly antedated the outbreak of pneumonia in December by months. No wonder now that he felt a 'deadly lassitude and inertia.' "

The book *Walt Whitman in Mickle Street* has an addendum in which it is stated that Whitman's brain was sent to the Anthropometric Society of Philadelphia. In Camden I was told that the brain slipped out of hand to the floor while being examined. This was the word of a Whitman enthusiast long familiar with the facts of Whitman's last days. Whether the brain was injured or in any way rendered beyond preservation by this accident I was not told. On seeing Doctor Macalister I asked about the brain and was told that it had been sent to the Wistar Institute of the University of Pennsylvania. The Wistar Institute replied to my letter of inquiry about the brain to the effect that it was never received there. The Anthropometric Society has no discoverable address. Obviously some unexplained contradiction and confusion exist here. If it could be cleared nothing much of moment might be discovered—and the matter may be allowed to pass. However, Doctor Macalister told me that Whitman's brain was sprinkled with tubercles, as in the case of miliary tuberculosis, yet that his organs were normal and in good condition for a man of his age.

On May 31, 1936, Doctor Longaker was interviewed, and

according to *The Philadelphia Record* of that date said: "Walt
Whitman's last sickness in reality dates from his years of hospital work in 1863-5, and originated at the time from two
causes—the first the emotional strain of those terrible years; the
second from blood poisoning, absorbed from certain gangre-
nous wounds in patients whom he at that time closely attended.
In 1864 and 1865 he had temporary breakdowns, and these
culminated in January, 1873, in an attack of paralysis which was
greatly aggravated during the same year by the death of his
mother. This paralysis more than once brought him to death's
door. It let up a little in the late seventies and early eighties,
then settled down thicker than ever in the late eighties, and
steadily deepened until the end. I wish to silence forever the
slanderous accusations that debauchery and excesses of various
kinds caused or contributed to his breakdown. There was
found no trace or reason to suspect either during his life or
after death, either alcoholism or syphilis. This statement is in
justice due the memory of one whose ideal of purity was high."

The fact that one of Whitman's brothers died of an aneurism
in 1875, and that his brother Edward was defective mentally
may indicate that there was vascular weakness in the Whitman
inheritance. Who can tell what was in the blood of the Whitmans, or of the Van Velsors back in the disordered days of the
Revolution? Whitman, apart from all questions of pathology,
seems to me after this study of the records, to have been loosely
constructed. His smooth skin and ruddy complexion give me
the impression of a body flabby and lymphatic, not hard and
athletic—all despite his great bulk. His shambling, rolling
walk, his drowsy and careless ways, his lack of system in daily
habits and in his thinking find their parallel in his sprawling
words and style, and in his handwriting—though that was legible
enough. But how untidy! Why did he elide the "e" in the past
tenses of words and lose the time thus saved by indicating the
elision by a caret? Whitman's manuscripts are as slatternly as
any in literary history. Whitman did not have tough fiber, he

was somehow flaccid, effeminate, dull, slack, and perhaps impotent.

Yet this Higginson detraction is a typical case of slanderous tongues. There is not any proof of a concrete nature that Whitman had syphilis. On the other hand what his physicians and Burroughs and others said is not conclusive. He could have been luetic and still have looked exactly as he did. However, a scientific autopsy can settle questions of this kind. Syphilis leaves unmistakable marks on the human cadaver. The fog and stir exist in denials that he was intemperate, that he was infected. It is a curious case of an affirmative getting a position by negatives denying what is baseless. Except for the fact that the intention of this book is to show Whitman in his life and work as he was, these matters would not be mentioned. For whether he drank, whether he fell a prey to paralysis through an amorous misfortune, has no bearing upon his work as a poet. De Quincey's opium produced his *Confessions,* Keats's consumption may have heightened the imaginative energy which created *Hyperion.* If we have read the story aright Whitman's poetry came out of the sun, the open air, the sea, and from watching crowds in cities. It was all sanity and health.

Whitman's tomb was finished and ready to hearse his body. A word may be said to nail down the false word of Whitman's mendicancy. His balance in the National State Bank was at his death $7,379.02. At the end of 1887 it was $6,084.68. On January 1, 1889, it was $5,670.51; at the end of 1889 it was $6,334.21, and by January 12, 1892, it was $6,962.77. He had deposited $416.25 between that date and the time of his death. These figures are taken from his bank book. Whitman's tomb was paid for and he owned 328 Mickle Street. For a poet he was well circumstanced and he seems to have always been able to pay for what he needed. It was fortunate for his art that he had no talent for making money, which might have tempted him to waste his concentration in business affairs.

On the day of the funeral his friends came together. Burroughs was there. Ingersoll delivered the oration with great beauty and eloquence. The services were held under a tent near the tomb where the air was charged with the perfume of the floral tributes. In the midst of Ingersoll's oration, as Burroughs recorded, a bluebird began to sing joyously in a tree that overhung the tent. The next day Burroughs, Traubel, and Warry, the nurse, went to the tomb and looked at its enduring masonry, and talked of the lamented dead. Over America men were getting ready for a political campaign. Historic forces were commencing that hour to change America from all that Whitman knew it to be, and altogether beyond what he ever could have dreamed about it, even in *Democratic Vistas*. The dear love of comrades, Whitman's dream of America, may have remained in the mighty drift of selfishness and materialism that was ensuing. But certainly they were lost to view as the great life stream rushed on to monopoly and imperialism, to the World War, to staggering national debt, and to national blindness and fumbling.

CHAPTER SEVENTEEN

WHITMAN has very largely survived
the criticisms that were made of him in his day. No one says
now with Emerson that Whitman is half song thrush and half
alligator. The judgment of today is expressed pretty much in
the same terms as in the estimate of Whitman by Bayard Taylor in 1866, namely that Whitman's poems sang the awe, reverence and beauty of life, as they are expressed in the human
body, with the physical attraction and delight of physical contact. "That tender and noble love of man for man which certainly
once existed, but now almost seems to have gone out of the experience of the race," found by Taylor in Whitman's poems, delighted him. "There is not one word of your large and beautiful
sympathy for men which I cannot take into my heart, nor
one of those subtle and wonderful physical affinities you describe which I cannot comprehend." Taylor was forty-one when
he wrote these words.

George Parsons Lathrop wrote to Burroughs in 1877, that
Whitman was America's greatest poet. As we have had occasion to see, Stedman was very friendly to Whitman's work.
These men may not stand at the apex of literary criticism,
but they are as high as Swinburne, whose savage attack on
Whitman at the last, after Swinburne had veered, is scarcely
remembered now. In *Studies in Prose and Poetry* Swinburne
wrote: "Did you ask dulcet rhymes from me, inquires Mr.
Whitman. No, my dear good sir, not in the wildest vision of
distempered slumber could I have dreamed of doing anything of the kind. . . . But metre, rhythm, cadence, not merely

296

appreciable but definable and reducible to rule and measurement, though we do not expect from you, we demand from all who claim, we discern in the work of all who have achieved, any place among poets of any class whatsoever. The question is whether you have any more right to call yourself a poet, or to be called a poet on the strength of your published writings than to call yourself or to be called a mathematician, a logician, a painter, a political economist, a sculptor, a dynamiter, an old parliamentarian hand, a civil engineer, a dealer in marine stores, an amphimacer, a triptych, a rhomboid, or a rectangular parallelogram."

Swinburne may have laughed as he wrote this; no one but a fool will laugh at it as he reads it. Swinburne had no word here for Whitman's thought, his vision, his passion for humanity and beauty, for nature. He passed by Whitman's music, his free rhythms, his lines long as sea waves, which wash in upon the ear bringing the deep susurrus of the deeps. It is too late to talk about Whitman's prosody. He chose the best form for his poems, his themes and his own diaphragm considered. He purposed to write "a book about new things," nothing on "a lady's sparrow" like Catullus. In 1888 Whitman said, as recorded by Traubel:

" 'For myself I have never had any difficulty in deciding what I should say and not say. First of all comes sincerity—frankness, openmindedness: that is the preliminary: to talk straight out. It was said of Pericles that each time before he went to speak he would pray (what was called praying then—what was it?) that he might say nothing to excite the wrath, the anger, of the people.' W. shook his head. 'That is a doubtful prescription: I should not like to recommend it myself. Emerson, for one, was an impeachment of that principle: Emerson, with his clear transparent soul: he hid nothing, kept nothing back, yet was not offensive: the world's antagonism softened Emerson's sweetness.' "

And again from a Whitman preface:

"The greatest poet is not he who has done the best; it is he who suggests the most; he, not all of whose meaning is at first obvious, and who leaves you much to desire, to explain, to study, much to complete in your turn. . . . The accepted notion of a poet would appear to be a sort of male odalisque, singing or piano-playing a kind of spiced ideas, second-hand reminiscence, or toying late hours at entertainments, in rooms stifling with fashionable scent. I think I haven't seen a new-publish'd, healthy, bracing, simple lyric in ten years. Not long ago, there were verses in each of three fresh monthlies, from leading authors, and in every one the whole central *motif* (perfectly serious) was the melancholiness of a marriageable young woman who didn't get a rich husband, but a poor one! . . .

"Never had real bard a task more fit for sublime ardor and genius than to sing worthily the songs these States have already indicated. Their origin, Washington, '76, the picturesqueness of old times, the war of 1812 and the sea-fights; the incredible rapidity of movement and breadth of area—to fuse and compact the South and North, the East and West, to express the native forms, situation, scenes, from Montauk to California, and from the Saguenay to the Rio Grande—the working out on such gigantic scales, and with such a swift and mighty play of changing light and shade, of the great problems of man and freedom,—how far ahead of the stereotyped plots, or gem-cutting, or tales of love, or wars of mere ambition! Our history is so full of spinal, modern, germinal subjects—one above all. What the ancient siege of Ilium, and the puissance of Hector's and Agamemnon's warriors proved to Hellenic art and literature, and all art and literature since, may prove the war of attempted secession of 1861-'65 to the future esthetics, drama, romance, poems of the United States."

It cannot be said too often that Whitman's great and really significant contribution to American poetry lies in the fact that he surveyed its future territory. When Texas has grown to twenty millions, when the country west of the Mississippi River is as populous as the Middle West is now, and when as accompaniments to such growth the thousand and one streams of American life and liberty are swept into national consciousness, what will be the significance of Robinson and his somber delineations, his word-splitting refinements, the near and thin utterance of Frost, and all mere Eastern schools of literature? It seems inconceivable that they can be anything but rocky headlands and peaks which a spiritual geology has deserted and left to their lonely sterility. Emerson will likely remain, since he was in his own way so American and so spiritually profound.

Let us examine more of Whitman's words to make the present point clearer. They are from his wonderful preface of 1872:

"I will therefore not conceal from any persons, known or unknown to me, who take an interest in the matter, that I have the ambition of devoting yet a few years to poetic composition. The mighty present age! To absorb and express in poetry, anything of it—of its world—America—cities and States —the years, the events of our Nineteenth century—the rapidity of movement—the violent contrasts, fluctuations of light and shade, of hope and fear—the entire revolution made by science in the poetic method—these great new underlying facts and new ideas rushing and spreading everywhere;—truly a mighty age! As if in some colossal drama, acted again like those of old under the open sun, the Nations of our time, and all the characteristics of Civilization, seem hurrying, stalking across, flitting from wing to wing, gathering, closing up, toward some long-prepared, most tremendous denouement. Not to conclude the infinite scenas of the race's life and toil and happiness and sorrow, but haply that the boards be clear'd from oldest, worst incumbrances, accumulations, and Man resume the eternal play anew, and under happier, freer auspices. To me, the United States are important because in this colossal drama they are unquestionably designated for the leading parts, for many a century to come. In them history and humanity seem to seek to culminate. Our broad areas are even now the busy theatre of plots, passions, interests, and suspended problems, compared to which the intrigues of the past of Europe, the wars of dynasties, the scope of kings and kingdoms, and even the development of peoples, as hitherto, exhibit scales of measurement comparatively narrow and trivial. And on these areas of ours, as on a stage, sooner or later, something like an *eclaircissement* of all the past civilization of Europe and Asia is probably to be evolved."

And more from this preface:

"Indeed the peculiar glory of our lands, I have come to see, or expect to see, not in their geographical or republican greatness, nor military or naval power, nor special, eminent names in any department, to shine with, or outshine, foreign special names in similar departments,—but more and more in a vaster, saner, more surrounding Comradeship, uniting closer and closer not only the American States, but all nations, and all humanity. That, O poets! is not that a theme worth chanting, striving for? Why not fix your verses henceforth to the gauge of the round globe? the whole race? Perhaps the most illustrious culmination of the modern may thus prove to be a signal growth of joyous, more exalted bards of adhesiveness, identically one in soul, but contributed by every nation, each after its distinctive kind. Let us, audacious, start it. Let the diplomats, as ever, still deeply plan, seeking advantages, proposing treaties between governments, and to bind them, on paper: what I seek is different, simpler. I would inaugurate from America, for this purpose, new formulas—international poems. I have thought that the invisible root out of which the poetry deepest in, and dearest to, humanity grows, is Friendship. I have thought that both in patriotism and song (even amid their grandest shows past) we have adhered too long to petty limits, and that the time has come to enfold the world. . . .

"Is there not such a thing as the philosophy of American history and politics? And if so, what is it? . . . Wise men say there are two sets of wills to nations and to persons—one set that acts and works from explainable motives—from teaching, intelligence, judgment, circumstance, caprice, emulation, greed, &c.—and then another set, perhaps deep, hidden, unsuspected, yet often more potent than the first, refusing to be argued with, rising as it were out of abysses, resistlessly urging on speakers, doers, communities, unwitting to themselves—the poet to his fieriest words—the race to pursue its loftiest ideal. Indeed, the paradox of a nation's life and career, with all its wondrous contradictions, can probably only be explain'd from these two wills, sometimes conflicting, each operating in its sphere, combining in races or in persons, and producing strangest results."

Whitman has this to say about sex:

"Indeed, might not every physiologist and every good physician pray for the redeeming of this subject from its hitherto relegation to the tongues and pens of blackguards, and boldly putting it for once at least, if no more, in the demesne of poetry and sanity—as something not in itself gross or impure, but entirely consistent with highest manhood and womanhood, and indispensable to both? Might not only every wife and every mother—not only every babe that comes into the world, if that were possible—not only all marriage, the foundation and *sine qua non* of the civilized state—bless and thank the showing, or taking for granted, that motherhood, fatherhood, sexuality, and all that belongs to them, can be asserted, where it comes to question, openly, joyously, proudly, without shame or the need of shame, from the highest artistic and human considerations—but, with reverence be it written, on such attempt to justify the base and start of the whole divine scheme in humanity, might not the Creative Power itself deign a smile of approval?"

And again: "The problems of the achievements of this

al Singers,

crowning stage through future first-class National Singers,
Orators, Artists, and others—of creating in literature an imaginative *New World,* the correspondent and counterpart of the
current Scientific and Political New Worlds,—and the perhaps
distant, but still delightful prospect, (for our children, if not
in our own day,) of delivering America, and, indeed, all Christian lands everywhere, from the thin moribund and watery,
but appallingly extensive nuisance of conventional poetry—
by putting something really alive and substantial in its place
—I have undertaken to grapple with, and argue, in the preceding *Democratic Vistas."*

The foregoing passages are in my judgment magnificent
prose, and if Emerson's essays are more subtle, more spiritual,
they are not more important to American culture than these
philosophies of Whitman, and they are not so close to the
practical ways of American nationality and achievement.

Whitman in his day had to contend with those who claimed
to speak with authority of the soul, those who somehow,
whether they exactly meant to or not, always stood in the
way of the new days, blocking the steps of wisdom and the
muses with Bibles and with solemn orthodoxy. One of the
absurd propositions of such thinkers, a proposition that contradicts such wise men as Goethe, is that something arises in
the human mind by introspection and by books, by religion,
so-called, too—which is superior to the flesh, to nature and to
normal impulses. As if any inner check could possibly be superior to the natural life of the mind and the body! This
cannot be, and Whitman is the great spokesman in America
of the impossibility of such a theory and for the life of freedom.

One of the ablest critics of Whitman has been George Santayana who in 1900 published *Interpretations of Poetry and Religion,* and in an essay contained in that book wrote of Browning
and Whitman as poets of barbarism, as poets who ignored the
past and did not accept life as an art, and history as a record of
life's experiments. Santayana called Whitman the prophet of a

lost cause, who made the initial and amorphous phases of
society his ideal, something that has often been said of Rousseau, but which I think cannot be justly charged against
Whitman. Whitman, according to Santayana, did not grasp
Spencer's principle of evolution, and his principle of the development of organisms and society as well, from the homo-
geneous to the heterogeneous. To Santayana, Whitman could
never be the spokesman of the tendencies of his country; he
could never be the poet of the people, because the people
look toward a higher life—perhaps that of Catholicism. He
called Whitman the poet of farmers and workers as Pan was
the patron of the shepherds of Arcadia.

In technical criticism Santayana accused Whitman of de-
ploying detail without its organization, of having a wealth of
perception without intelligence, and of imagination without
taste. He said that in all of Whitman's work there was not a
single character or story, and that his only hero was himself.
There is truth in some of this. Indeed Whitman was the architect of a building for which he was incapable of making a
blueprint, lacking as he did the art to draw the details of
its decoration. Since Whitman's day poets have come on in
America who have done this work of fine artistry much better than Whitman was gifted to do it. The reader knows from
what I have already granted that I subscribe to what Santayana said about Whitman's lack of taste, and also about his
inability to draw a character, tell a story or write a dramatic
poem.

However, I think that Whitman had intelligence to direct
the course and compass of his perceptions and that his imagination was very powerful or he could not have roamed the world
in thought as he did. Here is something Santayana said that,
therefore, I do not agree with: "With Whitman the surface is
absolutely all, and the underlying structure is without interest and almost without existence. . . . The world has no
inside; it is a phantasmagoria of continuous visions, vivid, im-

pressive, but monotonous and hard to distinguish in memory like the waves of the sea." These statements are refuted by Whitman's prefaces and by many poems, and the reader is left to see that such is the fact by referring to what I have quoted from them. At the same time I admit that Whitman did not penetrate into secrets as Browning did; for his mind was not as subtle as Browning's—but for that matter neither was Homer's.

The school of poetry called Imagists was undoubtedly influenced by Whitman. Santayana remarked of Whitman, "We find the swarm of men and objects rendered as they might strike the retina in a sort of waking dream. It is the most sincere possible confession of the lowest—I mean the most primitive—type of perception." There is truth in this judgment if one overlooks the larger matter that Whitman's swarms of men, and descriptions of nature and of his country inside and outside, aggregate themselves into a vast vision. The reader has to have patience to see this, he must overlook the fault that Whitman's imagination is not precise, that it lacks the Shakespearean or even the Shelleyan power to capture the fiery climax, the brief and essential summation and the high note and music. Such poems as the one he wrote on Columbus, in which he dramatized himself, are not successful in my estimation because of Whitman's limitations in these particulars.

But Whitman could not be everything, he could only be what the passion of his heart made him. It is much that he sang the dignity of the individual, that he depicted the ideal man who was the comrade, that thus singing he was the poet of democracy, and a very acute prophet speaking of the problems of America. No other poet gives us in such wealth of detail the labors and joys of men, the traffic of cities, the crowds on the streets, and the movement of ships and trains, with such poetic feeling—and all because he loved men and loved his America. No other poet entered with such loving sympathy into the hearts of every description of people. He made catalogues because he wanted to show how his heart comprehended human life in all its aspects; and he did this with emotion, which is the basis of poetry and its rhythms.

The catalogue of the ships in the Iliad may be dull to those who do not see that Homer knew Greece and could speak with feeling of the ships that came from rocky Pytho and lovely Augeiai, and from Epidauros full of vines. Homer does not sing the crises of the soul as Shakespeare does. He has no lines like "I have lived long enough." Rather he says simply "death and sleep bore him away." Modern art is full of realism, of Rodin lines. Whitman with all his details leaves the reader to grasp the significance of the recitation behind the exterior form. Tennyson's sonorous "Mort d'Arthur" may deceive the casual reader into believing that there is more in it than Whitman's "A Sight in the Camp at Daybreak." But let the reader reflect upon it and see if this be true. To get the full effect of Whitman's poetry is almost comparable to penetrating the arcanum of an esoteric secret.

Whitman was not, like Shakespeare, everything and nothing. He was not like Keats, without an individuality and determined character. He was a definite creed and voice—and that because of his democratic passion and love of the American nation and its prospect as well as because of his complete lack of the dramatic imagination. He could feel with masses and with specimens of people in mass; he could not explore and depict a human soul. Whitman saw human beings as blacksmiths hammering, carpenters planing, ferrymen running ferries, and busmen running buses. Shakespeare and Browning saw the soldier, courtier or painter in their souls as loving and suffering, aspiring and being defeated, wondering and doubting and solving nothing.

Whitman's vision of America is big if America is big. If America fails he fails; and the defects of his performance in that case become more evident. He was a prophet, and if not a

305

true one he must stand on his utterance as poetry. Then he must be judged along with Tennyson and others of general and traditional outlook but of excellent art. It is not because Whitman is a better poet than Emerson that he may be called the father of American poetry—it is because Whitman wrote for the American tribe and the American idea. Whitman's points of view, his wisdoms, his philosophical verses, are less gnomic than Emerson's and less lyrical. They are more matter-of-fact. They are roots and stems, not flowers. Whitman's "Eidolons" is quite inferior to Emerson's "The Sphinx." Whitman is to Browning and Tennyson as roots, stalks, leaves, to fruit—as all these are to apples or pomegranates.

This will do as answer to the question whether Browning and Tennyson are superior to Whitman. Neither of these English poets had a national vision, or perhaps any definite vision for the betterment of their country or the world. Neither celebrated the tribe. Whitman was the tribal prophet and poet. In some aspects of a full appraisement this makes Whitman more important than his English compeers—always supposing that his vision is realized and that he is himself uplifted by that fact.

Whitman's catalogues and observations seem obvious and matter-of-fact, but think of making them for the first time! Think of him reflecting on how to express for the first time the image of a whole new land! Think of the vision, thought, comprehension that these catalogues imply and accomplish! There is hardly a sentence of epigrammatic philosophy in Whitman from beginning to end. His

Only themselves understand themselves and the like of themselves
As souls understand souls,

is a kind of paraphrase of Goethe's, "You are like that spirit which you comprehend."

Whitman's richness of feeling, his suggestiveness and his

moral fervor must answer for all his failings as a poet. There may never be a time when excellent and cultivated minds will not prefer Milton's "Lycidas," Tennyson's "In Memoriam" and even Arnold's "Thyrsus" to Whitman's "When Lilacs Last in the Dooryard Bloom'd." They will prefer the classicism of Milton, the monotony of Tennyson's weeping in a cambric handkerchief, as Taine said; the second-hand music and paid-mournership of Arnold to the deep poignancy, the tear-blurred vision and the genuine heart-hurt of Whitman in this genuine threnody, which mourns as simple hearts can mourn and cry out when the springs of expression are loosened.

Whitman had the right idea, namely, that poetry, the real written word, must come out of life—not out of books or erudition. It must come out of the earth. When it speaks for a land and celebrates a tribe it has done the greatest work that poetry can do. Without invention, as that word is understood in poetry, he relied upon realities. It is no wonder that a man as sincere as Whitman, whose sincerity chose prosody without rhyme, meter or ornament, had to endure the sneers and the chatter of New York critics in magazines and newspaper columns. These are educated and traditional minds who expatiate upon the work-overs, the repaintings of descents from the cross, the ephemeral and well-worded stuff, and often miss the important, the real and the truly American art.

Whitman has not failed in the way that Santayana said he failed. He is a false prophet, if false, because his America did not live up to its possibilities. America departed from its path. The dear love of comrades may be put aside as visionary and unworkable like the doctrine of turning the other cheek. In America today there are more hatred, cynicism, dishonesty, and injustice than existed in Whitman's day. Still America might have persisted and even grown in strength. Whitman would be immensely great if he could have inspired his country to climb to purer heights and if he could have lifted it out of the dreadful filth following the War of the States—filth that he wrote of with such spirit and indignation in *Democratic Vistas*.

"Drum Taps" and "Passage to India" are the songs of a soul which has betaken itself to the hills. They are songs of sublimation and escape. What Whitman would have done if the war had not deflected him from writing the second part of *Leaves of Grass,* none can say. What he would have done if he had escaped paralysis and the neglect of him that persisted partly because of the preoccupations of a people living through the postlude of a war with lowered spirituality which affected and lowered him—none can predict. Where is the dear love of comrades today? Where the "gigantic embryo of personality" that Whitman purposed to map out for "these States"? If he didn't put this over in *Leaves of Grass* he didn't do it at all—not in "Drum Taps" and not in the "Passage to India."

Robinson Jeffers, who in courage, power, originality and in Americanism may be called one of Whitman's spiritual sons, thus sings in "Shine Perishing Republic":

While this America settles in the mould of its vulgarity, heavily
  thickening to empire,
And protest, only a bubble in the molten mass, pops and sighs out,
  and the mass hardens.

And boys, be in nothing so moderate as in love of man, a clever
  servant, insufferable master.
There is the trap that catches noblest spirits, that caught — they
  say — God when he walked on earth.

Immoderate love must be said to have caught Whitman, too, if America cannot be set right toward liberty and justice.

What has brought us to the pass where special privilege has America by the throat in tariffs and tax favors—where life, liberty and the pursuit of happiness are practically gone—where the public debt is staggering and absentee farm landlordism is in control to the extent of seventy-five per cent in some states—where the Democratic Party of Jefferson has resorted to doles and can carry elections by these doles to the populares as the Republican Party for years carried elections by feeding the taxing power through tariffs to merchants, manufacturers and banks? The truth is that there was profound symbolism in the fact that the Independence bell cracked when it was rung for the funeral of John Marshall. His decisions cracked the Constitution and ruined the American experiment. Through Marshall the old political economy of Europe took to its breast the young American Republic.

The War of the States was a *coup de grace,* ending, as it did, in the Fourteenth Amendment which imperialized the republic, and became at once the breeding place, as it was the fortress, of special privilege. The Fourteenth Amendment was the product of the Bible and the banks. There can be no good will, no fair and friendly democracy of equal liberty, not to say no dear love of comrades, where such engines of greed and hate are in control of a people. There can be no songs of liberty, no songs celebrating the America of a new day, as it was intended to be by Jefferson and Paine, where such things have come to pass. The definite and legalistic way in which a free government such as America was before the War of the States, was turned into a despotic plutocracy and made a feeding place for swine has no parallel in history. Whitman marked the beginning of this transformation and much of its consummation. He execrated it in *Democratic Vistas.* He scarcely foresaw the piling up of people in cities, the ruin of the farms and the consequent corruption of the spirit of the people— all of which Jefferson predicted as the result of mercantilism and centralization. It is not strange that Whitman had no sons dedicated to carrying on his work. It is logical, however, that he had sons bent on avenging the ruin of the America to which Whitman gave his life. These by their satire and anathema bewail and curse the state to which the republic and the people were reduced by deliberate executions against the last hope of liberty in this world, as Jefferson called the United States.

The bearing that all this has on poetry is clear enough.
What happens is that plotters get all the money by legalized
privileges and partial laws. They then go on and make the
culture of the country, both by surrounding every one with
materialism, and by further laws and court decisions to make
their possessions secure and on the increase. Soon the thinker
finds himself cramped and in want. The creator, the poet, the
minds who can save the country, are struck down or rendered
dumb or bitter. Budding Virgils and Homers are nipped, but
Juvenals grow up. For resistance, not to say revolution, is out-
lawed in America. Free speech is banned, and protesters must
steal through the interplexus of things forbidden. To do that
they must pick words which deceive the swine or which are
regarded by them as mere poetry and of no dangerous moment.
All this has happened in America, and much of it since Whitman died.

Notice Whitman's sordid picture of America as given in
Respondez:

(Stifled, O days! O lands! in every public and private corruption!
Brazen effrontery, scheming, rolling like ocean's waves around and
 upon you, O my days! my lands!
For not even those thunderstorms, nor fiercest lightnings of the
 war, have purified the atmosphere;)
—Let the theory of America still be management, caste, comparison! (Say! what other theory would you?)
Let them that distrust birth and death still lead the rest! (Say!
 why shall they not lead you?)
Let the crust of hell be neared and trod on! let the days be darker
 than the nights! let slumber bring less slumber than waking
 time brings!
Let the world never appear to him or her for whom it was all made!
Let the heart of the young man still exile itself from the heart of
 the old man! and let the heart of the old man be exiled from
 that of the young man!
Let the sun and moon go! let scenery take the applause of the
 audience! let there be apathy under the stars!

Let freedom prove no man's inalienable right! every one who can tyrannize, let him tyrannize to his satisfaction!

Let none but infidels be countenanced!

Let the eminence of meanness, treachery, sarcasm, hate, greed, indecency, impotence, lust, be taken for granted above all! let writers, judges, governments, households, religions, philosophers, take such for granted above all!

Let the worst men beget children out of the worst women!

Let the priest still play at immortality!

Let death be inaugurated!

Let nothing remain but the ashes of teachers, artists, moralists, lawyers, and learn'd and polite persons!

Let him who is without my poems be assassinated!

Let the cow, the horse, the camel, the garden-bee — let the mudfish, the lobster, the mussel, eel, the sting-ray, and the grunting pigfish — let these, and the like of these, be put on a perfect equality with man and woman!

Let churches accommodate serpents, vermin, and the corpses of those who have died of the most filthy of diseases!

Let marriage slip down among fools, and be for none but fools!

Let men among themselves talk and think forever obscenely of women! and let women among themselves talk and think obscenely of men!

Let the earth desert God, nor let there ever henceforth be mention'd the name of God!

Let there be no God!

Let there be money, business, imports, exports, customs, authority, precedents, pallor, dyspepsia, smut, ignorance, unbelief!

Let judges and criminals be transposed! let the prison-keepers be put in prison! let those that were prisoners take the keys! (Say! why might they not just as well be transposed?)

Let the slaves be masters! let the masters become slaves!

Let the reformers descend from the stands where they are forever bawling! let an idiot or insane person appear on each of the stands!

When Whitman was beginning his career England was still sneering at our literature. It really mattered very little that America won its governmental independence, if America remained an intellectual province controlled by England. To hold on to the New England States, while those states, in fealty to English traditions in literature and to English economics, maligned and opposed first Jefferson and then Jackson, gave to England a control fully as complete as would have come from victory in battle. The emancipation from this foreign rulership, for which Whitman wrote so many brave words in verse and prose, has not yet by any means come to pass. In his time he had to contend with New England and its influences over the country and with the English traditions for which many professional minds chirped incessantly, even as they do now.

Jefferson's labors and philosophy, Noah Webster's efforts for an American language, and in our own day the more thorough and philosophical work in the same direction of H. L. Mencken, have not been enough to keep back the deeply seated and ever active virus in our veins which we inherited from England and Europe. But in spite of everything we have had Emerson, Mark Twain, Whitman, and some lesser men, to save our literature from utter ruin, and to make it new, original and expressive of an American culture. Whitman thought that Bryant, Emerson, Whittier, and Longfellow belonged on any list that England could boast, topped by Chaucer and Shakespeare, and running down to Wordsworth, Byron, Shelley, and Keats.

Yet we got into colonialism as England smiled us into it, and as Kipling sang us into it. Kipling was a far more influential factor in our political course than ever Whitman was. And then England got us into the World War, ruining us for still more years to come. But after all, how is mere man to impugn the course of history? He can see his own present hopes ruined and the career of his country stayed in what seems to him its true and predestined course. He knows about the decline of Rome and the passing of Athens, but he does not know what the future pattern of the life around him is.

He has nothing to say by way of demonstrating these things as evils except that they are evil to him and his generation and to his country as he loves it and hopes for it. Meanwhile there is nature and the life forces that are never destroyed or reduced.

CHAPTER EIGHTEEN

WHITMAN undertook to sing himself "a simple separate person, yet utter the word Democratic, the word en masse." But he did more than that: he sang nature, and as a mystic, a transcendentalist. He may have derived clues and guides from what he gathered from Kant, Fichte, Schelling, and Hegel in particular; he may have been influenced by Emerson. Whitman knew Emerson's works much earlier then he confessed he knew them. In fact he reviewed *Emerson's Spiritual Laws* in *The Brooklyn Eagle* in its issue of December 15, 1847.

Early in life he was influenced by deism and English natural theology, by Rousseau and by Jefferson. Nevertheless Whitman was a close observer, a mystical lover of nature. But it may be doubted if he had the cast of mind to enter into nature's spirituality as fully as Wordsworth did, certainly he did not express his worship with equal beauty of words, nor in strophes of such music and memorableness. Still such questions may be left for every reader to decide for himself.

Whitman saw in nature beneath all shows and appearances, spirit and creative thought. This was the only absolute substance. He kept saying that he saw this. Good and evil, the opposing forces of positive and negative, were as waves of the ocean which are contained within its body, and do not change its body by any movement. Life is the law of the whole visible scheme of things; death is only the sinking of a wave. Truth and health proceed always from the changeless laws of the moral universe. Disease, vice, disaster, the fall of nations,

314

wars, all man-made as well as nature-made destroyers of human life and happiness are but the interplay of waves which do not affect the life process, nor the order of the universe. There is something of Spinoza here too. Let us look at Whitman's own words:

"Lo! *Nature* (the only complete, actual poem) existing calmly in the divine scheme, containing all, content, careless of the criticisms of a day, or these endless and wordy chatterers. And lo! to the consciousness of the soul, the permanent identity, the thought, the something, before which the magnitude even of Democracy, art, literature, etc., dwindles, becomes partial, measurable—something that fully satisfies (which those do not). That something is the *All* and the idea of *All,* with the accompanying idea of eternity, and of itself, the soul, buoyant, indestructible, sailing Space forever, visiting every region, as a ship the sea. And again lo! the pulsations in all matter, all spirit, throbbing forever—the eternal beats, eternal systole and dyastole of life in things—wherefrom I feel and know that death is not the ending, as we thought, but rather the real beginning—and that nothing ever is or can be lost, nor even die, nor soul nor matter."

And again:

"As far as I have sought any, not the best laid out garden or parterre has been my model—but Nature has been. I know that in a sense the garden is Nature too, but I had to choose— I could not give both. Besides, the gardens are well represented in poetry; while Nature (in letter and in spirit, in the divine essence) little if at all.

"Certainly (while I have not hit it by a long shot), I have aim'd at the most ambitious, the best—and sometimes feel to advance that aim (even with all its arrogance) as the most redeeming part of my books. I have never so much cared to feed the esthetic or intellectual palates—but if I could arouse from its slumbers that eligibility in every soul for its own true exercise! if I could only wield that lever!"

Whitman's nature poems mark a real departure in that field of poetry. They are not idyllic. He derived nothing from Virgil, from Bion or from Moschus. His worship of nature is earthly and rich. It is as artless as the mood of a man looking over a scene of fields, of hills and sea water. In its broad sweep and simplicity it is like the Homeric hymns. Even Shelley with a feeling for nature all different from that of the classical poets translated some of the fragments of Bion and Moschus, and some of the Eclogues and Georgics of Virgil. English literature through the neo-classicists imitated Virgil and other ancient poets. They too celebrated shepherds and shepherdesses, and redramatized Meliboeus and Tityrus. These poems are sensuous and musical, but they do not touch the inner heart of Nature. With Keats a new note of nature was struck, a note of rich and orginal description. But Whitman passed them all by. Wordsworth did not influence him, nor Bryant. He looked with fresh eyes upon Nature. He didn't live in the city and celebrate the country. Rather he studied the country by actual contact with it, around Brooklyn, in upper New York, near Washington and Camden, and through the Far West. He was in the country when he was in the city, and his youthful days were so impregnated with the hills and the sea that wherever he was in later years the country was with him. He was not a recluse singing of nature in his study. He roamed the streets and went riding in busses. But while he loved the stir of New York he spent hours alone in the Battery looking at the ships. He wandered away from the thoroughfares to walk like Chyrses by the shore of the many-voiced sea. People were to him but one more phase of nature, and Nature to him was the mother of people. He gathered together enough material for lyrics and sonnets to nature for the hands of a hundred lesser poets. The temple he erected to Nature could be robbed here and there of a bit of the capital or frieze for delicate lyricizing without damagaing the temple. All in all there is no poet of Nature to surpass him for compass. His depth, at least the depth of his expression, is something else.

To mention again Whitman's keen eye for scrutinizing objects and phases of outdoor life, words may be taken from his works, which are memorial of the happy days when he wandered by the shores of Long Island: "Sea cabbage, salt hay, sea rushes, ooze, sea-gluten, sea-scum, spawn, surf, salt-perfume, mud, sound of walking barefoot ankle deep in the edge of the water by the sea." Little escapes his observation.

All through his prose, as well as in his verse, may be found his worship of nature. It never occurred to him to say whether nature betrays or does not betray the heart that loves her. He could only love her. In *Democratic Vistas* he wrote:

"Nature, true Nature, and the true idea of Nature, long absent, must above all become fully restored, enlarged, and must furnish the pervading atmosphere to poems, and the test of all high literary and esthetic compositions. I do not mean the smooth walks, trimmed hedges, posys and nightingales of the English poets, but the whole orb, with its geologic history, the cosmos, carrying fire and snow, that rolls through the illimitable areas, light as a feather, though weighing billions of tons. Furthermore, as by what we now partially call Nature is intended, at most, only what is entertainable by the physical conscience, the sense of matter, and of good animal health —on these it must be distinctly accumulated, incorporated, that man, comprehending these, has in towering superaddition, the moral and spiritual consciences, indicating his destination beyond the ostensible, the mortal. To the heights of such estimate of Nature indeed ascending, we proceed to make observations for our Vistas, breathing rarest air. What is I believe called Idealism seems to me to suggest (guarding against extravagance, and ever modified even by its opposite) the course of inquiry and desert of favour for our New World metaphysics, their foundation of and in literature, giving hue to all."

And as a footnote to this utterance Whitman wrote: "The

317

culmination and fruit of literary and artistic expression, and its final fields of pleasure for the human soul, are in metaphysics, including the mysteries of the spiritual world, the soul itself, and the question of the immortal continuation of our identity. In all ages the mind of man has brought up here—and always will. . . . Though little or nothing can be absolutely known, perceived, except from a point of view which is evanescent, yet we know at least one permanency, that Time and Space, in the will of God, furnish successive chains, completions of material births and beginnings, solve all discrepancies, fears and doubts, and eventually fulfil happiness—and that the prophecy of those births namely spiritual results, throws the true arch over all teaching, all science."

No such faith for the purposes of poetry is to be found in Wordsworth or in any other poet. Wordsworth in his preface to the *Lyrical Ballads* stated his principal object in those poems to be to sing the humble man amid rustic surroundings, to portray situations from common life. Nature to him, as shown by his poems, was interpenetrated by an immortal beauty, a spiritual power. He did not expressly say what the worship of that power was to have as an influence upon liberty, and his country. Byron's apostrophes to Nature are great bursts of eloquence; Shelley sank his being into Nature by an idealistic pantheism; Bryant sang hymns to the forests and the prairies; Whitman with heartiness, yet with wonderful spirituality, identified himself with the good earth—with Nature as the visible embodiment of creative thought and mind, all good. Whitman's philosophy in this is unique and without any parallel in poetry. It was a philosophy that sustained him in sickness and in suffering old age.

Wordsworth mused on "Man, on Nature and on Human Life." That was Whitman's diapason whose "spirit has passed in compassion and around the whole earth" who never walked under trees but "large and melodious thoughts," descended upon him. "Nature is rude and incomprehensible at first," he

said. "Be not discouraged, keep on, there are divine things
envelop'd. . . . I swear the earth shall be complete to him
or her who shall be complete." Then he asks the secret of
making the best poems, and answers, "It is to grow in the
open air and to eat and sleep with the earth."

Out of Whitman's love of nature came the great beauty
of "Pioneers, O Pioneers," "Patroling Barnegat," and such
phrasing as "the yellow moon sagging down." Whitman's
titles are sometimes excellent, as "Give me the Splendid Shining Sun," and "Rise O Days from Your Fathomless Deeps."
Would that some of these best poems were not marred, as
by a false note in the midst of a symphony, by such words as
"camerado"—"allons"—"respondez."

When his feelings were wrought to the highest his figures
came forth like stars from behind clouds, his music became
ethereal or of organ volume. As:

O western orb, sailing the heaven,
Now I know what you must have meant as a month since I walk'd,
As I walk'd in silence the transparent shadowy night.

These lines are from his threnody on Lincoln. In the same
poem his passion for nature produced these beautiful verses:

In the distance the flowing glaze, the breast of the river, with a
    wind-dapple here and there,
With ranging hills on the banks, with many a line against the sky,
    and shadows,
And the city at hand with dwellings so dense, and stacks of
    chimneys,
And all the scenes of life and the workshops, and the workmen
    homeward returning.

Pictures of growing spring and farms and homes,
With the Fourth-month eve at sundown, and the grey smoke lucid
    and bright,
With floods of the yellow gold of the gorgeous, indolent, sinking
    sun, burning, expanding the air,

319

With the fresh sweet herbage under foot, and the pale green leaves
of the trees prolific.

And then from nature he could turn to man and to war:

And I saw askant the armies,
I saw as in noiseless dreams hundreds of battle-flags,
Borne through the smoke of the battles and pierc'd with missiles
I saw them,
And carried hither and yon through the smoke, and torn and
bloody,
And at last but a few shreds left on the staffs (and all in silence),
And the staffs all splinter'd and broken.

In "Give me the Splendid Silent Sun" he deserted nature for a
time to look upon people:

Keep your splendid silent sun,
Keep your woods, O Nature, and the quiet places by the woods,
Keep your fields of clover and timothy, and your corn-fields and
orchards,
Keep the blossoming buckwheat fields where the Ninth-month
bees hum;
Give me faces and streets — give me these phantoms incessant and
endless along the trottoirs!
Give me interminable eyes — give me women — give me comrades
and lovers by the thousand!
Let me see new ones every day — let me hold new ones by the
hand every day!
Give me such shows — give me the streets of Manhattan!
Give me Broadway, with the soldiers marching — give me the
sound of the trumpets and drums!

Whitman's poems of the sea and the rivers are rich with
feeling and descriptive touches. Yet again I say he does not rise
to such "purple patches" as Wordsworth and Shelley do.
The way to get Whitman's beauty in such passages is to consider his comprehension, the multiverse that he sees, the love
for nature that stirs him with such mystical simplicity of heart.
He crossed Brooklyn ferry and marked the "twelfth month

sea gulls, floating with motionless wings," and the "glisten-ing yellow lit up by parts of their bodies." He "look'd on the haze on the hills southward and south-westward; look'd on the vapour as it flew in fleeces tinged with violet," all amid the "swinging motion of the hulls, the white sails of schooners and sloops." This is not like "There is a pleasure in the pathless woods, There is a rapture on the lonely shore"; it is not "some-thing far more deeply interfused, Whose dwelling is the light of setting suns, And the round ocean and the living air"; it is not the onomatopoetic rendition of waters that wash the sands such as Shelley could accomplish, it is plainness, without fig-ures, without ornamentation, in obedience to the rules which Whitman set down for himself. It is his idea of American poetry, plain as the prairies, level as the quiet sea. He chose to sing for "These States"—America—and for a new day, free and vast.

But this method and conception of the art of poetry had marvellous possibilities. Whitman demonstrated them in "Out of the Cradle Endlessly Rocking." That, moreover, is one of his happy titles. In this poem his imagination became fluent and his words obeyed his passion:

Out of the cradle endlessly rocking,
Out of the mocking-bird's throat, the musical shuttle,
Out of the Ninth-month midnight,
Over the sterile sands, and the fields beyond, where the child leav-
    ing his bed wander'd alone, bareheaded, barefoot,
Down from the shower'd halo,
Up from the mystic play of shadows twining and twisting as if they
    were alive,
Out from the patches of briers and blackberries,
From the memories of the bird that chanted to me,
From your memories, sad brother, from the fitful risings and
    fallings I heard,
From under that yellow half-moon late-risen and swollen as if with
    tears,
From those beginning notes of yearning and love there in the mist,
From the thousand responses of my heart never to cease,

From the myriad thence-arous'd words,
From the word stronger and more delicious than any,
From such as now they start the scene revisiting,
Borne hither, ere all eludes me, hurriedly,
A man, yet by these tears a little boy again,
Throwing myself on the sand, confronting the waves,
I, chanter of pains and joys, uniter of here and hereafter,
Taking all hints to use them, but swiftly leaping beyond them,
A reminiscence sing.

This immediate discussion may be closed by quoting some lines from Whitman's "Kosmos" in which he describes himself and all those who see spirituality in nature, and through worship of nature identify themselves with the eternity and the immortality which is nature:

Who includes diversity, and is Nature,
Who is the amplitude of the earth, and the coarseness and sexuality of the earth, and the great charity of the earth, and the equilibrium also,
Who has not look'd forth from the windows, the eyes, for nothing, or whose brain held audience with messengers for nothing;
Who contains believers and disbelievers — who is the most majestic lover;
Who holds duly his or her triune proportion of realism, spiritualism, and of the æsthetic, or intellectual,
Who, having consider'd the Body, finds all its organs and parts good;
Who, out of the theory of the earth, and of his or her body, understands by subtle analogies all other theories,
The theory of a city, a poem, and of the large politics of These States;
Who believes not only in our globe, with its sun and moon, but in other globes, with their suns and moons;
Who, constructing the house of himself or herself, not for a day, but for all time, sees races, eras, dates, generations,
The past, the future, dwelling there, like space, inseparable together.

This is the vocal soul of Whitman in the strong, passionate, clear-eyed days when he was forty-one. In reading Whitman it is of advantage to know the age at which he wrote any given poem. For not all will seem the work of the gray-bearded, patriarchal man, prematurely old, though this association is often made. He was fifty when he produced "Passage to India" and "Gods."

This, then, is Whitman the man and the poet. He was in many ways a mystery, as all men of complex mind and vision are, and that in spite of a voluminous utterance. His was a specific purpose to sing himself, not a "simple separate person," but a soul who ranged the country and the earth in search of meanings and with the desire to expound them. He was accepted and rejected in his own day, and that is still the case. The common man could not understand him then or now, not as he can understand Burns, for example. Yet Whitman has meant much to the common man.

He was a great influence in inaugurating this better respect for the body which we know today. He stood for sanity in matters of sex and for the outspoken championship of sexual delight as one of the blessings of human life. Long before the days of Havelock Ellis, Whitman fought for the modern point of view which has discarded chastity as the perverted ideal of Asiatic mysticism. And he did this for America where it was needed as much, if not more than, any place in the world. He spoke for sensuality, not the life of wayward and hedonistic indulgence, but for man's and woman's spirit playing through the body and thereby ministering to the spirit and finding itself.

The evil dualism of soul and body, of the soul as good and the body as vile, which was opposed by the artists and thinkers of the Renaissance, Luther, Erasmus, and Rabelais, has had no more influential poet of protest than Walt Whitman. The doctrine that the deepest secrets of happiness lie in this spiritualized sensuality was never more subtly or more beautifully expounded than in John Cowper Powys's *In Defense of Sensuality*. It is a poem, and marshals arguments which Whitman in

323

his cosmic view of things was too far-sighted to see. Powys, a great admirer of Whitman, thus advanced the line that Whitman flung to the enemy of beauty and happiness. Granted that wars have diverted the course of America, and that a merchant philosophy has degraded its life—it remains true that the high souls of America keep their vision and march ahead. Walt Whitman is their prophet. They look to him for encouragement and strength.

For Whitman made a spiritual survey of America. It may be a rough survey, the notes may be crude at times, but it is a survey just the same. He went his way into the wilderness singing and surveying and prophesying of singers to come, who should be greater than he. What he surveyed needs to be fenced, reduced to cultivation, tested as to its particular productiveness in wisdom and beauty. Whitman dreamed with heavy-lids, with half open eyes; he saw a vast country and a great possibility for poetry. He left to posterity the outlines of poems and suggestions for poems. He bequeathed the spirit in which American poems should be written. He boasted that he would sing the songs of America, at the same time that he confessed he was only giving hints and directions.

The distinctive American poetry which Whitman wanted sung required a genius that he did not possess. That genius has a vision that penetrates into the heart of things, a creative and constructive power of logic, and of architecture, that his desultory, expansive mind was incapable of commanding. American material must be dramatized, lyricized, deeply realized, before the songs that Whitman forecast can be sung. By such methods and processes the poet extracts the essential from landscapes and the souls of men and women in their daily life and in heroic moments.

Whitman, despite his cosmic consciousness and mysticism, sang the seen—not the unseen. He sat at a loom throwing the shuttle and guiding the threads without any pattern other than that the fabric should be unmistakably American. When one says that a poem, a work of art, must be a finished thing, one means fundamentally that the material under careful artistry must have been wrought into the finest product of which the material is capable. Its truth and its beauty must be more than suggested and not merely outlined. Whitman saw in the large, and he worked with hands that meant to catch broad effects. Hence editors and critics saw in much of his work nothing beyond improvisations. In "By Blue Ontario's Shore," Whitman wrote:

The immortal poets of Asia and Europe have done their work
    and pass'd to other spheres,
A work remains, the work of surpassing all that they have done.

Very truly, but Whitman did not do it, and perhaps no one can ever do it. Whitman's spiritual self-assurance, boasting and promising is of a piece with the mind cures of his day and the spiritual quackeries that chanted the infinite possibilities of the mind to cure, save and achieve whatever the mind proposed to itself to do. He could say that "these states are the amplest poem." It does not make them a poem to assert this. The poem has to be written. Did he sing the song of the states, of their origin and growth? He did not. Did he celebrate Washington? His poem "The Centenarian's Story" shows that he did not have the genius to celebrate Washington. Did he portray the picturesqueness of old times, the War of 1812 or battles by land and sea? If he had done so he would have written American songs.

Browning in "Hervé Riel," and Tennyson in "The Revenge" made England immortal land and spirit. Lesser men, like Noyes and Masefield, have done for England what Whitman did not do for America. In this connection "Morte d'Arthur," the ballads in Percy's *Reliques,* Campbell's poems and many other heroic lyrics come to mind. Yet Whitman saw the material for such work and urged the necessity of its being done. "The Star-Spangled Banner" voices America, and does it with swift lyricism. Whitman did not write anything that has the power of communicating its effects so dramatically or so emotionally.

What did Whitman do to compact the North and the South, to "express native scenes," to fashion American material in such a way that the poetry of "Old plots, gem cutting, tales of love" would be driven out from the poetry of the New World? If the "War of Secession" was greater than the Trojan War, if Agamemnon and Achilles could be cancelled from the vocabulary of poetry by celebrating Grant, Meade, Lee, Jackson, and singing Chancellorsville, the Wilderness, Shiloh and Appomattox, why did not Whitman sing them? He could not have done so any more than he could have written Newton's *Principia*. Whitman's criticism of *Paradise Lost* is sound enough on the whole. But that production indicates methods, machinery and music by which the War of the States could be made into the epic of the New World. Nothing in Whitman's invention, nothing in his music meets the requirements of such a work. Yet America must thank Whitman that he enjoined us to create an "imaginative New World" and to make it the counterpart of the science and politics of America.

Nothing could be better by which to rid poetry of the "thin moribund and watery." These are the themes he contemplated, but did not touch,—suggestions to poets to come which he did not follow himself. As a great liberal living and writing in America when the land was cursed by superstition and churches—by obscenity and taboos—he cannot be too much thanked and remembered for what he wrote. As a lover, as a prophet of democracy, as a voice raising itself in behalf of comradeship and against that spirit which withdraws, stands aside, is ashamed of tenderness, communion, fellowship—Whitman may prove to be the chief figure in the pattern of American development. This he may be without doing more than he has already done for American poetry. For as things stand, when we read Whitman's declarations that he would sing the songs of America, we are compelled to say for the most part, "very well, go ahead, we are listening."

If Emerson, as Arnold said, was not a poet, not a philosopher, not a stylist in the sense that Cicero was a stylist, but only a thinker who helped men to live in the spirit—it may be said of Whitman that he was a pioneer, that his "Song of the Broad Axe" was a symbol of his own work, that he felled to some extent the encumbering forest and let later eyes see in part what the lay of the land was, what its resources were under the hills, and what its fertility was on top. That had to be done in order that later poets could build beautiful cities of song, always definitely harmonious with the American landscape, always original and of a new age and a new land, and incapable of being known by any other designation save that they were American.

Index

INDEX

INDEX

INDEX

INDEX

INDEX

340